MW00562089

ESSAYS ON ETHICS
A WEEKLY READING OF THE JEWISH BIBLE

MAGGID   OUPRESS

Other works by the author

Rabbi Jonathan Sacks

ESSAYS ON ETHICS

A Weekly Reading of the Jewish Bible

The Brickman Edition

Maggid Books & The Orthodox Union

Essays on Ethics
A Weekly Reading of the Jewish Bible

First Edition, 2016

Maggid Books
An imprint of Koren Publishers Jerusalem Ltd.

POB 8531, New Milford, CT 06776-8531, USA
& POB 4044, Jerusalem 9104001, Israel
www.maggidbooks.com

The publication of this book was made possible
through the generous support of *Torah Education in Israel*.

ISBN 978-1-59264-449-0, *hardcover*

A CIP catalogue record for this title is
available from the British Library

Printed and bound in the United States

This sefer is dedicated in loving memory
and in commemoration of the tenth yahrzeit of

Rabbi Seymour Brickman ז״ל

הרב שמואל צבי בן יוסף הלוי ז״ל

י״ט בכסלו תשס״ו

whose exemplary character and boundless love of
learning continue to guide and inspire us every day

הוֹלֵךְ תָּמִים וּפֹעֵל צֶדֶק וְדֹבֵר אֱמֶת בִּלְבָבוֹ

(תהלים טו, ב)

Devora Brickman

Sharon and Josh Brickman
NICOLE, TALIA, AND ADI

Rena and Victor Fein
MARC, JACOB, AND ZACHARY

Sharon and Sinclair Haberman
LAUREN, ALEXANDER, ANDREW
JONATHAN, AND SAMUEL

Contents

Foreword

Ethicising Religion

Joseph I. Lieberman[*]

As someone who believes in public service and knows how much leaders affect people's lives for better or worse, I have been embarrassed and deeply troubled by the number of current leaders who are guilty of unethical or immoral behaviour – leaders in government, politics, business, sports, and even religion. In one sense, there is nothing new about this. Since the Garden of Eden, people have struggled with the choice between good and evil. But, in our time, too many leaders seem to lose their way and make bad choices, which are in turn quickly communicated by modern telecommunications and social media to people

---

[*] Now Senior Counsel at the law firm of Kasowitz, Benson, Torres, and Friedman in New York, Joseph I. Lieberman was for twenty-four years a member of the US Senate from Connecticut. At the end of his service in January 2013, he was Chairman of the Homeland Security and Governmental Affairs Committee, and a senior member of the Armed Services Committee. Before his election to the Senate in 1988, Senator Lieberman served ten years in the Connecticut State Senate and six years as Connecticut's Attorney General. In 2000 he was the Democratic candidate for Vice President of the United States. Senator Lieberman is married to Hadassah Freilich Lieberman. Together they have four children and ten grandchildren.

all over the world. The result is a wide and deep distrust of leadership in general and a resulting popular insecurity about the present and future.

Onto this muddy field of ethical failures now comes Rabbi Lord Jonathan Sacks with a pen that is mightier than all the immorality. In this wonderful volume of essays drawing ethical lessons from each weekly portion of the Hebrew Bible, Rabbi Sacks speaks in a strong, principled, and eloquent voice. His insights will enrich the reader's understanding of the Torah and guide the daily efforts each of us makes to choose good over evil.

In Genesis, Rabbi Sacks observes, religion is for the first time "ethicised." Abraham is the first monotheist, but he is also the first ethical monotheist. He is instructed by God to keep the way of the Lord by teaching his children to do what is right and just.

A central theme of this book and elsewhere in Rabbi Sacks's work is that ethical behaviour is the essence of Jewish life and Jewish destiny. Religious observances and rituals have been critical to protecting the mandates of the Bible and enabling the miracle of Jewish survival over the millennia. However, the Jewish people's ultimate reason for being is to bring to the world the values that were codified and transmitted by God to man at Sinai. Rabbi Sacks advances that mission brilliantly in this book.

There is a powerful message in the biblical journey the Children of Israel took from slavery in Egypt to receiving the Ten Commandments at Sinai. It is that freedom alone usually leads to immorality, violence, or chaos. People need rules. They need law. In Egypt, Moses appeals to Pharaoh not just to "let my people go" but to "let my people go to serve the Lord." The divinely guided Exodus from Egypt is only the beginning of the journey; it leads inevitably to the Ten Commandments and the requirement to serve God by upholding the values expressed in those commandments and in the Torah.

Because people are inherently imperfect, the Ten Commandments – like all good laws since – are aspirational. They set a standard for what we aspire to be but often are not.

Rabbi Sacks's insights in this book would have been appreciated by the wise men who founded America. They were learned in the Hebrew Bible. Perhaps that is why they understood that they had a responsibility not only to secure their freedom, but to adopt rules to encourage better behaviour among their citizens. Because they were made sceptical of central authority by their experiences with the English monarch (I apologise for mentioning this in the foreword to a book written by an English lord), they wanted the reach of their new government to be limited. They therefore knew there was a need for non-governmental motivators of good conduct and they believed, as Rabbi Sacks does, that there is no better motivator than religion.

Look at the wise words of President George Washington in his Farewell Address:

> Of all the dispositions and habits which lead to political prosperity, religion and morality are indispensable supports…. The mere politician, equally with the pious man, ought to respect and cherish them. A volume could not trace all their connections with private and public felicity…. Let it simply be asked who is the security for property, for reputation, for life, if the sense of religious obligation desert the oaths…. And let us with caution indulge the supposition that morality can be maintained without religion.[1]

Washington's insights are as true and necessary today (particularly for "mere politicians") as they were in 1796 when he delivered them.

One of the big lessons that emerges in this book from the biblical text and Rabbi Sacks's explication of it is that belief in the Creator leads naturally to an ethic of egalitarianism. All of us – kings and knaves, presidents and paupers – are equally blessed and deserve to be treated ethically because we are all children of the same God. But there is another way in which the Torah makes clear that we are not all equal, that more is required of some of us. The greater an individual's position, power, or authority, the higher the standards to which he or she is held. We are all called to live according to the law, but leaders especially must be moral and ethical exemplars because the impact of unethical conduct by a king or president is greater than the impact of bad behaviour by a knave or pauper.

1. Philadelphia's *American Daily Advertiser*, September 19, 1796.

In the Bible, there are many examples of this higher standard for leaders, including Aaron the high priest, King Saul, and King David. But the most poignant is surely Moses, who was so great a person and leader that God spoke to him "face to face" (Ex. 33:11) – but because of one instance of loss of self-control, one instance of loss of faith, Moses was not allowed to enter the Promised Land.

Everyone who reads this book will benefit from it. Those in positions of leadership should be compelled to read it; hopefully they will then choose to apply its ethical and moral advice to their work.

As Rabbi Sacks writes in his commentary on the Torah portion *Emor* ("Speak") in the book of Leviticus:

> Long ago we were called on to show the world that religion and morality go hand in hand. Never was that more needed than in an age riven by religiously motivated violence in some countries, rampant secularity in others. To be a Jew is to be dedicated to the proposition that loving God means loving His image, humankind. There is no greater challenge, nor, in the twenty-first century, is there a more urgent one.[2]

2.   P. 199.

Introduction

Seven Features of Jewish Ethics

Towards the end of his *Civilization: The West and the Rest*, Harvard historian Niall Ferguson tells a remarkable story of how the Chinese Academy of Social Sciences was charged with the task of discovering how the West became the preeminent force in the modern world. Until the sixteenth century, China had been the world's most advanced civilisation but it was then overtaken and left behind. What was it about the West that gave it the ability to develop so rapidly?

One Chinese scholar told the story. At first, he said, we thought it was because the West had better guns than we had. They were militarily stronger. Then we searched deeper and concluded that it was their political system. They developed democracy while we did not. We went deeper still and came to the conclusion that it was their economic system. They developed the free market and we did not. But for the past twenty years we have known the real answer. It was their religion. That is what gave the West its critical advantage. It was what made possible the development, first of capitalism, and then of democratic politics – and these fuelled the rest.[1]

The religion in question was, of course, Christianity. But Christianity was not born in the sixteenth century when the West began its precipitous growth. To the contrary, it was already more than a millennium and a half old, and had been the dominant power in Europe since the conversion of Roman Emperor Constantine in the early fourth century. Something happened in the sixteenth century to turn European culture into the force that produced the rapid acceleration that made it the intellectual, economic, and political leader of the world.

What happened was the Reformation, which especially in its Calvinist form, brought Christians back to reading what they called the Old Testament and we know as Tanakh, the Hebrew Bible. It was this re-engagement with the Judaic tradition, brought about by the Christian Hebraists of the sixteenth and seventeenth centuries, that had a decisive impact on the politics and economics of the West. This was when the constellation of values that has come to be called the Judaeo-Christian heritage began to have a transformative impact on the West, launching it on its flight to greatness.

That civilisation is now in danger throughout most of Europe and in many parts of the United States. In 1869 in high Victorian England, Matthew Arnold argued that British culture was the result of the combined impact of two ancient civilisations, Athens and Jerusalem; he called them, respectively, Hellenism and Hebraism. Greece, he said, gave the world philosophy and science, while the Hebrew Bible gave it its moral code. As he put it, "The uppermost idea with Hellenism is to see things as they really are; the uppermost idea with Hebraism is conduct and obedience."[2] This meant that "as long as the world lasts, all who want to make progress in righteousness will come to Israel for inspiration, as to the people who have had the sense for righteousness most glowing and strongest." For Arnold, if you seek to understand morality, you must read the Hebrew Bible.

In his view, in his day the spirit of Hebraism was in the ascendant, and there was not enough Hellenism in British culture. Today the

1.   Niall Ferguson, *Civilization: The West and the Rest* (London: Allen Lane, 2011), 287.
2.   Matthew Arnold, *Culture and Anarchy* (London: 1869), ch. 4.

situation has been reversed. In countless ways, in its focus on the body, in its emphasis on material goods and physical sports, in its prioritising of politics over personal morality as the way to change the world, in its approach to sexual ethics, abortion, and euthanasia, the West today has reverted to the values and practices of pre-Christian Greece and Rome. This is how Ferdinand Mount puts it:

> Often without our being in the least aware of it, the ways in which we live our rich and varied lives correspond, almost eerily so, to the ways in which the Greeks and Romans lived theirs. Whether we are eating and drinking, bathing or exercising or making love, pondering, admiring or enquiring, our habits of thought and action, our diversions and concentrations recall theirs. It is as though the 1,500 years after the fall of Rome had been time out from traditional ways of being human.[3]

It may be that this is sustainable, but the likelihood is that it is not. Greece in the age of the Stoics and Epicureans and Rome in the first and second centuries were societies on the brink of decay. Their cultural achievements, especially those of Athens, were unsurpassed. But they lacked the ability to survive, recover from catastrophe, and renew themselves. They declined and fell. There is something about the way of life begun by Abraham, given shape and structure by the Revelation at Mount Sinai and moral voice by the prophets, that touched the imagination of a small and otherwise undistinguished people, lifting it time and again to spiritual greatness. At its heart was a moral vision of what it is to be human under the sovereignty of God, a vision that still has the capacity to inspire and to lift us individually and collectively.

I am not one of those who believe, like Dostoevsky, that "if God does not exist, all is permitted." You do not need to be religious to be moral. Plato, Aristotle, and the Stoics all had profound moral insights. Hinduism and Buddhism have their own traditions and codes. There are the great Chinese heritages of Confucianism and Taoism. None of these

---

3. Ferdinand Mount, *Full Circle: How the Classical World Came Back to Us* (London: Simon and Schuster, 2010), 1.

was an Abrahamic monotheism. Every society needs a code of conduct that allows its members to live constructively and collaboratively. There is honour even among thieves, as Judah HaLevi noted. Some form of morality is a universal characteristic of human groups.

Evolutionary biology and neuroscience have helped us understand how and why this works. All social animals are capable of acting for the benefit of the group as a whole. We pass on our genes as individuals but we survive as the members of a group. Computer simulations have shown that cooperation requires a pattern of behaviour known as reciprocal altruism, meaning, roughly, if you behave well towards me, I will behave well towards you. From this come the two almost universal features of the moral life, the so-called golden rule, "Act towards others as you would wish them to act towards you," and the principle of measure-for-measure justice, "As you do, so you will be done to." These flow from the logic of cooperation itself.

What is more, we can locate this within the brain. Social animals have a feature that makes for moral behaviour: the so-called mirror neurons that make us wince when we see someone else in pain. These are the basis of empathy (feeling with) and sympathy (feeling for). So we are, by nature and independently of religious convictions, inclined to be moral animals. But not all moral systems are the same. I want in this introduction to focus on seven features of the ethic of the Torah that make it transformative and uniquely sustainable over time. Great civilisations come and go. Judaism came and stayed. These are among the reasons why.

1. *The dignity of the individual*

First is the unprecedented dignity of the individual, signalled in the statement of the Torah's first chapter: "Let us make mankind in our image, in our likeness" (Gen. 1:26). Every human being, regardless of class, colour, culture, or creed, carries within him or her the image of God. This, according to the Mishnaic sage Ben Azzai, is the essential principle of the Torah.[4]

4. *Sifra, Kedoshim* 4:12.

The idea that a human being could be in the image of God was not new to the ancient Near East. That is what Mesopotamian kings, Assyrian emperors, and Egyptian pharaohs were believed to be: the children of the gods, or the chief intermediaries with the gods. It was a standard description of royalty. What was revolutionary to the Bible was the proposition that this applies equally to all of us. The concept of human rights was not born until the seventeenth century, yet it is fair to say that its possibility was created in those words.

The rabbis spelled out some of the implications. A mishna in Sanhedrin (4:5) states that humans were created singly (the Torah speaks of the creation of the first man and woman) to teach that a single life is like a universe. When a person destroys a life, it is as if he destroyed a universe. When a person saves a life, it is as if he saved a universe. They were also created singly for the sake of peace so that no one could say to others, "My ancestor was greater than yours." Lastly, the mishna concludes, it was to show the greatness of the Holy One, Blessed Be He, for when humans make many coins from one mould, they all emerge alike, but God makes each person in the same image, His image, and they are all different. Therefore we are each obliged to say, "For my sake the world was created."

There is an important point worth noting here. Monotheism is not just a set of beliefs about God. It has deep implications for our understanding of humanity as well. *Discovering God, singular and alone, humans discovered the significance of the individual, singular and alone.* Hence remarks like that of Moses, "Shall one man sin and will You be angry with the whole congregation?" (Num. 16:22). Hence also the appearance for the first time in literature of sharply individuated characters like Moses, David, Elijah, and Jeremiah alongside women like Deborah, Ruth, Naomi, and Hannah. These are not the two-dimensional representational figures of myth but rather, complex individuals who think and act as individuals.

2. Human freedom

Second is the emphasis the Torah places on personal and collective freedom. This too flows from the logic of monotheism. The gods of the ancient world were part of nature. They were more powerful than humans and they did not die, but they existed within the natural world. God of the Torah *transcends* nature because He created nature as a free act of will. Because God is free and endowed us with His image, we too are free.

This gift of freedom defines the human drama as set out in the early chapters of Genesis because it meant, fatefully, that humans could disobey God. Adam and Eve, the first humans, disobeyed the first command. Cain, the first human child, became the first murderer. By the time of Noah the world was full of violence. God "regretted that He had made human beings on the earth, and His heart was deeply troubled" (Gen. 6:6). Despite this, there is no suggestion anywhere in Tanakh that God ever considered taking back the gift of freedom. Implicit in the Torah is the radical idea that the free God seeks the free worship of free human beings.

Freedom is one of the fundamental principles of Jewish faith. Rambam codifies it as such.[5] We are each, he said, capable of becoming as righteous as Moses or as wicked as Jeroboam. The point is made both near the beginning and end of the Torah. At the beginning it is contained in a short speech by God to Cain, who He knows is in the grip of anger and about to commit an act of violence: "Why are you angry? Why is your face downcast? If you do what is right, will you not be accepted? But if you do not do what is right, sin is crouching at your door; it desires to have you, but you must master it" (Gen. 4:6–7). In other words: it is human nature to be subject to deep-seated drives that may, at times, be necessary for survival but at others are dysfunctional and destructive. We have to be able to control our passions. As Freud said, civilisation is marked by the ability to defer the gratification of instinct. Much of Torah law is dedicated to inculcating this.

At the end of the Torah, Moses, having recapitulated the history of the Israelites, poses a supreme choice: "This day I call heaven and earth as witnesses against you that I have set before you life and death, blessings and curses. Now choose life, that you and your children may live"

---

5. *Mishneh Torah, Hilkhot Teshuva* 5:3.

(Deut. 30:19). Individually and collectively we are free to choose between good and evil and *our fate is determined by our choices*. We are moral agents, and therefore responsible and called to account for what we do.

This emphasis on freedom is one of the defining characteristics of Judaism. Most other civilisations have to some extent denied it. We are, thought the Greeks, subject to fate and forces beyond our control. That is the basis of Greek tragedy. We are, said Paul, in the grip of sin, still scarred by the disobedience of the first humans. Therefore we need someone else's sacrificial act to atone for us. The Jewish belief that we are untainted by original sin, and capable of choosing between good and evil without special divine help, is not shared by all forms of Christianity, where it is known as the Pelagian heresy.

Note that Judaism does not take freedom for granted. It is not easy at either the individual or collective level. As God said to Cain, sin is crouching at the door and desires to dominate us. In neuro-scientific terms, the prefrontal cortex allows us to understand the consequences of our actions, and thus choose the good, but the limbic system – faster and more powerful – means that we are often in the grip of strong emotion. Hence the importance of the life of self-discipline engendered by the commands. Hence also the centrality of the family as the matrix of moral education. God chose Abraham, the Torah tells us, "so that he will instruct his children and his household after him that they may keep the way of the Lord by doing what is right and just" (Gen. 18:19). It takes strong families, cohesive communities, and a shared moral code to yield individuals with the strength to be free.

The same is true at the collective level. The entire burden of the Torah from the beginning of Exodus to the end of Deuteronomy is about what it is to create a free society, as opposed to the slavery the Israelites experienced in Egypt. "There is nothing more arduous than the apprenticeship of liberty," said Alexis de Tocqueville.[6] God, who created the universe in freedom, wants humankind, to whom He gave the gift of choice, to create a social universe where all can live in liberty.

6. *Democracy in America* (New York: Vintage Books, 1954), 1:256.

3. *The sanctity of life*

Third is the principle set out in the Noahide covenant – the covenant God made with Noah after the Flood, and through him with all humanity: "Whoever sheds the blood of man, by man shall his blood be shed, for in the image of God has God made man" (Gen. 9:6). Life is sacred. We are each in God's image, His only image since making images is otherwise absolutely forbidden. Therefore murder is more than a crime. It is an act of sacrilege, a dishonouring of God Himself.

In general, the Torah is a protest against the use of violence to attain human ends. The human drama can be summed up as follows: *God is free. God creates order. God gives man freedom. Man then creates chaos.* Hence the question to which the Torah, the Hebrew Bible, and Judaism as a whole, are directed: Can freedom and order coexist? The answer is the moral life as the Torah envisages it. *Morality is that shared system of self-imposed restraints that allow my freedom to coexist with yours.*

The alternative to morality is violence. Violence is the attempt to satisfy my desires at the cost of yours. I want X; you have X; you stand in the way of my having X; therefore if I am to have what I desire, I must force you to relinquish X. Violence is the imposition, by force, of my will on the world. Thus is born the rule of might. As the Athenians said to the Melians, "You know as well as we do that right, as the world goes, is only in question between equals in power, while the strong do what they can and the weak suffer what they must."[7] Or as Thrasymachus says in Plato's *Republic*, justice is whatever serves the interests of the stronger party. This is what Nietzsche saw as the fundamental principle of human existence: the will to power.

Judaism is a sustained protest against this way of life. Even God Himself, creator of the universe, rules by right, not might. That is the meaning of the story of the Exodus and why it is central to the Torah. *The supreme power intervenes in history to liberate the supremely powerless.* The reason God sent plagues against Egypt, the most powerful empire of the ancient world, was to show Egypt that *those who rule by*

7. Thucydides, "The Melian Dialogue," 5.84–116.

power are defeated by power. The reason God chose a tiny and otherwise inconsequential nation to be the bearers of His covenant was, at least in part, to show *the power of the powerless* when they have right, not might, on their side.

The alternative to power is law: law freely accepted and freely obeyed. Only by observing the rule of law – law that applies equally to the rich and poor, the powerful and powerless – do we escape the tragic cycle of freedom that begets conflict that leads to chaos, resulting in the use of force that generates tyranny, the freedom of the few and the enslavement of the many. *God reveals Himself in the form of law, because law is the constitution of liberty.* That is the moral shape of a society of freedom under the sovereignty of God.

4. Guilt, not shame

All societies need a shared moral code. They all therefore need a process of socialisation. But not all do this in the same way. The anthropologist Ruth Benedict made a fundamental distinction between *shame cultures* and *guilt cultures.* In shame cultures the highest value is honour. In guilt cultures it is righteousness, "doing what is right because it is right." In shame cultures, morality functions through a sense of what others expect from you. Shame itself is the sense of the disgrace we would suffer if others found out what we have done. Guilt has nothing to do with opinions of others and everything to do with the voice of conscience. Shame cultures are other-directed. Guilt cultures are inner-directed.[8]

This has significant consequences. One who has been shamed has been marked, tainted, stigmatised. The only way of escaping shame is to leave and live elsewhere or, in extremis, to commit suicide. Guilt cultures are different because they draw a sharp distinction between the agent and the act, the sinner and the sin. The act may be wrong, but the agent remains untainted, intact. As we say in our morning prayers, "The soul You gave me is pure," even if I have done things

---

8. *The Chrysanthemum and the Sword: Patterns of Japanese Culture* (Boston: Houghton Mifflin, 1946).

that are impure. Thus, in guilt cultures, there is always the possibility of remorse, repentance, atonement, and forgiveness. We can mend broken relationships. We can atone for sins. We can apologise and be forgiven. What we did does not hold us eternally captive. What we do in the future can atone for what we did in the past. A guilt culture is a morality of freedom. A shame culture is a morality of conformity and social control.

Much has been written about Genesis 2–3, the story of the first humans in the Garden of Eden and the first sin, eating from the fruit of the Tree of Knowledge. Few, however, have understood that it is actually a story about the difference between guilt and shame. Bernard Williams, in *Shame and Necessity*,[9] points out that shame is essentially a visual phenomenon. When you feel shame, you are experiencing or imagining what it is like to be seen doing what you did by others. The first instinct on feeling shame is to wish to be invisible or elsewhere. Guilt, by contrast, is more a phenomenon of hearing than one of seeing. It represents the inner voice of conscience. Becoming invisible or transported to somewhere else may assuage shame, but it has no effect on guilt. The voice goes with you, wherever you are.

Read the story of Adam and Eve and the forbidden fruit carefully and you will see that it is about visual phenomena and shame. At first the couple were naked and "not ashamed" (Gen. 2:25). Eve then saw that the fruit was "pleasing to the eyes" (Gen. 3:6). The couple ate the fruit and "the eyes of both of them were opened" (Gen. 3:7). They sought to cover their nakedness. For the first time they saw themselves as they might be seen by others and they experienced shame. Then they heard "the voice of God" (Gen. 3:8) and tried to hide. All of these are unmistakable signs of a shame culture. The story of Adam and Eve is not about original sin or about knowledge as such. It is about the danger of following the eyes rather than listening to the word of God with the ears. The Hebrew verb *shema*, a key term of Jewish faith, means both to "listen" or "hear" and "to obey." Judaism, the religion of the-God-who-cannot-be-seen, is a morality of guilt, not shame.

9. Berkeley: University of California Press, 1993.

5. *Loyalty and love*

The fifth principle becomes apparent as soon as we notice a strange feature of the book of Genesis. We normally think of Judaism as Abrahamic monotheism, and monotheism itself as a rejection of and protest against the polytheism of the ancient world. Yet Genesis contains not a single polemic against idolatry. Other than an obscure reference to Rachel stealing her father's *terafim*, "household gods" or "fetishes" (Gen. 31:19), there is not even one mention of it. Yet there is no doubt that the story of Genesis from chapter 12 to the end is about a single and singular family that lives differently from the nations and cultures that surround it. Of what does this difference consist?

There is a connecting theme. Whenever a member of the covenantal family leaves the matrix of the family, he or she encounters a world of sexual anomie. Three times Abraham and Isaac are forced to leave home because of famine and on each occasion feel themselves to be in danger of their lives. They will be killed so that their wives can be taken into the royal harem (Gen. 12, 20, 26). When two strangers, who turn out to be angels, visit Lot in Sodom, the people of the town surround Lot's house demanding that he bring them out for the purpose of homosexual rape. When Dina goes out to visit Shechem, she is abducted and raped by the local prince. When Joseph, in Egypt, is left alone with his master's wife, she attempts to seduce him and when he resists has him imprisoned on a false charge of rape.

Even the members of Abraham's family themselves become corrupted when they live among the people. Lot's daughters get their father drunk and have an incestuous relationship with him. Judah, who has left his brothers to live among the Canaanites, feels no qualms about having sex with a woman he takes to be a prostitute.

A truly remarkable idea is being formulated here: that there is a connection between idolatry and sexual lawlessness. And there is a corollary principle about the Abrahamic faith, that the relationship between God and humanity, and specifically between God and the people of the covenant, is one of love – love moralised, love as deed, love as commitment and mutual obligation. The biblical word *emuna*, usually translated as "faith," does not mean this at all. It is not a cognitive attribute, meaning something you believe to be true. It belongs to an entirely different sphere of discourse. It is a moral attribute and means *faithfulness*, as in a marriage. Faith in the Hebrew Bible is the story of a love – the love of God for creation, for humanity, and for a particular family, the children of Abraham, a love full of passion but one that is not always, or even often, reciprocated. Sometimes, as in the Mosaic books, it is described like the relationship between a parent and a child. At other times, particularly in the prophetic literature, it is envisaged as the love between a husband and an often faithless wife. But it is never less than love.

Judaism was the first moral system to place interpersonal love at the centre of the moral life: love of God "with all your heart, with all your soul, and with all your might" (Deut. 6:5), love of "your neighbour as yourself" (Lev. 19:18), and love of the stranger because "you know what it feels like to be a stranger" (Ex. 23:9). This was later adopted by Christianity and remains a distinctive element of the Judaeo-Christian ethic. All moral systems have at their heart a principle of justice, or reciprocal altruism: do as you would be done by. But love is something different and more demanding.

Hence the fundamental importance of sexual ethics in Judaism, and of the sanctity of marriage and the family as the matrix of society and the place where children are inducted into the moral life. This is announced early in the biblical story. In the only place where the Torah states why Abraham was chosen, it says, "For I have chosen him so that he will instruct his children and his household after him that they may keep the way of the Lord by doing what is right and just" (Gen. 18:19). Hence also the significance of circumcision as the sign of the covenant, as if to say that holiness has a direct connection with the way we conduct our sexual relations. It seems that the Torah sees the Darwinian drive to pass on one's genes to the next generation, and with it the phenomenon of the alpha male who dominates access to females, as one of the prime causes of violence within a society. Judaism is as much about the moralisation of sex as it is about the moralisation of power, and the two are connected.

6. *The ethics of covenant*

What makes marriage fundamental to the ethics of the Torah is its covenantal nature. It was Nietzsche in *The Genealogy of Morals* who argued that the primary act of the moral life is making a promise. A promise is an obligation I place myself under. It thus reconciles freedom and order – freedom, because I have chosen to obligate myself, and order because if I am trustworthy, I can be relied upon to keep my word. Covenant is essentially an exchange of promises. Two or more parties agree to be bound by certain undertakings, pledging themselves to one another in an open-ended relationship of mutual care.

Covenants were a familiar feature of the politics of the ancient Near East. They were usually peace agreements between potentially conflicting powers. The Torah takes this device and puts it to an entirely new use, to define the relationship between human beings and God and to establish the shape of the moral life. There are three covenants between God and humans in the Torah – the first with Noah and through him all humanity, the second with Abraham and his descendants, and the third with Moses and the Israelites at Mount Sinai. It was the third of these that gave Judaism its constitution of liberty under the sovereignty of God.

At Sinai the Israelites agreed to become a nation bound by a covenant with God which involved their adoption of a detailed moral and social code. They were to construct a society of justice and compassion, of freedom and human dignity, whose logic lay, in part, in their memories of exile and enslavement in Egypt. They were, in effect, charged with constructing a kind of anti-type to Egypt, one free of oppression and exploitation. At the same time they agreed to be bound by an ethic of holiness whose purpose was to remind them that the Divine Presence was in their midst. A society based on covenant is one in which individual and collective responsibility belongs to the people as a whole, and history is seen as an ongoing commentary on the moral state of the nation. Morality itself is seen not simply as a natural law inherent in creation, nor as the arbitrary will of a God who demands blind obedience, but as an agreement between God and a people in the light of their relationship over time.

Covenant generates an ethic of social responsibility. It is rooted in a sense of history and identity. It is predicated on the belief that a free society is a moral achievement and one for whose maintenance all the people share responsibility.

7. *The dual covenant*

Finally we come to the unique feature of Judaic ethics, one much mis-understood and criticised, namely the dual ethic generated by the covenant with Noah on the one hand, and with the Israelites at Sinai on the other. The first is universal, the second particular. The Noah covenant applies to all humans in virtue of their humanity, the covenant of Sinai specifically to the members of the covenanted community. This reflects the duality of the human situation.

On the one hand we recognise a special affinity towards kin – towards members of our family. This is, in fact, where the moral bond is first formed. As we grow, our sense of obligation widens to include friends, neighbours, community members, and fellow citizens. All human groups have this form, that we are duty-bound to help those within our group. Darwin recognised this, writing in *The Descent of Man*:

> A tribe including many members, who from possessing in a high degree the spirit of patriotism, fidelity, obedience, courage and sympathy, were always ready to give aid to each other and to sacrifice themselves for the common good, would be victorious over most other tribes; and this would be natural selection.[10]

We favour kin over non-kin, friends over strangers, in-group over out-group. Without this, groups would not exist at all. And we need them, because we are social animals, not isolated individuals: "It is not good for man to be alone" (Gen. 2:18). Belonging to a group is essential to the sense of identity.

On the other hand, a moral system that failed to acknowledge duties to strangers would simply generate endlessly warring tribes. Indeed, it seems to be implicit in the Torah that the Israelites experienced exile and enslavement in order to engrave this truth in collective memory: "You must not oppress strangers. You know what it feels like to be a stranger, for you yourselves were once strangers in the land of Egypt" (Ex. 23:9).

10. Darwin, *The Descent of Man* (Princeton, NJ: Princeton University Press, 1981), 166.

That is what Judaism's dual covenant represents. On the one hand we are human, and we share a set of basic obligations to one another by virtue of that fact. We are all in the image and likeness of God. We are all bound by the basic rules of justice and fairness. Every life is sacred. Violence and murder are assaults against the human condition. This is what Abraham meant when he explained to Avimelekh, king of Gerar, why he said that Sarah was his sister, not his wife: "I said to myself, 'There is surely no fear of God in this place, and they will kill me because of my wife'" (Gen. 20:11). Fear of God – identified as *Elokim* rather than *Hashem* – is assumed in Genesis to be a basic, shared set of principles as to what morality requires, even between strangers.

On the other hand, the covenant of Sinai is not addressed to humanity as a whole. It is addressed specifically to the Israelites in their role as "a kingdom of priests and a holy nation" (Ex. 19:6). This is more demanding than the Noah covenant, both because the Israelites are expected to be exemplars and role models of the holy life, and because there are strong ties of kinship between them. They share a past, a set of memories, and a fate. They are like an extended family. Much of the social legislation, for example in Leviticus 25, uses the language of kinship: "When *your brother* becomes poor...."

There have been ages in which the primary group has been the tribe. The result was war. There have also been attempts to abolish groups altogether in favour of the universal. The classic example was the European Enlightenment. However, group identity returned in the nineteenth century, in the form of the nation-state and the race. The result of European nation-states was two world wars. The worship of race brought about the Holocaust. We cannot escape identity, and hence the tension between in-group and out-group. The only solution known to me that addresses this issue clearly and in a principled way is that of the Torah with its two covenants, one representing our duties to humanity as a whole, the other our duties to our fellow members of the community of fate and faith. This unusual duality represents the two great features of the moral life: the universality of justice and the particularity of love.[11]

---

11. On this, see Jonathan Sacks, *Not in God's Name* (New York: Schocken, 2015), and Avishai Margalit, *The Ethics of Memory* (Cambridge, MA: Harvard University Press, 2002).

The eclipse of biblical morality

Those are the seven features that make biblical ethics different from other ethical systems: human dignity, freedom, the sanctity of life, repentance and forgiveness, the centrality of marriage and the family, covenant as the basis of moral obligation, and a dual ethic of justice on the one hand and love on the other. Many – perhaps all – of these beliefs are currently at risk in the contemporary West.

First, human dignity. One result of Darwinian biology has been to erode the differences between humans and other animals. We share 98 per cent of our genes with the primates. A group of distinguished scientists declared, in a statement about human cloning in 1997: "Humankind's rich repertoire of thoughts, feelings, aspirations, and hopes seems to arise from electrochemical brain processes, not from an immaterial soul that operates in ways no instrument can discover."[12] Nietzsche was the first to see that the higher our scientific achievements, the lower our self-evaluation as humans. In a prescient passage he wrote: "Gone, alas, is [man's] faith in his dignity, uniqueness, irreplaceableness, in the rank ordering of beings – he has become animal, literally, unqualifiedly and unreservedly an animal."[13] Human dignity, it seems, cannot survive the loss of the concept of the image of God.

The idea of freedom of the will has eroded in favour of a series of scientific and social-scientific determinisms: what we do is caused by social conditions, economic forces, unconscious drives, our genes, or our encoded, hard-wired instincts. It is not clear that a scientific account can or ever could be given of human freedom, since science deals with causal relationships rather than purposeful behaviour. Freedom, on this account, is an illusion. If so, it is difficult to see how the ideal of a free society could be sustained in the long run, for why should we seek collective liberty if individual freedom is nothing but an illusion?

12. The International Academy of Humanism, "Declaration in Defense of Cloning and Integrity of Scientific Research," *Free Inquiry* 17, no. 3 (Summer 1997): 11–12.
13. Nietzsche, *On the Genealogy of Morality*, ed. Keith Ansell-Pearson, trans. Carol Diethe (Cambridge, NY: Cambridge University Press, 2007), 115.

I once had a conversation, on television, with an Oxford neuroscientist who was a determinist, convinced that nothing we did, including his taking part in the television programme, was the result of a free choice. I asked him why, if this was so, we should continue to have laws, courts, trials, and a concept of justice. If someone is found breaking the law, the logical thing to do would be to treat him with psychotropic drugs or neurosurgery. He replied, "Well, I can see how in totalitarian societies people might be tempted to do that." He simply could not see that if free will does not exist, there would be no reason to *object* to totalitarianism. I prefer the witty remark of Yiddish novelist Isaac Bashevis Singer who said, "We *must* be free. We have no choice."

Third, with the legalisation of abortion for reasons other than saving the mother's life, and the campaign – already successful in a number of countries – for voluntary euthanasia and assisted dying, the West has largely lost the concept of the sanctity of life. Instead it has adopted the principle of autonomy. In this view, my life belongs to me and I can dispose of it as I wish. This is a return to the ethics of pre-Christian Greece and Rome, cultures that had no qualms about abortion, even infanticide, and euthanasia.

Fourth, with the spread of social media, the ethic of shame has returned, vividly described in Jon Ronson's book *So You've Been Publicly Shamed*.[14] Trial by media is a regression to old stigmatisation rituals. In a shame morality, what matters is appearances. The ultimate command is "Thou shalt not be found out." In a shame society it is difficult to create space for confession, repentance, forgiveness, and rehabilitation. Shame cultures tend to be deeply conformist, and can lead to rule of the mob or, as at present, the electronic crowd.

Fifth, the sanctity of marriage has disappeared from large swathes of the West. In Britain and America, almost half of all children are born outside of marriage, fewer people are marrying, those who do are marrying later, and half of all marriages end in divorce. The price has been paid by children. In the space of two generations there has been a massive rise in drug and alcohol abuse, eating disorders, stress-related syndromes,

14. London: Picador, 2015. See also Jennifer Jaquet, *Is Shame Necessary? New Uses for an Old Tool* (London: Allen Lane, 2015).

depression, and attempted suicide. There has also been a rise in child poverty, caused by the prevalence of single-parent families. It may be that in the long run the single most significant consequence will be the fall of birthrates – already below replacement levels in every European country. Europe is ageing, shrinking, and slowly dying, its population sustained only by unprecedented levels of immigration.

Sixth, the covenantal basis of society has grown weak in much of the West. In *The Home We Build Together,*[15] I argued that the idea of society-as-home has been displaced by society-as-a-hotel. Citizens pay taxes much as guests pay hotel charges, in return for which we have our room in which we can do as we choose so long as we do not disturb others. The idea that we are bound by bonds of identity, belonging, shared morality, and collective loyalty to our fellow citizens was weakened by the individualism of the 1960s and further damaged by the ill-thought-out multiculturalism of the 1980s.

Lastly, the idea of a dual covenant was rarely considered by the West, with the exception of an ethic of war: there are certain things that are morally impermissible even in a state of military conflict, because our opponents are also human and therefore possess certain inalienable rights. That concept died in the Holocaust, was resurrected in the 1948 United Nations Universal Declaration of Human Rights, and has been destroyed again in our time by groups like Al Qaeda and ISIS, who make no distinction between combatants and non-combatants and follow none of the classic rules of war.

In short, the moral tradition that shaped the West for many centuries – that, according to the Chinese Academy of Social Sciences, gave it its unique capacity to lead the world in science, technology, market economics, and democratic politics – is in real and present danger of eclipse. What will replace it will not be a free, open, tolerant, rights-respecting society, but barbarism. Plato's scenario in *The Republic* will be played out: democracy will give way to anarchy which will yield to tyranny.

A free society is a moral achievement. That is the central insight of the Torah. It depends on the existence of a shared moral code, a code we are taught by our parents, a code we internalise in the course of

15. London: Continuum, 2007.

growing up, a code for whose maintenance we are collectively responsible. Today, throughout much of the West, morality has been largely outsourced to governments and regulatory bodies. The state deals with the consequences of the breakdown of marriage and the almost total absence of a sexual ethic. Regulatory bodies become responsible for the implementation of professional ethics. People slide imperceptibly from "I have a right to do X" to "I am right to do X," meaning that whatever is not forbidden by legislation is morally permissible and therefore morally reasonable. The end result is that there is little work for morality-as-the-voice-of-conscience to do. Such a system has never succeeded for long in the past, and there is no reason to suppose that it will do so in the future.

What was born in the Torah was a remarkable moral vision. Parts of this vision may be opaque to us today and other elements have been reinterpreted by the Oral Law; however, in its basic principles it taught us to value the individual, cherish as sacred the bonds between husband and wife, parent and child, and honour the covenant binding together society as a whole. If the West loses this, people will not cease to be moral, but they will move to a moral system similar to the one that prevailed in third-century pre-Christian Greece, the age of the Epicureans and Stoics, or first-century Rome, about which Livy said, "We can endure neither our vices nor their cure." These were societies in decline.

It is therefore important that we reflect on, and open ourselves to, the Torah's ethical vision, which I have tried to do in these studies of the weekly *parasha*. Clearly they are not a systematic presentation of the subject, more a set of insights and impressions. But they remain "a Tree of Life," teaching us, at best, to love, to give, and to forgive, to seek justice and practise compassion, and to seek to do the right and the good in the sight of God and our fellow humans.

At the end of his *History of the Jews*, Paul Johnson wrote the following:

> To [the Jews] we owe the idea of equality before the law, both divine and human; of the sanctity of life and the dignity of the human person; of the individual conscience and so of personal redemption; of the collective conscience and so of social responsibility; of peace as an abstract ideal and love as the foundation of

justice, and many other items which constitute the basic moral furniture of the human mind.[16]

The moral system initiated by the Torah, honed and refined by the Oral Tradition and more than three thousand years of reflection and elucidation, remains our greatest heritage of wisdom and insight into the human condition under the sovereignty of God – and His challenge remains: to become His partner in the work of creation and healing the wounds of a fractured world.

It is not always easy to write books in the midst of the pressures of public life, which means that I have always been dependent on my office team. I have been especially blessed by my present team of Joanna Benarroch, Dan Sacker, and Debby Ifield, for whom I thank the Almighty daily. They are a joy to work with, and without their calm efficiency and devotion beyond the call of duty I doubt whether I could have written this book or any of the others these past few years.

In one of the most beautiful of Psalms, King David wrote: "Who can discern their own errors? Forgive my unperceived faults." It is always easy to get things wrong, and I have to thank two people in particular for pointing out mistakes in this as in other works: David Frei, registrar of the London Beth Din, and Professor Leslie Wagner. I am hugely in their debt. David has a range of knowledge that is simply breathtaking, and Leslie can spot faulty logic at a hundred yards. No one could ask for better or gentler friends.

My thanks as always to my publisher, Matthew Miller, my editor Gila Fine, and the team at Maggid Books – Deena Glickman, Nechama Unterman, Tali Simon, and Tomi Mager – for their wonderful enthusiasm and professionalism. It's a privilege working with them.

I owe an immense debt of thanks to Senator Joe Lieberman not only for his lovely preface to the book, but also for the way he and Hadassah have been role models in their life in the public square as well as within the Jewish community. They have been a *kiddush Hashem*. They have shown the moral beauty of our faith and its concern for justice and

16. Paul Johnson, *A History of the Jews* (New York: HarperCollins, 1987), 585.

compassion, freedom and dignity, living all that I have tried to articulate in this book. Elaine and I cherish their friendship.

I save my deepest thanks for my wife Elaine, and our children, Joshua, Dina, and Gila and their respective families. They have taught me more than I have taught them. I have watched and admired how they have lived lives of moral principle. They have inspired me by their integrity and courage, their "firmness in the right as God gives us to see the right." The world they face in this troubled century will call for the highest moral ideals. May Hashem give them and us the strength to live for what matters, to do the right thing even if it is the difficult thing, and to become, through our deeds and lives, a blessing to the world.

Jonathan Sacks
London
Tammuz 5776

Genesis
בראשית

Bereshit

The Genesis of Justice

There are words that change the world, none more so than two sentences that appear in the first chapter of the Torah:

> Then God said, "Let us make mankind in our image, in our likeness, so that they may rule over the fish in the sea and the birds in the sky, over the livestock and all the wild animals, and over all the creatures that move along the ground."
> *So God created mankind in His own image,*
> *in the image of God He created them;*
> *male and female He created them.* (Gen. 1:26–27)

The idea set forth here is perhaps the most transformative in the entire history of moral and political thought. It is the basis of the civilisation of the West with its unique emphasis on the individual and on equality. It lies behind Thomas Jefferson's words in the American Declaration of Independence, "We hold these truths to be self-evident, that all men are created equal [and] are endowed by their Creator with certain inalienable rights." These truths are anything *but* self-evident. They would have been regarded as absurd by Plato, who held that society should be based on the myth that humans are divided into people of gold, silver, and bronze and it is this that determines their status in society. Aristotle believed that some are born to rule and others to be ruled.

Revolutionary utterances do not work their magic overnight. As Rambam (Rabbi Moses ben Maimon, or Maimonides; 1135–1204) explained in *The Guide for the Perplexed*, it takes people a long time to change. The Torah functions in the medium of time. It did not abolish slavery, but it set in motion a series of developments – most notably Shabbat, when all hierarchies of power were suspended and slaves had a day a week of freedom – that were bound to lead to its abolition in the course of time. People are slow to understand the implications of ideas. Thomas Jefferson, champion of equality, was a slave owner. Slavery was not abolished in the United States until the 1860s and not without a civil war. And as Abraham Lincoln pointed out, slavery's defenders as well as its critics cited the Bible when discussing their cause. But eventually people change, and they do so because of the power of ideas, planted long ago in the Western mind.

What exactly is being said in the first chapter of the Torah? The first thing to note is that it is not a standalone utterance, an account without a context. It is in fact a polemic, a protest, against a certain way of understanding the universe. In all ancient myth the world was explained in terms of battles of the gods in their struggle for dominance. The Torah dismisses this way of thinking totally and utterly. God speaks and the universe comes into being. This, according to the great nineteenth-century sociologist Max Weber, was the end of myth and the birth of Western rationalism.

More significantly, it created a new way of thinking about the universe. Central to both the ancient world of myth and the modern world of science is the idea of power, force, energy. That is what is significantly absent from Genesis 1. God says, "Let there be," and there is. There is nothing here about power, resistance, conquest, or the play of forces. Instead, the key word of the narrative, appearing seven times, is utterly unexpected. It is the word *tov*, good.

Tov is a moral word. The Torah in Genesis 1 is telling us something radical. The reality to which Torah is a guide (the word "Torah" itself means guide, instruction, or law) is *moral* and *ethical*. The question Genesis seeks to answer is not "How did the universe come into being?" but "How then shall we live?" This is the Torah's most significant paradigm shift. The universe that God made and that we inhabit is not about power or dominance but about *tov* and *ra*, good and evil.[1] For the first time, religion was ethicised. God cares about justice, compassion, faithfulness, loving-kindness, the dignity of the individual, and the sanctity of life.

This same principle, that Genesis 1 is a polemic, part of an argument with a background, is essential to understanding the idea that God created humanity in His image, in His likeness. This language would not have been unfamiliar to the first readers of the Torah. It was a language they knew well. It was commonplace in the first civilisations, Mesopotamia and ancient Egypt. Certain people were said to be in the image of God. They were the kings of the Mesopotamian city-states and the pharaohs of Egypt. Nothing could have been more radical than to say that not just kings and rulers are God's image. We all are. Today the idea is still daring; how much more so must it have been in an age of absolute rulers with absolute power.

Understood thus, Genesis 1:26–27 is not so much a metaphysical statement about the nature of the human person as it is *a political protest against the very basis of hierarchical, class- or caste-based societies*, whether in ancient or modern times. That is what makes it the most incendiary idea in the Torah. In some fundamental sense we are all equal in dignity and ultimate worth, for we are all in God's image regardless of colour, culture, or creed.

A similar idea appears later in the Torah, in relation to the Jewish people, when God invites them to become a kingdom of priests and a holy nation. All nations in the ancient world had priests, but none was "a kingdom of priests" (Ex. 19:6). All religions have holy individuals – but

1. What I take to be the meaning of the story of Adam and Eve and the Tree of Knowledge must wait for another time. In the meantime, see Rambam, *The Guide for the Perplexed*, I:2.

none claim that every one of their members is holy. This too took time to materialise. During the entire biblical era there were hierarchies. There were priests and high priests, a holy elite. But after the destruction of the Second Temple, every prayer became a sacrifice, every leader of prayer a priest, and every synagogue a fragment of the Temple. A profound egalitarianism is at work just below the surface of the Torah, and the rabbis knew it and lived it.

A second idea is contained in the phrase, "so that they may rule over the fish in the sea and the birds in the sky." Note that there is no suggestion that anyone has the right to have dominion over any other human being. In *Paradise Lost*, Milton, like the Midrash, states that this was the sin of Nimrod, the first great ruler of Assyria and by implication the builder of the Tower of Babel (see Gen. 10:8–11). Milton writes that when Adam was told that Nimrod would "arrogate dominion undeserved," he was horrified:

> O execrable son so to aspire
> Above his Brethren, to himself assuming
> Authority usurped, from God not given:
> He gave us only over beast, fish, fowl
> Dominion absolute; that right we hold
> By his donation; but man over men
> He made not lord; such title to himself
> Reserving, human left from human free.[2]

To question the right of humans to rule over other humans without their consent was at that time utterly unthinkable. All advanced societies were like this. How could they be otherwise? Was this not the very structure of the universe? Did the sun not rule the day? Did the moon not rule the night? Was there not a hierarchy of the gods in heaven itself? Already implicit here is the deep ambivalence the Torah would ultimately show towards the very institution of kingship, the rule of "man over men."

2. *Paradise Lost*, 12.64–71.

The third implication lies in the sheer paradox of God saying, "Let us make mankind in our image, in our likeness." We sometimes forget, when reading these words, that in Judaism *God has no image or likeness*. To make an image of God is to transgress the second of the Ten Commandments and to be guilty of idolatry. Moses emphasised that at the Revelation at Sinai, "You saw no likeness, you only heard the sound of words" (Deut. 4:12).

God has no image because He is not physical. He transcends the physical universe because He created it. Therefore He is free, unconstrained by the laws of matter. That is what God means when He tells Moses that His name is "I will be what I will be" (Ex. 3:14), and later when, after the sin of the Golden Calf, He tells him, "I will have mercy on whom I will have mercy" (Ex. 33:19). God is free, and by making us in His image, He gave us also the power to be free.

This, as the Torah makes clear, was God's most fateful gift. Given freedom, humans misuse it – as we noted earlier, Adam and Eve disobey God's command; Cain murders Abel. By the end of the *parasha* we find ourselves in the world before the Flood, filled with violence to the point where God regretted that He had ever created humanity. This is the central drama of Tanakh and of Judaism as a whole. Will we use our freedom to respect order or misuse it to create chaos? Will we honour or dishonour the image of God that lives within the human heart and mind?

These are not only ancient questions. They are as alive today as ever they were in the past. The question raised by serious thinkers – ever since Nietzsche argued in favour of abandoning both God and the Judaeo-Christian ethic – is whether justice, human rights, and the unconditional dignity of the human person are capable of surviving on secular grounds alone. Nietzsche himself thought not.

In 2008, Yale philosopher Nicholas Wolterstorff published a magisterial work arguing that our Western concept of justice rests on the belief that "all of us have great and equal worth: the worth of being made in the image of God and of being loved redemptively by God."[3] There is, he insists, no secular rationale on which a similar framework of justice can be built. That is surely what John F. Kennedy meant in

3. *Justice: Rights and Wrongs* (Princeton, NJ: Princeton University Press, 2008), 393.

his Inaugural Address when he spoke of the "revolutionary beliefs for which our forebears fought," that "the rights of man come not from the generosity of the state, but from the hand of God."[4]

Momentous ideas made the West what it is, ideas like human rights, the abolition of slavery, the equal worth of all, and justice based on the principle that right is sovereign over might. All of these ultimately derived from the statement in the first chapter of the Torah that we are made in God's image and likeness. No other text has had a greater influence on moral thought, nor has any other civilisation ever held a higher vision of what we are called on to be.

4. Washington, DC, January 20, 1961.

Noaḥ

Beyond Nature

Are we naturally good or naturally bad? On this great minds have argued for a very long time indeed. Hobbes believed that we have naturally "a perpetuall and restlesse desire of Power after power, that ceaseth onely in Death."[1] We are bad, but governments and police can help limit the harm we do. Rousseau, to the contrary, believed that naturally we are good. It is society and its institutions that make us bad.[2]

The argument continues today among the neo-Darwinians. Some believe that natural selection and the struggle for survival make us, genetically, hawks rather than doves. As Michael T. Ghiselin puts it, "Scratch an 'altruist' and watch a 'hypocrite' bleed."[3] By contrast, naturalist Frans de Waal in a series of delightful books about the primates,

1. *Leviathan* (Cambridge: Cambridge University Press, 1996), 48.
2. See *Discourse on the Origin and Foundations of Inequality Among Men* (*Discours sur l'origine et les fondements de l'inégalité parmi les hommes*), 1754.
3. *The Economy of Nature and the Evolution of Sex* (Berkeley: University of California Press, 1974), 247.

including his favourite, the bonobos, shows that they can be empathic, caring, and even altruistic.[4] So by nature are we.

T. E. Hulme called this the fundamental divide between Romantics and Classicists throughout history. Romantics believed that "man was by nature good, that it was only bad laws and customs that had suppressed him. Remove all these and the infinite possibilities of man would have a chance."[5] Classicists believed the opposite, that "man is an extraordinarily fixed and limited animal whose nature is absolutely constant. It is only by tradition and organisation that anything decent can be got out of him."[6]

In Judaism, according to the sages, this was the argument between the angels when God consulted them as to whether He should or should not create humans. The angels were the "us" in "Let us make mankind." The angels of *ḥesed* (mercy) and *tzedek* (righteousness) said, "Let him be created because humans do merciful and righteous deeds." The angels of *shalom* (peace) and *emet* (truth) said, "Let him not be created because he is full of falsehood and never ceases quarrelling." What did God do? He created humans anyway and had faith that we would gradually become better and less destructive.[7] That, in secular terms, is what Harvard neuroscientist Steven Pinker argues in *The Better Angels of Our Nature*.[8]

The Torah suggests we are both destructive and constructive, and evolutionary psychology tells us why. We are born to compete and cooperate. On the one hand, life is a competitive struggle for scarce resources – so we fight and kill. On the other hand, we survive only within groups. Without habits of cooperation, altruism, and trust, we

4. See, for example, *Good-Natured: The Origins of Right and Wrong in Humans and Other Animals* (Harvard University Press, 1996); *Primates and Philosophers: How Morality Evolved* (Princeton University Press, 2006); *Chimpanzee Politics* (Johns Hopkins University Press, 2007); *The Age of Empathy: Nature's Lessons for a Kinder Society* (Broadway Books, 2009); *The Bonobo and the Atheist* (W. W. Norton, 2013); *Are We Smart Enough to Know How Smart Animals Are?* (W. W. Norton, 2016).
5. T. E. Hulme, "Romanticism and Classicism," in *T. E. Hulme: Selected Writings*, ed. Patrick McGuiness (New York: Routledge, 2003), 69.
6. Ibid., 70.
7. See Bereshit Rabba 8:5.
8. New York: Viking, 2011.

would have no groups and we would not survive. That is part of what the Torah means when it says, "It is not good for man to be alone" (Gen. 2:18).

But the Torah is much too profound to leave it at the level of the old joke: a rabbi, hearing both sides of a domestic argument, tells the husband, "You are right," and the wife, "You are right"; when his disciple says, "They can't both be right," the rabbi replies, "You are also right." The Torah states the problem, but it also supplies an answer that is not obvious. This is the clue that helps us decode a very subtle argument running through the previous *parasha* and this one.

The basic structure of the story that begins with creation and ends with Noah is this: In the beginning God created a universe of order. He then created human beings, who created a universe of chaos – "the land was filled with violence" (Gen. 6:11). So God, as it were, deleted creation by bringing the Flood, thus returning the earth to the way it was at the very beginning when "the earth was formless and empty, darkness was over the surface of the deep, and the spirit of God hovered over the waters" (Gen. 1:2). He then begins again, with Noah and his family as the new Adam and Eve and their children.

Genesis 8–9 is thus a kind of second version of Genesis 1–3, but with two differences. The first is that in both accounts a keyword appears seven times: in Genesis 1 the word is "good"; in Genesis 9 it is "covenant." The second is that in both cases, reference is made to the fact that humans are in the image of God – but the two sentences have different implications. In Genesis 1 we are told that "God created mankind in His own image, in the image of God He created them, male and female He created them" (Gen. 1:27). In Genesis 9 we read, "Whoever sheds the blood of man, by man shall his blood be shed, for in the image of God has God made man" (Gen. 9:6).

The difference is striking. Genesis 1 tells me that "I" am in the image of God. Genesis 9 tells me that "you," my potential victim, are in the image of God. Genesis 1 tells us about human *power*. We are able, says the Torah, to "rule over the fish of the sea and the birds of the air" (Gen. 1:28). Genesis 9 tells us about *the moral limits of power*. We *can* kill but we *may* not. We have the power, but not the permission.

Reading the story closely, it seems that God created humans in the faith that they would *naturally* choose the right and the good. They would not need to eat the fruit of the Tree of Knowledge of Good and Evil because instinct would lead them to behave as they should. Calculation, reflection, decision – all the things we associate with knowledge – would not be necessary. They would act as God wanted them to act, because they had been created in His own image.

It did not turn out that way. Adam and Eve sinned, Cain committed murder, and within a few generations the world was reduced to chaos. That is when we read:

> The Lord saw how great the wickedness of the human race had become on the earth, and that *every inclination of the thoughts of the human heart was only evil all the time.* The Lord regretted that He had made human beings on the earth, and His heart was deeply troubled. (Gen. 6:6)

Everything else in the universe was *tov,* "good." But humans are not naturally good. That is the problem. The answer, according to the Torah, is *covenant.*

Covenant introduces the idea of a moral law. A moral law is not the same as a natural, scientific law. Scientific laws are observed regularities in nature: drop an object and it will fall. A moral law is a rule of conduct: do not rob or steal or deceive. Scientific laws *de*scribe, whereas moral laws *pre*scribe. When a natural event does not accord with the current state of science, when it "breaks" the law, that is a sign that there is something wrong with the law. That is why Newton's laws were replaced by those of Einstein. But when a human act breaks the law, when people do rob and steal and deceive, the fault is not in the law but in the act. So we must keep the law and condemn – and sometimes punish – the act. Scientific laws allow us to predict. Moral laws help us to decide. Scientific laws apply to entities without free will. Moral laws presuppose free will. That is what makes humans qualitatively different from other forms of life.

So, according to the Torah, a new era began, centred not on the idea of natural goodness but on the concept of covenant – that is, moral law. Civilisation began in the move from what the Greeks called *physis,* nature, to *nomos,* law. That is what makes the concept of being "in the

image of God" completely different in Genesis 1 and Genesis 9. Genesis
1 is about nature and biology. We are in the image of God in the sense
that we can think, speak, plan, choose, and dominate. Genesis 9 is about
law. Other people are in God's image. Therefore we must respect them
by banning murder and instituting a system of justice. With this simple
move, morality was born.

What is the Torah telling us about morality?

First, that it is *universal*. The Torah places God's covenant with
Noah and through him all humanity *prior* to His particular covenant with
Abraham and His later covenant with his descendants at Mount Sinai.
Our universal humanity precedes our religious differences. This may well be
the single most important contribution of monotheism to civilisation.
All societies, ancient and modern, have had some form of morality but
by and large they concern only relations within the group. Hostility to
strangers is almost universal in both the animal and human kingdoms.
Between strangers, power rules. As the Athenians said to the Melians,
"The strong do what they can and the weak suffer what they must."[9]

The idea that *even the people not like us have rights*, and that we
should "love the stranger" (Deut. 10:19), would have been considered
utterly alien to most people at most times. It took the recognition that
there is one God sovereign over all humanity ("Do we not all have one
father? Did not one God create us?"; Mal. 2:10) to create the momentous
breakthrough to the principle that there are moral universals, among
them the sanctity of life, the pursuit of justice, and the rule of law.

Second, God Himself recognises that we are not naturally good.
After the Flood, He says: "I will never again curse the ground because
of humankind, even though the inclination of their minds is evil from
childhood on" (Gen. 8:21). The antidote to the *yetzer*, the inclination
to evil, is covenant.

We now know the neuroscience behind this. We have a prefrontal
cortex that evolved to allow humans to think and act reflectively, considering the consequences of their deeds. But this is slower and weaker
than the amygdala (what the Jewish mystics called the *nefesh habehemit*,
the animal soul), which produces, even before we have had time to think,

9. Thucydides, *The Peloponnesian War* 5.89.

13

the fight-or-flight reactions without which humans before civilisation would simply not have survived.

The problem is that these reactions can be deeply destructive. Often they lead to violence – not only the violence between species (predator and prey) that is part of the order of nature, but also to the more gratuitous violence that is a feature of the life of most social animals, not just humans. It is not that we only do evil. Empathy and compassion are as natural to us as are fear and aggression. The problem is that fear lies just beneath the surface of human interaction, and it threatens all else.

Daniel Goleman calls this an *amygdala hijack.* "Emotions make us pay attention right now – this is urgent – and give us an immediate action plan without having to think twice. The emotional component evolved very early: Do I eat it, or does it eat me?"[10] Impulsive action is often destructive because it is undertaken without thought of the consequences. That is why Rambam argued that many of the laws of the Torah constitute a training in virtue by making us think before we act.[11]

So the Torah tells us that naturally we are neither good nor bad but have the capacity for both. We have a natural inclination to empathy and sympathy, but we have an even stronger instinct for fear that leads to violence. That is why, in the move from Adam to Noah, the Torah shifts from nature to covenant, from *tov* to *brit*, from power to the moral limits of power. Genes are not enough. We also need the moral law.

10. Daniel Goleman, *Emotional Intelligence* (London: Bloomsbury, 1996), 13ff.
11. *Mishneh Torah, Hilkhot Temura* 4:13.

Lekh Lekha

How Perfect Were the Patriarchs and Matriarchs?

In an extraordinary series of observations on *Parashat Lekh Lekha*, Ramban (Rabbi Moses ben Nahman Girondi, or Nahmanides; 1194–1270), delivers harsh criticisms of Abraham and Sarah. The first has to do with Abraham's decision, after arriving at the land of Canaan, to leave and go to Egypt because "there was a famine in the land" (Gen. 12:1). On this Ramban says:

> Know that Abraham our father unintentionally committed a great sin by bringing his righteous wife to a stumbling block of sin on account of his fear for his life. He should have trusted that God would save him and his wife and all his belongings, for God surely has the power to help and to save. His leaving the land concerning which he had been commanded from the beginning, on account of the famine, was also a sin he committed, for in famine God would redeem him from death. It was because of this deed

that the exile in the land of Egypt at the hand of Pharaoh was decreed for his children.[1]

According to Ramban, Abraham should have stayed in Canaan; he should have had faith in God that He would sustain him despite the famine. Abraham's decision to leave was not his only error; he also put Sarah in a position of moral hazard because, as a result of going to Egypt, she was forced to tell a lie. In saying that she was Abraham's sister and not his wife, she was taken into Pharaoh's harem where she might have been forced to commit an act of adultery. This is a very harsh judgement, made more so by Ramban's further assertion that it was because of this lack of faith that Abraham's children were sentenced to exile in Egypt centuries later.

Further in the *parasha*, Ramban criticises Sarah. Despairing of having a child, she asks Abraham to sleep with her handmaid Hagar in the hope that she might bear him a child. Abraham does so, and Hagar becomes pregnant. The text then says that Hagar "began to despise her mistress" (Gen. 16:4). Sarah complains to Abraham and then "afflict[s] Hagar" (16:6) who flees from her into the desert. On this, Ramban writes:

> Our mother [Sarah] transgressed by this affliction, as did Abraham by allowing her to do so. So God heard her [Hagar's] affliction and gave her a son who would be *a wild ass of a man* to afflict the seed of Abraham and Sarah with all kinds of affliction. (Commentary to Gen. 16:6)

Here the moral judgement is easier to understand. Sarah's conduct does seem volatile and harsh. The Torah itself says that Sarah "afflicted" Hagar. Yet Ramban seems to be saying that it is this episode in the ancient past that explains Jewish suffering at the hands of Muslims (the descendants of Ishmael) in a much later age.

It is not difficult to defend Abraham and Sarah in these incidents and other commentators did so. Abraham was not to know that God would perform a miracle and save him and Sarah from famine had they

---

1. Ramban, commentary to Genesis 12:10, based on the Zohar, *Tazria*, 52a.

stayed in Canaan. Nor was he to know that the Egyptians would endanger his life and place Sarah in a moral quandary. Neither of them had been to Egypt before. They did not know in advance what to expect.

As for Sarah and Hagar, although an angel sent Hagar back, later when Ishmael and Isaac were born, Sarah once again banished Hagar. This time, though Abraham protested, God told him to do what Sarah said. So Ramban's criticisms are easily answered. Why then did he make them?

Ramban surely did not make these comments lightly. He was, I believe, driven by another consideration altogether, namely the justice of history. Why did the Israelites suffer exile and slavery in Egypt? Why in Ramban's own age were Jews subject to attack by radical Islamists, the Almohads, who brought to an end the Golden Age of Spain they had enjoyed under the more tolerant rule of the Umayyads?

Ramban believed, as we say in our prayers, that "because of our sins we were exiled from our land," but what sins had the Israelites committed in the days of Jacob that merited exile? He also believed that "the acts of the fathers are a sign for the children" (Commentary to Gen. 12:6), and that what happened in the lives of the patriarchs foreshadowed what would happen to their descendants. What had they done to Ishmael to earn the scorn of Muslims? A close reading of the biblical text pointed Ramban in the direction of Sarah's treatment of Hagar.

So Ramban's comments make sense within his reading of Jewish history, but this too is not without its difficulties. The Torah states explicitly that God may punish "the children and their children for the sin of the parents to the third and fourth generation" (Ex. 34:7) but not beyond. The rabbis further restricted this to cases where "the children continue the sins of the parents" (Rashi [Rabbi Shlomo Yitzhaki; 1040–1105], Ex. 34:7). Jeremiah (31:28) and Ezekiel (18:2) both said that no one would any more say, "The parents have eaten sour grapes and their children's teeth are set on edge." The transfer of sins across the generations is problematic, Jewishly and ethically.

What is deeply interesting about Ramban's approach to Abraham and Sarah is his willingness to point out flaws in their behaviour. This answers a fundamental question as far as our understanding of the narratives of Genesis is concerned. How are we to judge the patriarchs when their behaviour seems problematic? How do we approach Jacob taking Esau's blessing in disguise, for example, or Simeon and Levi's brutality in the course of rescuing their sister Dina?

The stories of Genesis are often morally perplexing. Rarely does the Torah pass an explicit, unequivocal verdict on people's conduct. This means that it is sometimes difficult to teach these narratives as a guide to how to behave. This state of affairs led to their systematic reinterpretation by rabbinic Midrash so that black and white take the place of subtle shades of grey. So, for example, the words "Sarah saw the son of Hagar the Egyptian ... mocking" (Gen. 21:9) were understood by the sages to mean that the thirteen-year-old Ishmael was guilty of idolatry, illicit sex, or murder. This is clearly not the plain sense of the verse. It is, instead, an interpretation that would justify Sarah's insistence that Ishmael be sent away.

Rabbi Zvi Hirsch Chajes explains that the tendency of Midrash to make the heroes seem perfect and the villains completely evil is entirely for educational reasons. The word *Torah* means "teaching" or "instruction," and it is difficult to teach ethics through stories whose characters are fraught with complexity and ambiguity. Yet the Torah *does* paint its characters in shades of grey. Why so? He gives three reasons.

The first is that the moral life is not something we understand in depth all at once. As children we hear stories of heroes and villains. We learn basic distinctions: right and wrong, good and bad, permitted and forbidden. As we grow, though, we begin to realise how difficult some decisions are. Do I go to Egypt? Do I stay in Canaan? Do I show compassion to my servant's child despite the risk that he may be a bad influence on my child who has been chosen by God for a sacred mission? Anyone who thinks such decisions are easy is not yet morally mature. So the best way of teaching ethics is to do so by way of stories that can be read at different levels at different times in our life.

Second, not only are decisions difficult. People are also complex. No one in the Torah is portrayed as perfect. Noah, the only person in Tanakh to be called righteous, ends drunk and dishevelled. Moses, Aaron, and Miriam are all punished for their sins. So is King David. Solomon, wisest of men, ends his life as a deeply compromised leader. Many of the prophets suffered dark nights of despair. "There is none so righteous on earth," says Ecclesiastes, "as to do only good and never sin" (Eccl. 7:20). No religious literature was ever further from hagiography, idealisation, and hero worship.

In the opposite direction, even the non-heroes have their saving graces. Esau is a loving son, and when he meets his brother Jacob after a long estrangement, they kiss, embrace, and go their separate ways. Levi, condemned by Jacob for his violence, counts Moses, Aaron, and Miriam among his grandchildren. Even Pharaoh, the man who enslaved the Israelites, had a moral heroine for a daughter. The descendants of Korah sang psalms in the Temple of Solomon. This too is moral maturity, light years removed from the dualism adopted by many religions – including some Jewish sects (like the Qumran sect of the Dead Sea Scrolls) – that divides humanity into children of light and children of darkness.

Lastly and most important, more than any other religious literature, the Torah makes an absolute distinction between earth and heaven, between God and human beings. Because God is God, there is space for humans to be human. In Judaism the line dividing them is never blurred. How rare this is was pointed out by Walter Kaufmann:

> In India, the Jina and the Buddha, founders of two new religions in the sixth century BCE, came to be worshipped later by their followers. In China, Confucius and Lao-tze came to be deified. To the non-Christian, Jesus seems to represent a parallel case. In Greece, the heroes of the past were held to have been sired by a god or to have been born of goddesses, and the dividing line between gods and men became fluid. In Egypt, the Pharaoh was considered divine.[2]

In Israel, says Kaufmann, "no man was ever worshipped or accorded even semi-divine status. This is one of the most extraordinary facts about the religion of the Old Testament."[3] There never was a cult of Moses or any other biblical figure. That is why "no man knows Moses' burial place to this day" (Deut. 34:6) – so that it could never become a place of pilgrimage.

2. *The Faith of a Heretic* (Princeton, NJ: Princeton University Press, 2015), 187–88.
3. Ibid., 188.

No religion has held a higher view of humanity than the book that tells us we are each in the image and likeness of God. Yet none has been more honest about the failings of even the greatest. God does not ask us to be perfect. He asks us, instead, to take risks in pursuit of the right and the good, and to acknowledge the mistakes we will inevitably make.

In Judaism the moral life is about learning and growing, knowing that even the greatest have failings and even the worst have saving graces. It calls for humility about ourselves and generosity towards others. This unique blend of idealism and realism is morality at its most demanding and mature.

Vayera

The Binding of Isaac

Take your son, your only son, the one you love – Isaac – and go to the land of Moriah. Offer him there as a burnt offering on a mountain I will show you" (Gen. 22:2). Thus begins one of the most famous episodes in the Torah, but also one of the most morally problematic. The conventional reading of this passage is that Abraham was being asked to show that his love for God was supreme. He would show this by being willing to sacrifice the son for whom he had spent a lifetime waiting. Why did God need to test Abraham, given that He knows the human heart better than we know it ourselves? Rambam answers that God did not need Abraham to prove his love for Him. Rather the test was meant to establish for all time how far the fear and love of God must go.[1]

On this principle there was little argument. The story is about the awe and love of God. Kierkegaard wrote a book about it, *Fear and Trembling*,[2] and made the point that ethics is universal. It consists of

---

1. *The Guide for the Perplexed*, III:24.
2. Søren Kierkegaard, *Fear and Trembling* and *The Sickness unto Death* (Garden City, NY: Doubleday, 1954).

general rules. But the love of God is particular. It is an I-Thou personal relationship. What Abraham underwent during the trial was, says Kierkegaard, a "teleological suspension of the ethical," that is, a willingness to let the I-Thou love of God overrule the universal principles that bind humans to one another.

Rabbi Soloveitchik explained the episode in terms of his own well-known characterisation of the religious life as a dialectic between victory and defeat, majesty and humility, man-the-creative-master and man-the-obedient-servant.[3] There are times when "God tells man to withdraw from whatever man desires the most."[4] We must experience defeat as well as victory. Thus the binding of Isaac was not a once-only episode but rather a paradigm for the religious life as a whole. Wherever we have passionate desire – eating, drinking, physical relationships – there the Torah places limits on the satisfaction of desire. Precisely because we pride ourselves on the power of reason, the Torah includes *ḥukkim*, statutes, that are impenetrable to reason.

These are the conventional readings and they represent the mainstream of tradition. However, since there are "seventy faces to the Torah," I want to argue for a different interpretation. The reason I do so is that one test of the validity of an interpretation is whether it coheres with the rest of the Torah, Tanakh, and Judaism as a whole. There are four problems with the conventional reading:

1. We know from Tanakh and independent evidence that the willingness to offer up your child as a sacrifice was not rare in the ancient world. It was commonplace. Tanakh mentions that Mesha, king of Moab, did so. So did Yiftaḥ, the least admirable leader in the book of Judges. Two of Tanakh's most wicked kings, Ahaz and Menashe, introduced the practice into Judah, for which they were condemned. There is archaeological evidence – the bones of thousands of young children – that child sacrifice was widespread in Carthage and other Phoenician sites. It was a pagan practice.

3. Joseph Soloveitchik, "Majesty and Humility," *Tradition* 17:2 (Spring 1978): 25–37.
4. Ibid., 36.

2. Child sacrifice is regarded with horror throughout Tanakh. Micah asks rhetorically, "Shall I give my firstborn for my sin, the fruit of my body for the sin of my soul?" (Mic. 6:7), and replies, "He has shown you, O man, what is good. And what does the Lord require of you? To act justly and to love mercy and to walk humbly with your God" (6:8). How could Abraham serve as a role model if what he was prepared to do is what his descendants were commanded not to do?

3. Specifically, Abraham was chosen to be a role model as a father. God says of him, "For I have chosen him *so that he will instruct his children and his household after him that they may keep the way of the Lord by doing what is right and just*" (Gen. 18:19). How could he serve as a model father if he was willing to sacrifice his child? To the contrary, he should have said to God: "If you want me to prove to You how much I love You, then take me as a sacrifice, not my child."

4. As Jews – indeed as humans – we must reject Kierkegaard's principle of the "teleological suspension of the ethical." This is an idea that gives carte blanche to a religious fanatic to commit crimes in the name of God. It is the logic of the Inquisition and the suicide bomber. It is not the logic of Judaism rightly understood.[5] God does not ask us to be unethical. We may not always understand ethics from God's perspective but we believe that "He is the Rock, His works are perfect; all His ways are just" (Deut. 32:4).

To understand the binding of Isaac we have to realise that much of the Torah, Genesis in particular, is a polemic against worldviews the Torah considers pagan, inhuman, and wrong. One institution to which Genesis is opposed is the ancient family as described by Fustel de Coulanges in *The Ancient City* (1864)[6] and recently restated by Larry Siedentop in *Inventing the Individual: The Origins of Western Liberalism*.[7]

---

5. For more on this subject, see Jonathan Sacks, *Not in God's Name* (New York: Schocken, 2015).
6. *The Ancient City: A Study on the Religion, Laws, and Institutions of Greece and Rome* (Garden City, NY: Doubleday, 1956).
7. London: Penguin, 2014.

Before the emergence of the first cities and civilisations, the fundamental social and religious unit was the family. As Coulanges puts it, in ancient times there was an intrinsic connection between three things: the domestic religion, the family, and the right to property. Each family had its own gods, among them the spirits of dead ancestors, from whom it sought protection and to whom it offered sacrifices. The authority of the head of the family, the paterfamilias, was absolute. He had the power of life and death over his wife and children. Authority invariably passed, on the death of the father, to his firstborn son. Meanwhile, as long as the father lived, children had the status of property rather than the status of persons in their own right. This idea persisted even beyond the biblical era in the Roman law principle of *patria potestas*.

The Torah is opposed to every element of this worldview. As anthropologist Mary Douglas notes, one of the most striking features of the Torah is that it includes no sacrifices to dead ancestors.[8] Seeking the spirits of the dead is explicitly forbidden. Equally noteworthy is the fact that in the early narratives, succession does *not* pass to the firstborn: not to Ishmael but Isaac, not to Esau but Jacob, not to the tribe of Reuben but to Levi (priesthood) and Judah (kingship), not to Aaron but to Moses.

The principle to which the entire story of Isaac, from birth to binding, is opposed is the idea that *a child is the property of the father*. First, Isaac's birth is miraculous. Sarah is already post-menopausal when she conceives. In this respect the Isaac story is parallel to that of the birth of Samuel to Hannah, who, like Sarah, is also unable naturally to conceive. That is why when Samuel is born Hannah says, "I prayed for this child, and the Lord has granted me what I asked of Him. So now I *give him to the Lord*. For his whole life he will be *given over to the Lord*" (I Sam. 1:27). This passage is the key to understanding the message from heaven telling Abraham to stop: "Now I know that you fear God, *because you have not withheld from Me your son*, your only son" (the statement appears twice, in Gen. 22:12 and 16). The test was not whether Abraham would sacrifice his son but whether he would *give him over* to God.

The same principle recurs in the book of Exodus. First, Moses' survival is semi-miraculous since he was born at a time when Pharaoh

8. *Leviticus as Literature* (Oxford: Oxford University Press, 1999).

had decreed that every male Israelite child should be killed. Secondly, during the tenth plague, when every firstborn Egyptian child died, the Israelite firstborn were miraculously saved. "Consecrate to Me every firstborn male. The first offspring of every womb among the Israelites *belongs to Me*, whether human or animal" (Ex. 13:2). The firstborn were originally designated to serve God as priests, but lost this role after the sin of the Golden Calf. Nonetheless, a memory of this original role still persists in the ceremony of *Pidyon HaBen*, redemption of a firstborn son.

What God was doing when He asked Abraham to offer up his son was not requesting a child sacrifice but something quite different. He wanted Abraham to *renounce ownership* of his son. He wanted to establish as a non-negotiable principle of Jewish law that *children are not the property of their parents*.

That is why three of the four matriarchs found themselves unable to conceive other than by a miracle. The Torah wants us to know that the children they bore were the children of God rather than the natural outcome of a biological process. Eventually, the entire nation of Israel would be called the children of God. A related idea is conveyed by the fact that God chose as His spokesperson Moses, who was "not a man of words" (Ex. 4:10). He was a stammerer. Moses became God's spokesman because people knew that the words he spoke were not his own but those placed in his mouth by God.

The clearest evidence for this interpretation is given at the birth of the very first human child. When she first gives birth, Eve says: "With the help of the Lord I have acquired [*kaniti*] a man" (Gen. 4:1). That child, whose name comes from the verb "to acquire," was Cain, who became the first murderer. If you seek to own your children, your children may rebel into violence.

If the analysis of Fustel de Colanges and Larry Siedentop is correct, it follows that something fundamental was at stake. *As long as parents believed they owned their children, the concept of the individual could not yet be born.* The fundamental unit was the family. The Torah represents the birth of the individual as the central figure in the moral life. Because children – all children – belong to God, parenthood is not ownership but guardianship. As soon as they reach the age of maturity (traditionally, twelve for girls, thirteen for boys) children become independent moral agents with their own dignity and freedom.[9]

Sigmund Freud famously had something to say about this too. He held that a fundamental driver of human identity is the Oedipus complex, the conflict between fathers and sons as exemplified in Sophocles' tragedy.[10] *By creating moral space between fathers and sons, Judaism offers a non-tragic resolution to this tension.* If Freud had taken his psychology from the Torah rather than from Greek myth, he might have arrived at a more hopeful view of the human condition.

Why then did God say to Abraham about Isaac: "Offer him up as a burnt offering"? So as to make clear to all future generations that the reason Jews condemn child sacrifice is not because they lack the courage to perform it. Abraham is the proof that they do not lack the courage. The reason they do not do so is because God is the God of life, not death. In Judaism, as the laws of purity and the rite of the Red Heifer show, death is not sacred. Death defiles.

The Torah is revolutionary not only in relation to society but also in relation to the family. To be sure, the Torah's revolution was not fully completed in the course of the biblical age. Slavery had not yet been abolished. The rights of women had not yet been fully actualised. But the birth of the individual – the integrity of each of us as a moral agent in our own right – was one of the great moral revolutions in history.

9. It is perhaps no accident that the figure who most famously taught the idea of "the child's right to respect" was Janusz Korczak, creator of the famous orphanage in Warsaw, who perished together with the orphans in Treblinka. See Tomek Bogacki, *The Champion of Children: The Story of Janusz Korczak* (New York: Frances Foster Books, 2009).
10. He argued, in *Totem and Taboo* (New York: Norton, 1952), that the Oedipus complex was central to religion also.

Ḥayei Sara

The Kindness of Strangers

In 1966 an eleven-year-old black boy moved with his parents and family to a white neighbourhood in Washington, DC.[1] Sitting with his two brothers and two sisters on the front step of the house, he waited to see how they would be greeted. They were not. Passersby turned to look at them but no one gave them a smile or even a glance of recognition. All the fearful stories he had heard about how whites treated blacks seemed to be coming true. Years later, writing about those first days in their new home, he says, "I knew we were not welcome here. I knew we would not be liked here. I knew we would have no friends here. I knew we should not have moved here."[2]

As he was thinking those thoughts, a white woman coming home from work passed by on the other side of the road. She turned to the children and, with a broad smile, said, "Welcome!" Disappearing into the house, she emerged minutes later with a tray laden with drinks and cream cheese and jelly sandwiches which she brought over to the

1. Stephen Carter, *Civility* (New York: Basic Books, 1999), 61–75.
2. Ibid., 62.

children, making them feel at home. That moment – the young man later wrote – changed his life. It gave him a sense of belonging where there was none before. It made him realise, at a time when race relations in the United States were still fraught, that a black family could feel at home in a white area and that there could be relationships that were colour-blind. Over the years, he learned to admire much about the woman across the street, but it was that first spontaneous act of greeting that became, for him, a definitive memory. It broke down a wall of separation and turned strangers into friends.

The young man, Stephen Carter, eventually became a law professor at Yale and wrote a book about what he learned that day. He called it *Civility*. The name of the woman, he tells us, was Sara Kestenbaum, and she died all too young. He adds that it was no coincidence that she was a religious Jew. "In the Jewish tradition," he notes, such civility is called *ḥesed* – "the doing of acts of kindness – which is in turn derived from the understanding that human beings are made in the image of God." Civility, he adds, "itself may be seen as part of [*ḥesed*]: it does indeed require kindnesses towards our fellow citizens, including the ones who are strangers, and even when it is hard." To this day, he adds, "I can close my eyes and feel on my tongue the smooth, slick sweetness of the cream cheese and jelly sandwiches that I gobbled on that summer afternoon when I discovered how a single act of genuine and unassuming civility can change a life forever."[3]

I never knew Sara Kestenbaum, but years after I had read Carter's book I gave a lecture to the Jewish community in the part of Washington where she had lived. I told them Carter's story, which they had not heard before. But they nodded in recognition. "Yes," one said, "that's the kind of thing Sara would do."

Something like this thought was surely in the mind of Abraham's servant, unnamed in the text but traditionally identified as Eliezer, when he arrived at Nahor in Aram Naharaim, northwest Mesopotamia, to find a wife for his master's son. Abraham had not told him to look for any specific traits of character. He had simply told him to find someone from his own extended family. Eliezer, however, formulated a test:

3. Ibid., 71–72.

Lord, God of my master Abraham, make me successful today, and show kindness to my master Abraham. See, I am standing beside this spring, and the daughters of the townspeople are coming out to draw water. May it be that when I say to a young woman, "Please let down your jar that I may have a drink," and she says, "Drink, and I will water your camels too" – let her be the one You have chosen for Your servant Isaac. By this I will know that You have shown kindness [*ḥesed*] to my master. (Gen. 24:12–14)

His use of the word *ḥesed* here is no accident, for it is the very characteristic he is looking for in the future wife of the first Jewish child, Isaac, and he found it in Rebecca.

It is the theme, also, of the book of Ruth. It is Ruth's kindness to Naomi, and Boaz's to Ruth, that the Tanakh seeks to emphasise in sketching the background to David, their great-grandson, who would become Israel's greatest king. Indeed the sages said that the three characteristics most important to Jewish character are modesty, compassion, and kindness.[4] *Ḥesed*, what I have defined elsewhere as "love as deed,"[5] is central to the Jewish value system.

The sages based it on the acts of God Himself. R. Simlai taught:

The Torah begins with an act of kindness and ends with an act of kindness. It begins with God clothing the naked – "The Lord God made for Adam and his wife garments of skin and clothed them" (Gen. 3:21) – and it ends with Him caring for the dead: "And He [God] buried [Moses] in the valley" (Deut. 34:6). (Sota 14a)

Ḥesed – providing shelter for the homeless, food for the hungry, or assistance to the poor; visiting the sick, comforting mourners, and providing a dignified burial for all – became constitutive of Jewish life. During the many centuries of exile and dispersion Jewish communities were built around these needs. There were *ḥevrot*, "friendly societies," for each of them.

---

4. Numbers Rabba 8:4.
5. Jonathan Sacks, *To Heal a Fractured World* (New York: Schocken, 2005), 44–56.

In seventeenth-century Rome, for example, there were seven societies dedicated to the provision of clothes, shoes, linen, beds, and warm winter bed coverings for children, the poor, widows, and prisoners. There were two societies providing trousseaus, dowries, and the loan of jewellery to poor brides. There was one for visiting the sick, another bringing help to families who had suffered bereavement, and others to perform the last rites for those who had died – purification before burial and the burial service itself. Eleven fellowships existed for educational and religious aims – study and prayer, another raised alms for Jews living in the Holy Land, and others were involved in the various activities associated with the circumcision of new-born boys. Yet others provided the poor with the means to fulfil commands such as mezuzot for their doors, oil for the Hanukka lights, and candles for Shabbat.[6]

Hesed, said the sages, is in some respects higher even than *tzedaka*:

> Our masters taught: loving-kindness [*hesed*] is greater than charity [*tzedaka*] in three ways. Charity is done with one's money, while loving-kindness may be done with one's money or with one's person. Charity is done only to the poor, while loving-kindness may be given both to the poor and to the rich. Charity is given only to the living, while loving-kindness may be shown to the living and the dead. (Sukka 49b)

Hesed in its many forms became synonymous with Jewish life and one of the pillars on which it stood. Jews performed kindnesses to one another because it was "the way of God" and also because they or their families had had intimate experience of suffering and knew they had nowhere else to turn. It provided an access of grace in dark times. It softened the blow of the loss of the Temple and its rites:

> Once, as R. Yohanan was walking out of Jerusalem, R. Yehoshua followed him. Seeing the Temple in ruins, he cried, "Woe to us that this place is in ruins, the place where atonement was made

---

6. Israel Abrahams, *Jewish Life in the Middle Ages* (London: Edward Goldston, 1932), 348–363.

for Israel's iniquities." R. Yoḥanan said to him: "My son, do not grieve, for we have another means of atonement which is no less effective. What is it? It is deeds of loving-kindness, about which Scripture says, 'I desire loving-kindness and not sacrifice'" (Hos. 6:6).[7]

Through *ḥesed*, Jews humanised fate as, they believed, God's *ḥesed* humanises the world. As God acts towards us with love, so we are called on to act lovingly to one another. The world does not operate solely on the basis of impersonal principles like power or justice, but also on the deeply personal basis of vulnerability, attachment, care and concern, recognising us as individuals with unique needs and potentialities.

It also added a word to the English language. In 1535 Myles Coverdale published the first-ever translation of the Hebrew Bible into English (the work had been begun by William Tyndale who paid for it with his life, burnt at the stake in 1536). It was when he came to the word *ḥesed* that he realised that there was no English word which captured its meaning. It was then that, to translate it, he coined the word "loving-kindness."

The late Rabbi Abraham Joshua Heschel used to say, "When I was young I admired cleverness. Now that I am old I find I admire kindness more." There is deep wisdom in those words. It is what led Eliezer to choose Rebecca to become Isaac's wife and thus the first Jewish bride. Kindness brings redemption to the world and, as in the case of Stephen Carter, it can change lives. Wordsworth was right when he wrote that the "best portion of a good man's [and woman's] life" is their "little, nameless, unremembered, acts / Of kindness and of love."[8]

7. *Avot DeRabbi Natan*, 4.
8. From his poem, "Tintern Abbey."

Toledot

Was Jacob Right to Take the Blessings?

Was Jacob right to take Esau's blessing in disguise? Was he right to deceive his father and to take from his brother the blessing Isaac sought to give him? Was Rebecca right in conceiving the plan in the first place and encouraging Jacob to carry it out? These are fundamental questions. What is at stake is not just biblical interpretation but the moral life itself. How we read a text shapes the kind of people we become.

Here is one way of interpreting the narrative: Rebecca was right to propose what she did and Jacob was right to do it. Rebecca knew that it would be Jacob, not Esau, who would continue the covenant and carry the mission of Abraham into the future. She knew this for two separate reasons. First, she had heard it from God Himself, in the oracle she received before the twins were born:

> Two nations are in your womb,
> and two peoples from within you will be separated;

one people will be stronger than the other,
and the elder will serve the younger. (Gen. 25:23)

Esau was the elder, Jacob the younger. Therefore it was Jacob who would emerge with greater strength, Jacob who was chosen by God.

Second, she had watched the twins grow up. She knew that Esau was a hunter, a man of violence. She had seen that he was impetuous, mercurial, a man of impulse rather than calm reflection. She had seen him sell his birthright for a bowl of soup. She had watched while he "ate, drank, rose, and left. So Esau despised his birthright" (Gen. 25:34). No one who despises his birthright can be the trusted guardian of a covenant intended for eternity.

Third, just before the episode of the blessing we read: "When Esau was forty years old, he married Judith daughter of Beeri the Hittite, and also Basemath daughter of Elon the Hittite. They were a source of grief to Isaac and Rebecca" (Gen. 26:34). This too was evidence of Esau's failure to understand what the covenant required. By marrying Hittite women he proved himself indifferent both to the feelings of his parents and to the self-restraint in the choice of marriage partner that was essential to being Abraham's heir.

The blessing had to go to Jacob. If you had two sons, one indifferent to art, the other an art-lover and aesthete, to whom would you leave the Rembrandt that has been part of the family heritage for generations? And if Isaac did not understand the true nature of his sons, if he was "blind" not only physically but also psychologically, might it not be necessary to deceive him? He was by now old, and if Rebecca had failed in the early years to get him to see the true nature of their children, was it likely that she could do so now?

This was, after all, not just a matter of relationships within the family. It was about God and destiny and spiritual vocation. It was about the future of an entire people, since God had repeatedly told Abraham that he would be the ancestor of a great nation who would be a blessing to humanity as a whole. And if Rebecca was right, then Jacob was right to follow her instructions.

This was the woman whom Abraham's servant had chosen to be the wife of his master's son, because she was kind, because at the well she had given water to a stranger and to his camels as well. Rebecca was not Lady Macbeth. She was the embodiment of loving-kindness. She was not acting out of favouritism or ambition. And if she had no other way of ensuring that the blessing went to one who would cherish it and live it, then in this case the end justified the means. This is one way of reading the story and it is taken by many of the commentators.

However, it is not the only way.[1] Consider, for example, the scene that transpired immediately after Jacob left his father. Esau returned from hunting and brought Isaac the food he had requested. We then read this:

> Isaac trembled violently and said, "Who was it, then, that hunted game and brought it to me? I ate it just before you came and I blessed him – and indeed he will be blessed!"
>
> When Esau heard his father's words, he burst out with a loud and bitter cry and said to his father, "Bless me – me too, my father!"
>
> But he said, "Your brother came deceitfully [*bemirma*] and took your blessing."
>
> Esau said, "Is he not rightly named Jacob? This is the second time he has taken advantage of me: he took my birthright, and now he has taken my blessing!" Then he asked, "Have you not reserved any blessing for me?" (Gen. 27:33–36)

It is impossible to read Genesis 27 – the text as it stands without commentary – and not to feel sympathy for Isaac and Esau rather than Rebecca and Jacob. The Torah is sparing in its use of emotion. It is completely silent, for example, on the feelings of Abraham and Isaac as they journeyed together towards the trial of the binding. Phrases like

---

1. Critical readings of Rebecca's or Jacob's conduct appear in several midrashic works: Genesis Rabba, *Tanḥuma* (Buber), *Yalkut Reuveni*, *Midrash HaNe'elam*, and *Midrash Shoḥer Tov* (to Ps. 80:6). Among critical commentators are Rabbi Eliezer Ashkenazi, *Tzeda LaDerekh*, and Rabbi Yaakov Tzvi Mecklenberg in *HaKetav VeHaKabbala*. All these interpretations are based on the textual clues cited in what follows.

"trembled violently" and "burst out with a loud and bitter cry" cannot but affect us deeply. Here is an old man who has been deceived by his younger son, and a young man, Esau, who feels cheated out of what was rightfully his. The emotions triggered by this scene stay with us long in the memory.

Then consider the consequences. Jacob had to leave home for more than twenty years in fear of his life. He then suffered an almost identical deceit practised against him by Laban when he substituted Leah for Rachel. When Jacob cried out, "Why did you deceive me [*rimitani*]?" Laban replied: "It is *not done in our place* to put the younger before the elder" (Gen. 29:25–26). Not only the act but even the words imply a punishment, measure for measure. "Deceit," of which Jacob accuses Laban, is the very word Isaac used about Jacob. Laban's reply sounds like a virtually explicit reference to what Jacob had done, as if to say, "We do not do in our place what you have just done in yours."

The result of Laban's deception brought grief to the rest of Jacob's life. There was tension between Leah and Rachel. There was hatred between their children. Jacob was deceived yet again, this time by his sons, when they brought him Joseph's bloodstained robe – another deception of a father by his children involving the use of clothes. The result was that Jacob was deprived of the company of his most beloved son for twenty-two years, just as Isaac was of Jacob.

Asked by Pharaoh how old he was, Jacob replied, "Few and evil have been the years of my life" (Gen. 47:9). He is the only figure in the Torah to make a remark like this. It is hard not to read the text as a precise statement of the principle of measure for measure: As you have done to others, so will others do to you. The deception brought all concerned great grief, and this persisted into the next generation.

My reading of the text is therefore this.[2] The phrase in Rebecca's oracle, *verav yaavod tzair* (Gen. 25:23), is in fact ambiguous. It may mean, "The elder will serve the younger," but it may also mean, "The younger will serve the elder." It is what the Torah calls a *hidda* (Num. 12:8), that is, an opaque, deliberately ambiguous communication. It suggested an

2. For a more detailed explanation, see *Covenant & Conversation: Genesis – The Book of Beginnings* (Jerusalem: Maggid, 2009), 153–158, 219–228.

ongoing conflict between the two sons and their descendants, but did not foretell who would win.

Isaac fully understood the nature of his two sons. He loved Esau but this did not blind him to the fact that Jacob would be the heir of the covenant. Therefore Isaac prepared two sets of blessings, one for Esau, the other for Jacob. He blessed Esau (Gen. 27:28–29) with the gifts he felt he would appreciate, wealth and power: "May God give you heaven's dew and earth's richness – an abundance of grain and new wine" – that is, wealth; "May nations serve you and peoples bow down to you. Be lord over your brothers, and may the sons of your mother bow down to you" – that is, power. These are *not* the covenantal blessings.

The covenantal blessings that God had given Abraham and Isaac were completely different. They were about *children* and a *land*. It was this blessing that Isaac later gave Jacob before he left home (Gen. 28:3–4): "May God Almighty bless you and make you fruitful and increase your numbers until you become a community of peoples" – that is, children; "May He give you and your descendants the blessing given to Abraham, so that you may take possession of the land where you now reside as a foreigner, the land God gave to Abraham" – that is, land. *This was the blessing Isaac had intended for Jacob all along.* There was no need for deceit and disguise.

Jacob eventually came to understand all this, perhaps during his wrestling match with the angel during the night before his meeting with Esau after their long estrangement. What happened at that meeting is incomprehensible unless we understand that Jacob was giving back to Esau the blessings he had wrongly taken from him. The massive gift of sheep, cattle, and other livestock represented "heaven's dew and earth's richness" – that is, wealth. The fact that Jacob bowed down seven times to Esau was his way of fulfilling the words, "May the sons of your mother bow down to you" – that is, power.

Jacob gave the blessing back. Indeed, he said so explicitly. He said to Esau: "Please accept the blessing [*birkati*] that was brought to you, for God has been gracious to me and I have all I need" (Gen. 33:11). In this reading of the story, Rebecca and Jacob made a mistake – a forgivable one, an understandable one, but a mistake nonetheless. *The blessing Isaac was about to give Esau was not the blessing of Abraham.* He intended to give Esau a blessing appropriate to him. In so doing, he was acting on the basis of precedent. God had blessed Ishmael with the words, "I will make him into a great nation" (Gen. 21:18). This was the fulfilment of a promise God had given Abraham many years before when He told him that it would be Isaac, not Ishmael, who would continue the covenant:

> Abraham said to God, "If only Ishmael might live under Your blessing!" Then God said, "Yes, but your wife Sarah will bear you a son, and you will call him Isaac. I will establish My covenant with him as an everlasting covenant for his descendants after him. As for Ishmael, I have heard you: *I will surely bless him*; I will make him fruitful and will greatly increase his numbers. He will be the father of twelve rulers, and I will make him into a great nation." (Gen. 17:18–21)

Isaac surely knew this because, according to midrashic tradition, he and Ishmael were reconciled later in life. We see them standing together at Abraham's grave (Gen. 25:9). It may be that this was a fact that Rebecca did not know. She associated blessing with covenant. She may have been unaware that Abraham wanted Ishmael blessed even though he would not inherit the covenant, and that God had acceded to the request.

If so then *it is possible all four people acted rightly as they understood the situation, yet still tragedy occurred.* Isaac was right to wish Esau blessed in the same way as Abraham had wanted Ishmael blessed. Esau acted honourably towards his father. Rebecca sought to safeguard the future of the covenant. Jacob felt qualms but did what his mother said, knowing she would not have proposed deceit without a strong moral reason for doing so.

Do we have here one story with two possible interpretations? Perhaps, but that is not the best way of describing it. What we have here, and there are other such examples in Genesis, is a story we understand one way the first time we hear it, and a different way once we have discovered and reflected on all that happened later. It is only after we have read about the fate of Jacob in Laban's house, the tension between Leah and Rachel, and the animosity between Joseph and his brothers that we can go back and read Genesis 27, the chapter of the blessing, in a new light and with greater depth.

There is such a thing as an honest mistake, and it is a mark of Jacob's greatness that he recognised it and made amends to Esau. In the great encounter twenty-two years later, the estranged brothers met, embraced, parted, and went their separate ways. But first, Jacob had to wrestle with an angel.

That is how the moral life is. We learn by making mistakes. We live life forwards, but we understand it only looking back. Only then do we see the wrong turns we inadvertently made. This discovery is sometimes our greatest moment of moral truth.

Each of us has a blessing that is our own. That was true not just of Isaac but also of Ishmael, not just of Jacob but also of Esau. The moral could not be more powerful. Never seek your brother's blessing. Be content with your own.[3]

---

3. This message later became the tenth of the Ten Commandments.

Vayetzeh

Love Is Not Enough

Judaism is supremely a religion of love: three loves. "You shall love the Lord your God with all your heart, with all your soul, and with all your might" (Deut. 6:5); "You shall love your neighbour as yourself" (Lev. 19:18); and "You shall love the stranger, for you were once strangers in the land of Egypt" (Deut. 10:19).[1]

Not only is Judaism a religion of love – it was the first civilisation to place love at the centre of the moral life. C. S. Lewis and others pointed out that all great civilisations contain something like the golden rule – act towards others as you would wish them to act towards you,[2] or, in Hillel's negative formulation, do not do to others what you would hate them to do to you (Shabbat 31a). This is what game theorists call reciprocal altruism or tit-for-tat. Some form of this (especially the variant devised by Martin Nowak of Harvard called

---

1. See also Leviticus 19:33–34.
2. C. S. Lewis, *The Abolition of Man* (New York: Macmillan, 1947).

41

"generous") has been proven by computer simulation to be the best strategy for the survival of any group.[3]

Judaism is also about justice. Albert Einstein spoke about the "almost fanatical love of justice" that made him thank his lucky stars that he was born a Jew.[4] The only place in the Torah to explain why Abraham was chosen to be the founder of a new faith states, "For I have chosen him so that he will instruct his children and his household after him that they may keep the way of the Lord by doing what is right and just" (Gen. 18:19). So why the combination of justice and love? Why is love alone not enough?

Parashat Vayetzeh contains a gripping passage of only a few words that gives us the answer. Recall the background: Jacob, fleeing home, is taking refuge with his uncle Laban. He falls in love with Rachel, Laban's younger daughter. He works for seven years so that he can marry her. The wedding night comes and a deception is practised on him. When he wakes up the next morning he discovers that he has married Rachel's elder sister Leah. Livid, he confronts Laban. Laban replies: "It is not done in our place to marry the younger before the elder" (Gen. 29:26). He tells Jacob he can marry Rachel as well, in return for another seven years of work.

We then read, or rather hear, a series of very poignant words. To understand their impact we have to recall that in ancient times until the invention of printing there were few books. Until then most people (other than those standing at the *bima*) *heard* the Torah in the synagogue. They did not *see* it in print. The phrase *Keriat HaTorah* really means not *reading* the Torah but *proclaiming* it, making it a public declaration.[5]

There is a fundamental difference between reading and hearing in the way we process information. Reading, we can see the entire

---

3. See for example Martin Nowak and Roger Highfield, *Super Cooperators: Altruism, Evolution and Mathematics (or, Why We Need Each Other to Succeed)* (Edinburgh: Canongate, 2011).
4. Albert Einstein, *The World As I See It*, trans. Alan Harris (San Diego: The Book Tree, 2007), 90.
5. This has halakhic implications. *Keriat HaTorah* is, according to most *Rishonim*, a *ḥovat hatzibbur*, a communal rather than an individual obligation (unlike the reading of the Megilla on Purim).

text – the sentence, the paragraph – at one time. Hearing, we cannot. We hear only one word at a time, and we do not know in advance how a sentence or paragraph will end. Some of the most powerful literary effects in an oral culture occur when the opening words of a sentence lead us to expect one ending and instead we encounter another.

These are the words we hear: "And he [Jacob] loved also Rachel" (Gen. 29:30). This is what we expected and hoped for. Jacob now has two wives, sisters, something that will be forbidden in later Jewish law. It is a situation fraught with tension. But our first impression is that all will be well. He loves them both.

That expectation is dashed by the next word, *miLeah*, "more than Leah." This is not merely unexpected. It is also grammatically impossible. You cannot have a sentence that says, "X *also* loved Y *more than* Z." "Also" and "more than" contradict one another. This is one of those rare and powerful instances in which the Torah deliberately uses fractured syntax to indicate a fractured relationship.[6]

Then comes the next phrase and it is shocking: "The Lord saw that Leah was hated" (Gen. 29:31). Was Leah hated? No. The previous sentence has just told us she was loved. What then does the Torah mean by "hated"? It means, that is how Leah felt. Yes she was loved, but less than her sister. Leah knew, and had known for seven years, that Jacob was passionately in love with her younger sister Rachel. The Torah says that he worked for her for seven years "but they seemed to him like a few days because he was so in love with her" (Gen. 29:20).

Leah was not hated. She was less loved. But someone in that situation cannot but feel rejected. The Torah forces us to hear Leah's pain in the names she gives her children. Her first she calls Reuben, saying "It is *because the Lord has seen my misery. Surely my husband will love me now.*" The second she calls Simeon, "Because *the Lord heard that I am not loved.*" The third she calls Levi, saying, "Now *at last my husband will become attached to me*" (Gen. 29:32–35). There is sustained anguish in these words.

---

6. The classic example is the untranslatable verse in Gen. 4:8, in which Cain kills Abel. The breakdown of words expresses the breakdown of relationship which leads to the breakdown of morality and the first murder.

We hear the same tone later when Reuben, Leah's firstborn, finds mandrakes in the field. Mandrakes were thought to have aphrodisiac properties, so he gives them to his mother hoping that this will draw his father to her. Rachel, who has been experiencing a different kind of pain, childlessness, sees the mandrakes and asks Leah for them. Leah then says: "Wasn't it enough that you took away my husband? Will you take my son's mandrakes too?" (Gen. 30:15). The misery is palpable.

Note what has happened. It began with love. It was about love throughout. Jacob loved Rachel. He loved her at first sight. In fact, there is no other love story quite like it in the Torah: Abraham and Sarah are already married by the time we first meet them; Isaac has his wife chosen for him by his father's servant. But Jacob loves. He is more emotional than the other patriarchs; that is the problem. Love unites but it also divides. It leaves the unloved, even the less-loved, feeling rejected, abandoned, forsaken, alone. That is why you cannot build a society, a community, or even a family on love alone. There must be justice-as-fairness also.

If we look at the eleven times the word "love," *ahava*, is mentioned in the book of Genesis we make an extraordinary discovery. Every time love is mentioned, it generates conflict. Isaac loved Esau but Rebecca loved Jacob. Jacob loved Joseph, Rachel's firstborn, more than his other sons. From these came two of the most fateful sibling rivalries in Jewish history.

Even these pale into insignificance when we reflect on the first time the word love appears in the Torah, in the opening words of the trial of the binding of Isaac: "Take now your son, your only one, the one you love" (Gen. 22:2). Rashi, following Midrash (itself inspired by the obvious comparison between the binding of Isaac and the book of Job), says that Satan, the accusing angel, said to God when Abraham made a feast to celebrate the weaning of his son: "You see, he loves his child more than You" (Rashi, Gen. 22:1). That, according to the midrash, was the reason for the trial, to show that Satan's accusation was untrue.

Judaism is a religion of love. It is so for profound theological reasons. In the world of myth the gods were at worst hostile, at best indifferent to humankind. In contemporary atheism the universe and life exist for no reason whatsoever. We are accidents of matter, the result of blind chance and natural selection. Judaism's approach is the most beautiful I know. We are here because God created us in love and forgiveness asking us to love and forgive others. Love, God's love, is implicit in our very being.

So many of our texts express that love: the paragraph before the *Shema* with its talk of "great" and "eternal love"; the *Shema* itself with its command of love; the priestly blessings to be uttered in love; *Shir HaShirim*, the Song of Songs, the great poem of love; Shlomo Albaketz's *Lekha Dodi*, "Come, My Beloved"; Eliezer Azikri's *Yedid Nefesh*, "Beloved of the Soul." If you want to live well, love. If you seek to be close to God, love. If you want your home to be filled with the light of the Divine Presence, love. Love is where God lives.

But love is not enough. You cannot build a family, let alone a society, on love alone. For that you need justice also. Love is partial, justice is impartial. Love is particular, justice is universal. Love is for this person, not that; justice is for all. Much of the moral life is generated by this tension between love and justice. It is no accident that this is the theme of many of the narratives of Genesis. Genesis is about people and their relationships while the rest of the Torah is predominantly about society.

Justice without love is harsh. Love without justice is unfair, or so it will seem to the less-loved. Yet to experience both at the same time is virtually impossible. As Niels Bohr, the Nobel Prize-winning physicist, put it when he discovered that his son had stolen an object from a local shop: he could look at him from the perspective of a judge (justice) and as his father (love), but not both simultaneously.[7]

At the heart of the moral life is a conflict with no simple resolution. There is no general rule to tell us when love is the right reaction and when justice is. In the 1960s the Beatles sang "All you need is love." Would that it were so, but it is not. Let us love, but let us never forget those who feel unloved. They too are people. They too have feelings. They too are in the image of God.

7. Jerome Bruner, *Actual Minds, Possible Worlds* (Cambridge, MA: Harvard University Press, 1986), 51.

Vayishlaḥ

The Parable of the Tribes

From beginning to end, Genesis 34 tells a terrifying story. Dina, Jacob's daughter – the only Jewish daughter mentioned in the entire patriarchal narrative – leaves the safety of home to go out to "look at the daughters of the land" (Gen. 34:1). She is raped and abducted by a local prince, Shechem, son of the king of the town known as Shechem.

Jacob learns of this fact but does nothing until his sons return. Simeon and Levi, Dina's brothers, immediately realise that they must act to rescue her. It is an almost impossible assignment. The hostage-taker is no ordinary individual. As the son of the king, he cannot be confronted directly. The king is unlikely to order his son to release her. The other townspeople, if challenged, will come to the prince's defence. It is Simeon and Levi against the town, two against many. Even were all of Jacob's sons to be enlisted, they would still be outnumbered.

Simeon and Levi therefore decide on a ruse. They agree to let Dina marry the prince but they make one condition. The members of the town must all be circumcised. The townspeople, seeing long-term advantages to an alliance with this neighbouring tribe, agree. The men of the town are weakened by the operation, and the pain is most acute on the third day. That day, Simeon and Levi enter the town and kill the entire male population. They rescue Dina and bring her home. The other brothers then plunder the town.

Jacob is horrified. "You have made me odious to the people of the land," he says (Gen. 34:30). What then were we supposed to do, ask the two brothers? "Should we have left our sister to be treated like a prostitute?" (Gen. 34:31). With that rhetorical question, the episode ends and the narrative moves elsewhere. But Jacob's horror at the action of his sons does not end there. He returns to it on his deathbed, and in effect curses them:

> Simeon and Levi are brothers –
> their swords are weapons of violence.
> Let me not enter their council,
> let me not join their assembly,
> for they have killed men in their anger
> and hamstrung oxen as they pleased.
> Cursed be their anger, so fierce,
> and their fury, so cruel!
> I will scatter them in Jacob
> and disperse them in Israel. (Gen. 49:5–7)

The story of Dina is an extraordinary passage. It seems to lack any kind of moral message. No one comes out of it well. Shechem, the prince, would seem to be the chief villain. It was he who abducted and raped Dina in the first place. Hamor, his father, fails to reprimand him or order Dina's release. Simeon and Levi are guilty of a horrendous act of violence. The other brothers engage in looting the town.[1] Jacob seems passive throughout. He neither acts nor instructs his sons on how to act. Even Dina herself seems at best to have been guilty of carelessness in going out into the town in the first place, in what was clearly a dangerous neighbourhood – recall that both Abraham and Isaac, her grandfather

---

1. An action that is disapproved of biblically; see Deut. 13:13–19; I Sam. 15:13–26; Est. 9:10, 15–16.

and great-grandfather, had feared for their own lives because of the law-lessness of the times.[2]

Who was in the right and who in the wrong are left conspicuously undecided in the text. Jacob condemns his sons. But his sons reject the criticism. The debate continued and was taken up by two of the greatest rabbis in the Middle Ages. Rambam takes the side of Simeon and Levi. They were justified in what they did, he says. The other members of the town saw what Shechem had done, knew that he was guilty of a crime, and yet neither brought him to court nor rescued the girl. They were therefore accomplices in his guilt. What Shechem had done was a capital crime, and by sheltering him the townspeople were implicated.[3] This is, incidentally, a fascinating ruling since it suggests that for Rambam the rule that "all Israel are responsible for one another" (Shevuot 39a) is not restricted to Israel. It applies to all societies. As Isaac Arama would write in the fifteenth century, any crime known about and allowed to continue ceases to be an offence of individuals only and becomes a sin of the community as a whole.[4]

Ramban disagrees (in his commentary to Gen. 34:13). The principle of collective responsibility does not, in his view, apply to non-Jewish societies. The Noahide covenant requires every society to set up courts of law, but it does not imply that a failure to prosecute a wrongdoer involves all members of the society in a capital crime.

The debate continues today among Bible scholars. Two in particular subject the story to close literary analysis: Meir Sternberg in his *The Poetics of Biblical Narrative*[5] and Rabbi Elchanan Samet in his studies on the *parasha*.[6] They too arrive at conflicting conclusions. Sternberg argues that the text is critical of Jacob for both his inaction and his criticism of his sons for acting. Samet sees the chief culprits as Shechem and Hamor. Both point out, however, the remarkable fact that the text

---

2. The Midrash is critical of Dina. See *Midrash Aggada* (Buber) to Gen. 34:1. *Midrash Sekhel Tov* 34:1 is even critical of her mother Leah for allowing her to go out.

3. Rambam, *Mishneh Torah, Hilkhot Melakhim* 9:14.

4. Arama, *Akedat Yitzḥak, Bereshit, Vayera*, gate 20, s.v. *UVeMidrash*.

5. *The Poetics of Biblical Narrative: Ideological Literature and the Drama of Reading* (Bloomington: Indiana University Press, 1985), 444–81.

6. *Iyyunim BeParashat HaShavua*, third series (Tel Aviv: Yediot Aharonot, 2012), 149–171.

deliberately deepens the moral ambiguity by refusing to portray even the apparent villains in an unduly negative light. Consider the chief wrongdoer, the young prince Shechem. The text tells us that "his heart was drawn to Dina daughter of Jacob; he loved the young woman and spoke tenderly to her. And Shechem said to his father Hamor, 'Get me this girl as my wife'" (Gen. 34:3–4). Compare this with the description of Amnon, son of King David, who rapes his half-sister Tamar. That story too is a tale of bloody revenge. But the text says about Amnon that after raping Tamar, he "hated her with intense hatred. In fact, he hated her more than he had loved her. Amnon said to her, 'Get up and get out!'" (II Sam. 13:15). Shechem is not like that at all. He falls in love with Dina and wants to marry her. The king, Shechem's father, and the people of the town readily accede to Simeon and Levi's request that they become circumcised.

Not only does the text not demonise the people of Shechem, it also does not paint any of Jacob's family in a positive light. It uses the same word – "deceit" (Gen. 34:13) – of Simeon and Levi that it has used previously about Jacob taking Esau's blessing and Laban substituting Leah for Rachel. In its description of all the characters – from the gad-about Dina to her excessively violent rescuers, to the plundering other brothers and the passive Jacob – the text seems written deliberately to alienate our sympathies.

The overall effect is a story with no irredeemable villains and no stainless heroes. Why then is it told at all? Stories do not appear in the Torah merely because they happened. The Torah is not a history book. It is silent on some of the most important periods of time. We know nothing, for example, about Abraham's childhood, or about thirty-eight of the forty years spent by the Israelites in the wilderness. *Torah* means "teaching," "instruction," "guidance." What teaching does the Torah want us to draw from this narrative out of which no one emerges well?

There is an important thought experiment devised by Andrew Schmookler known as the parable of the tribes.[7] Imagine a group of

---

7. Andrew Bard Schmookler, *The Parable of the Tribes: The Problem of Power in Social Evolution* (Berkeley: University of California, 1984).

tribes living close to one another. All choose the way of peace except one that is willing to use violence to achieve its ends. What happens to the peace-seeking tribes? One is defeated and destroyed by the violent tribe. A second is conquered and subjugated. A third flees to some remote and inaccessible place. If the fourth seeks to defend itself it too will have to have recourse to violence. "The irony is that successful defence against a power-maximising aggressor requires a society to become more like the society that threatens it. Power can be stopped only by power."[8]

There are, in other words, four possible outcomes: (1) destruction, (2) subjugation, (3) withdrawal, and (4) imitation. "*In every one of these outcomes the ways of power are spread throughout the system. This is the parable of the tribes.*"[9] Recall that all but one of the tribes seek peace and have no desire to exercise power over their neighbours. Nonetheless, if you introduce a single violent tribe into the region, violence will eventually prevail, however the other tribes choose to respond. That is the tragedy of the human condition.

As I was writing this essay in the summer of 2014, Israel was engaged in a bitter struggle with Hamas in Gaza in which many people died. The State of Israel had no more desire to be engaged in this kind of warfare than did our ancestor Jacob. Throughout the campaign I found myself recalling the words earlier in *Parashat Vayishlaḥ* about Jacob's feelings prior to his meeting with Esau: "Jacob was very afraid and distressed" (Gen. 32:8), about which the sages said, "Afraid, lest he be killed, distressed lest he be forced to kill" (quoted by Rashi ad loc.). What the episode of Dina tells us is not that Jacob, or Simeon and Levi, were right, but rather that there can be situations in which there is no simple right course of action. Whatever you do will be considered wrong; every option will involve the compromise of some moral principle.

That is Schmookler's point, that "power is like a contaminant, a disease, which once introduced will gradually but inexorably become universal in the system of competing societies."[10] Shechem's single act

---

8. Ibid., 21.
9. Ibid., 22.
10. Ibid.

of violence against Dina forced two of Jacob's sons into violent reprisal and in the end everyone was either contaminated or dead. It is indicative of the moral depth of the Torah that it does not hide this terrible truth from us by depicting one side as guilty, the other as innocent.

Violence defiles us all. It did then. It does now.

Vayeshev

The Heroism of Tamar

This is a true story that took place in the 1970s. Rabbi Dr. Nachum Rabinovitch, then principal of Jews' College, the rabbinic training seminary in London where I was a student and teacher, was approached by an organisation that had been given an unusual opportunity to engage in interfaith dialogue. A group of African bishops wanted to understand more about Judaism. Would the principal be willing to send his senior students to engage in such a dialogue, in a chateau in Switzerland?

To my surprise, he agreed. He told me that he was sceptical about Jewish-Christian dialogue in general because he believed that over the centuries the Church had been infected by an anti-Semitism that was very difficult to overcome. At that time, though, he felt that African Christians were different. They loved Tanakh and its stories. They were – at least in principle – open to understanding Judaism on its own terms. He did not add – though I knew it was in his mind since he was one of the world's greatest experts on Rambam – that the great twelfth-century sage held an unusual attitude to dialogue.

Rambam believed that Islam was a genuinely monotheistic faith while Christianity in those days was not. Nonetheless, he held that it was permissible to study Tanakh with Christians but not Muslims, since Christians believed that Tanakh (what they called the Old Testament) was the word of God while Muslims believed that Jews had falsified the text.[1]

So we went. It was an unusual group: the *semikha* class of Jews' College, together with the top class of the yeshiva in Montreux where the late Rabbi Yechiel Weinberg, author of *Seridei Esh* and one of the world's foremost halakhists, had taught. For three days the Jewish group *davened* and *bentsched* with special intensity. We learned Talmud each day. For the rest of the time we had an unusual, even transformative, encounter with the African bishops, ending with a hasidic-style *tisch* during which we shared with the Africans our songs and stories and they taught us theirs. At three in the morning we finished by dancing together. We knew we were different, we knew that there were deep divides between our respective faiths, but we had become friends. Perhaps that is all we should seek. Friends do not have to agree in order to stay friends. And friendships can sometimes help heal the world.

On the morning after our arrival, however, an event occurred that left a deep impression on me. The sponsoring body, a global Jewish organisation, was a secular one, and to keep within their frame of reference the group had to include at least one non-Orthodox Jew, a woman studying for the rabbinate. We, the *semikha* and yeshiva students, were *davening* the *Shaḥarit* service in one of the lounges in the chateau when the Reform woman entered, wearing *tallit* and *tefillin*, and sat herself down in the middle of the group.

This is something the students had not encountered before. What were they to do? There was no *meḥitza*. There was no way of separating themselves. How should they react to a woman wearing *tallit* and *tefillin* and praying in the midst of a group of men? They ran up to Rabbi Rabinovitch in a state of great agitation and asked what

---

1. Rambam, *Teshuvot HaRambam* (Responsa of the Rambam), Blau Edition (Jerusalem: Mekitzei Nirdamim, 1960), no. 149.

they should do. Without a moment's hesitation he quoted to them the saying of the sages: a person should be willing to throw himself into a furnace of fire rather than shame another person in public (Berakhot 43b; Ketubbot 67b). With that he ordered them back to their seats, and the prayers continued.

The moral of that moment never left me. The rabbi, for the past thirty-two years head of the yeshiva in Maale Adumim, was and is one of the great halakhists of our time. He knew immediately how serious were the issues at stake: men and women praying together without a barrier between them and the complex question about whether women may or may not wear a *tallit* and *tefillin*. The issue was anything but simple.

But he knew also that halakha is a systematic way of turning the great ethical and spiritual truths into a tapestry of deeds and that one must never lose the larger vision in an exclusive focus on the details. Had the students insisted that the woman pray elsewhere they would have put her to shame, the way Eli did when he saw Hannah praying and thought she was drunk (I Sam. 1:13–17). Never, ever shame someone in public. That was the transcending imperative of the hour. That is the mark of a great-souled man. I count as one of the great privileges of my life having been his student for more than a decade.

The reason I tell this story here is that it is one of the powerful and unexpected lessons of *Parashat Vayeshev*. Judah, the brother who proposed selling Joseph into slavery (Gen. 37:26), had "gone down" to Canaan where he married a local Canaanite woman (38:1). The phrase "gone down" was rightly taken by the sages as full of meaning.[2] Just as Joseph had been brought down to Egypt (39:1), so Judah had been morally and spiritually brought down. Here was one of Jacob's sons doing what the patriarchs insisted on not doing: marrying into the local population. It is a tale of sad decline.

---

2. According to midrashic tradition (*Midrash Aggada, Pesikta Zutreta, Sekhel Tov*), Judah was "sent down" or excommunicated by his brothers for advising them to sell Joseph after the grief they saw their father suffer. See also Rashi ad loc.

Judah married his firstborn son, Er, to a local woman, Tamar.[3] An obscure verse tells us that he sinned and died. Judah then married his second son, Onan, to her, under a pre-Mosaic form of levirate marriage whereby a brother is bound to marry his sister-in-law if she has been widowed without children. Onan, reluctant to father a child that would be regarded as not his but his deceased brother's, practised a form of coitus interruptus that to this day carries his name. For this, he too died. Having lost two of his sons, Judah was reluctant to give his third, Shelah, to Tamar in marriage. The result was that she was left as a "living widow," bound to marry her brother-in-law whom Judah was withholding, but unable to marry anyone else.

After many years, seeing that her father-in-law (by this time a widower himself) was reluctant to marry her to Shelah, she decided on an audacious course of action. She removed her widow's clothes, covered herself with a veil, and positioned herself at a point where Judah was likely to see her on his way to the sheep-shearing. Judah saw her, took her to be a prostitute, and engaged her services. As surety for the payment he had promised her, she insisted that he leave his seal, cord, and staff. Judah duly returned the next day with the payment, but the woman was nowhere to be seen. He asked the locals the whereabouts of the temple prostitute (the text at this point uses the word *kedesha*, "cult prostitute," rather than *zona*, thus deepening Judah's offence), but no one had seen such a person in the locality. Puzzled, Judah returned home.

Three months later he heard that Tamar was pregnant. He leapt to the only conclusion he could draw, namely that she had had a physical relationship with another man while bound in law to his son Shelah. She had committed adultery, for which the punishment was death. Tamar was brought out to face her sentence. She came, holding the staff and seal that Judah instantly recognised as his own. She said, "I am pregnant by the person to whom these objects belong."

---

3. *Targum Yonatan* identifies her as the daughter of Noah's son, Shem. Others identify her as a daughter of Abraham's contemporary Melchizedek. The truth is, though, that she appears in the narrative without lineage, a device often used by the Torah to emphasize that moral greatness can often be found among ordinary people. It has nothing to do with ancestry. See Alshikh ad loc.

Judah realised what had happened and said, "She is more righteous than I" (Gen. 38:26).

This moment is a turning point in history. Judah is the first person in the Torah to explicitly admit he was wrong.[4] We do not realise it yet, but this seems to be the moment at which he acquired the depth of character necessary for him to become the first real *baal teshuva*. We see this years later, when he – the man who proposed selling Joseph as a slave – becomes the man who is willing to spend the rest of his life in slavery so that his brother Benjamin can go free (Gen. 44:33). I have argued elsewhere that it is from here that we learn the principle that a penitent stands higher than even a perfectly righteous individual (Berakhot 34b).[5] Judah the penitent becomes the ancestor of Israel's kings while Joseph, the righteous, is only a viceroy, *mishneh lemelekh*, second to the king.

Thus far Judah. But the real hero of the story was Tamar. She had taken an immense risk by becoming pregnant. Indeed she was almost killed for it. She had done so for a noble reason: to ensure that the name of her late husband was perpetuated. But she took no less care to avoid Judah being put to shame. Only he and she knew what had happened. Judah could acknowledge his error without loss of face. It was from this episode that the sages derived the rule articulated by Rabbi Rabinovitch that morning in Switzerland: it is better to risk being thrown into a fiery furnace than shame someone else in public.

It is thus no coincidence that Tamar, a heroic non-Jewish woman, became the ancestor of David, Israel's greatest king. There are striking similarities between Tamar and the other heroic woman in David's ancestry, the Moabite woman we know as Ruth.

---

4. The text here is full of verbal allusions. As we noted, Judah has "gone down" just as Joseph has been "brought down." Joseph is about to rise to political greatness; Judah will eventually rise to moral greatness. Tamar's deception of Judah is similar to Judah's deception of Jacob – both involve clothes: Joseph's blood-stained coat, Tamar's veil. Both reach their climax with the words *haker na*, "please examine." Judah forces Jacob to believe a lie. Tamar forces Judah to recognise the truth.
5. Jonathan Sacks, *Covenant & Conversation: Genesis – The Book of Beginnings* (Jerusalem: Maggid, 2009), 303–314.

The ancient Jewish custom on Shabbat and festivals to cover the ḥallot (or matza) while holding the glass of wine over which Kiddush is being made is performed so as not to put the ḥalla to shame while it is being, as it were, passed over in favour of the wine. There are religious Jews who will go to great lengths to avoid shaming an inanimate loaf of bread but have no compunction about putting their fellow Jews to shame if they regard them as less religious than they are. That is what happens when we remember the halakha but forget the underlying moral principle behind it.

Never put anyone to shame. That is what Tamar taught Judah and what a great rabbi of our time taught those who were privileged to be his students.

Miketz

Appearance and Reality

Finally, after twenty-two years and many twists and turns, Joseph and his brothers meet. We sense the drama of the moment. The last time they were together, the brothers planned to kill Joseph and eventually sold him as a slave. One of the reasons they did so was that they were angry at his reports about his dreams; he had twice dreamed that his brothers would bow down to him. To them that sounded like hubris, excessive confidence, and conceit.

Hubris is usually punished by nemesis and so it was in Joseph's case. Far from being a ruler, his brothers turned him into a slave. That, however, turned out not to be the end of the story but only the beginning. Unexpectedly, now in *Parashat Miketz*, the dream has just come true. The brothers do bow down to him, "their faces to the ground" (Gen. 42:6). Now, we feel, the story has reached its end. Instead it turns out only to be the beginning of another story altogether, about sin, repentance, and forgiveness. Biblical stories tend to defy narrative conventions.

The reason, though, that the story does not end with the brothers' meeting is that only one person present at the scene, Joseph himself, knew that it was a meeting. "As soon as Joseph saw his brothers, *he recognised them,* but he pretended to be a stranger and spoke harshly to them.... *Joseph recognised his brothers, but they did not recognise him"* (Gen. 42:7–8).

There were many reasons they did not recognise him. They did not know he was in Egypt. They believed he was still a slave while the man before whom they bowed was a viceroy. Besides which, he looked like an Egyptian, spoke Egyptian, and had an Egyptian name, Tzofnat Paane'aḥ. Most importantly, though, he was wearing the uniform of an Egyptian of high rank. That had been the sign of Joseph's elevation at the hand of Pharaoh when he interpreted his dreams:

> So Pharaoh said to Joseph, "I hereby put you in charge of the whole land of Egypt." Then Pharaoh took his signet ring from his finger and put it on Joseph's finger. He dressed him in robes of fine linen and put a gold chain round his neck. He made him ride in a chariot as his second-in-command, and people shouted before him, "Make way." Thus he put him in charge of the whole land of Egypt. (Gen. 41:41–43)

We know from Egyptian wall paintings and from archaeological discoveries like Tutankhamen's tomb how stylised and elaborate were Egyptian robes of office. Different ranks wore different clothes. Early pharaohs had two headdresses, a white one to mark the fact that they were kings of Upper Egypt, and a red one to signal that they were kings of Lower Egypt. Like all uniforms, clothes told a story, or as we say nowadays, "made a statement." They proclaimed a person's status. Someone dressed like the Egyptian before whom the brothers had just bowed could not possibly be their long-lost brother Joseph. Except that he was.

This seems like a minor matter. I want in this essay to argue the opposite. It turns out to be a very major matter indeed. The first thing we need to note is that the Torah as a whole, and Genesis in particular, has a way of focusing our attention on a major theme: It presents us with recurring episodes. Robert Alter calls them "type scenes."[1] There

---

1. Robert Alter, *The Art of Biblical Narrative* (New York: Basic Books, 1981), 55–78.

is, for example, the theme of sibling rivalry that appears four times in Genesis: Cain and Abel, Isaac and Ishmael, Jacob and Esau, and Joseph and his brothers. There is the theme that occurs three times: the patriarch forced to leave home because of famine, and then realising that he will have to ask his wife to pretend she is his sister for fear that he will be murdered so that she can be taken into the royal harem. And there is the theme of finding-future-wife-at-well, which also occurs three times: Rebecca, Rachel, and Yitro's daughter Tzippora.

The encounter between Joseph and his brothers is the fifth in a series of stories in which clothes play a key role. The first is Jacob who dresses in Esau's clothes while bringing his father a meal so that he can take his brother's blessing. The second is Joseph's finely embroidered robe or "coat of many colours," which the brothers bring back to their father stained in blood, saying that a wild animal must have seized him. The third is the story of Tamar taking off her widow's dress, covering herself with a veil, and making herself look as if she were a prostitute. The fourth is the robe Joseph leaves in the hands of Potiphar's wife while escaping her attempt to seduce him. The fifth is the one in *Parashat Miketz* in which Pharaoh dresses Joseph as a high-ranking Egyptian, with clothes of linen, a gold chain, and the royal signet ring.

What all five cases have in common is that they facilitate deception. In each case, they bring about a situation in which things are not as they seem. Jacob wore Esau's clothes because he was worried that his blind father would feel him and realise that the smooth skin did not belong to Esau but to his younger brother. In the end it was not only the texture but also the smell of the clothes that deceived Isaac: "Ah, the smell of my son is like the smell of a field the Lord has blessed" (Gen. 27:27).

Joseph's stained robe was produced by the brothers to disguise the fact that they were responsible for Joseph's disappearance. Jacob "recognised it and said, 'It is my son's robe! A wild animal has devoured him. Joseph has surely been torn to pieces'" (Gen. 37:33).

Tamar's appearance dressed as a veiled prostitute was intended to deceive Judah into sleeping with her since she wanted to have a child to "raise up the name" of her dead husband Er. Potiphar's wife used the evidence of Joseph's robe to substantiate her claim that he had tried to rape her, a crime of which he was wholly innocent. Lastly, Joseph used the fact that his brothers did not recognise him to set in motion a series of staged events to test whether they were still capable of selling a brother as a slave or whether they had changed.

So the five stories about garments tell a single story: *things are not necessarily as they seem*. Appearances deceive. It is therefore with a frisson of discovery that we realise that the Hebrew word for garment, B-G-D, is also the Hebrew word for "betrayal," as in the confession formula, *Ashamnu, bagadnu,* "We have been guilty, we have betrayed."

Is this a mere literary conceit, a way of linking a series of otherwise unconnected stories? Or is there something more fundamental at stake?

It was the nineteenth-century Jewish historian Heinrich Graetz who pointed out a crucial difference between other ancient cultures and Judaism:

> The pagan perceives the Divine in nature through the medium of the eye, and he becomes conscious of it as something to be looked at. On the other hand, to the Jew who conceives God as being outside of nature and prior to it, the Divine manifests itself through the will and through the medium of the ear…. The pagan beholds his god, the Jew hears Him; that is, apprehends His will.[2]

In the twentieth century, literary theorist Erich Auerbach contrasted the literary style of Homer with that of the Hebrew Bible.[3] In Homer's prose we see the play of light on surfaces. *The Odyssey* and *The Iliad* are full of visual descriptions. By contrast, biblical narrative has very few such descriptions. We do not know how tall Abraham was, the colour of Isaac's hair, or what Moses looked like. Visual details are minimal, and are present only when necessary to understand what follows. We are told for example that Joseph was good-looking (Gen. 39:6) only to explain why Potiphar's wife conceived a desire for him.

2. Heinrich Graetz, *The Structure of Jewish History, and Other Essays* (New York: Ktav Publishing House, 1975), 68.
3. Erich Auerbach, *Mimesis: The Representation of Reality in Western Literature* (Garden City, NY: Doubleday, 1957), 3–23.

The key to the five stories occurs later on in Tanakh, in the biblical account of Israel's first two kings. Saul looked like royalty. He was "head and shoulders above" everyone else (I Sam. 9:2). He was tall. He had presence. He had the bearing of a king. But he lacked self-confidence. He followed the people rather than leading them. Samuel had to rebuke him with the words, "You may be *small in your own eyes* but you are head of the tribes of Israel" (I Sam. 15:17). Appearance and reality were opposites. Saul had physical but not moral stature.

The contrast with David was total. When God told Samuel to go to the family of Yishai to find Israel's next king, no one even thought of David, the youngest of the family. Samuel's first instinct was to choose Eliav who, like Saul, looked the part. But God told him, "Do not consider his appearance or his height, for I have rejected him. The Lord does not look at the things people look at. *People look at the outward appearance but the Lord looks at the heart*" (I Sam. 16:7).

Only when we have read all these stories are we able to return to the first story of all in which clothes play a part: the story of Adam and Eve and the forbidden fruit, after eating which they see they are naked. They are ashamed and they make clothes for themselves. That is a story for another occasion but its theme should now be clear. It is about eyes and ears, seeing and listening. Adam and Eve's sin had little to do with fruit, or sex, and everything to do with the fact that they let what they saw override what they had heard.

"Joseph recognised his brothers, but they did not recognise him." The reason they did not recognise him is that, from the start, they allowed their feelings to be guided by what they saw, the "coat of many colours" that inflamed their envy of their younger brother. Judge by appearances and you will miss the deeper truth about situations and people. You will even miss God Himself, for God cannot be seen, only heard. That is why the primary imperative in Judaism is *Shema Yisrael*, "Listen, O Israel," and why, when we say the first line of the *Shema*, we place our hand over our eyes so that we cannot see.

Appearances deceive. Clothes betray. Deep understanding, whether of God or of human beings, needs the ability to listen. In order to choose between right and wrong, between good and bad – in order to live the moral life – we must make sure not only to look, but also to listen.

Vayigash

The Birth of Forgiveness

Tここ here are moments that change the world: 1439, when Johannes Gutenberg invented the movable-type printing press (though the Chinese had developed it four centuries before); 1821, when Faraday invented the electric motor; or 1990, when Tim Berners-Lee created the World Wide Web. There is such a moment in *Parashat Vayigash*, and in its way it may have been no less transformative than any of the above. It happened when Joseph finally revealed his identity to his brothers. While they were silent and in a state of shock, he went on to say these words:

> I am your brother Joseph, whom you sold into Egypt! And now, do not be distressed and do not be angry with yourselves for selling me here, because it was to save lives that God sent me ahead of you. For two years now there has been famine in the land, and for the next five years there will be no ploughing and reaping. But God sent me ahead of you to preserve for you a remnant on earth and to save your lives by a great deliverance. So then, it was not you who sent me here, but God. (Gen. 45:4–8)

This is the first recorded moment in history in which one human being forgives another.

According to the Midrash, God had forgiven before this,[1] but not according to the plain sense of the text. Forgiveness is conspicuously lacking as an element in the stories of the Flood, the Tower of Babel, and Sodom and the cities of the plain. When Abraham prayed his audacious prayer for the people of Sodom, he did not ask God to forgive them. His argument was about justice, not forgiveness. Perhaps there were innocent people there, fifty or even ten. It would be unjust for them to die. Their merit should therefore save the others, said Abraham. That is quite different from asking God to forgive.

Joseph forgave. That was a first in history. Yet the Torah hints that the brothers did not fully appreciate the significance of his words. After all, he did not explicitly use the word "forgive." He told them not to be distressed. He said, "It was not you but God." He told them their act had resulted in a positive outcome. But all of this was theoretically compatible with holding them guilty and deserving of punishment. That is why the Torah recounts a second event, years later, after Jacob had died. The brothers sought a meeting with Joseph fearing that he would now take revenge. They concocted a story:

> They sent word to Joseph, saying, "Your father left these instruc-
> tions before he died: 'This is what you are to say to Joseph: I ask
> you to *forgive* your brothers for the sins and the wrongs they
> committed in treating you so badly.' Now please *forgive* the sins
> of the servants of the God of your father." When their message
> came to him, Joseph wept. (Gen. 50:16–17)

What they said was a white lie, but Joseph understood why they said it. The brothers used the word "forgive" – this is the first time it

---

1. There are midrashic suggestions that God partially forgave, or at least mitigated the punishments of, Adam and Eve and Abel. Ishmael was said to have become a penitent, and there are midrashic interpretations that identify Ketura, the woman Abraham married after the death of Sarah, with Hagar, implying that Abraham and Isaac were reunited and reconciled with Sarah's maidservant and her son.

appears explicitly in the Torah – because they were still unsure about what Joseph meant. Does someone truly forgive those who sold him into slavery? Joseph wept that his brothers had not fully understood that he had forgiven them long before. He no longer felt ill will towards them. He had no anger, no lingering resentment, no desire for revenge. He had conquered his emotions and reframed his understanding of events.

Forgiveness does not appear in every culture. It is not a human universal, nor is it a biological imperative. We know this from a fascinating study by American classicist David Konstan, *Before Forgiveness: The Origins of a Moral Idea*.[2] In it he argues that there was no concept of forgiveness in the literature of the ancient Greeks. There was something else, often mistaken for forgiveness: *appeasement of anger*.

When someone does harm to someone else, the victim is angry and seeks revenge. This is clearly dangerous for the perpetrator and he or she may try to get the victim to calm down and move on. He or she may make excuses: it wasn't me, it was someone else; it was me but I couldn't help it; it was me but it was a small wrong, and I have done you much good in the past, so on balance you should let it pass.

Alternatively, or in conjunction with these other strategies, the perpetrator may beg, plead, and perform some ritual of abasement or humiliation. This is a way of saying to the victim, "I am not really a threat." The Greek word *sugnome*, sometimes translated as forgiveness, really means, says Konstan, *exculpation* or *absolution*. It is not that I forgive you for what you did, but that I understand why you did it – you could not really help it, you were caught up in circumstances beyond your control – or, alternatively, I do not need to take revenge because you have now shown by your deference to me that you hold me in proper respect. My dignity has been restored.

There is a classic example of appeasement in the Torah: Jacob's behaviour towards Esau when they meet again after a long separation. Jacob had fled home after Rebecca overheard Esau resolving to kill him after Isaac's death (Gen. 27:41). Prior to the meeting Jacob sent him a huge gift of cattle, saying "I will *appease* him with the present that goes before me, and afterwards I will see his face; perhaps he will accept me." (32:21).

2. Cambridge, NY: Cambridge University Press, 2010.

When the brothers meet, Jacob bows down to Esau seven times, a classic abasement ritual. The brothers meet, kiss, embrace, and go their separate ways – not because Esau has forgiven Jacob but because either he has forgotten or he has been placated.

Appeasement as a form of conflict management exists even among non-humans. Frans de Waal, the primatologist, has described peacemaking rituals among chimpanzees, bonobos, and mountain gorillas.[3] There are contests for dominance among the social animals, but there must also be ways of restoring harmony to the group if it is to survive at all. So there are forms of appeasement and peacemaking that are pre-moral and have existed since the birth of humanity.

Forgiveness has not. Konstan argues that its first appearance is in the Hebrew Bible and he cites the case of Joseph. What he does not make clear is *why* Joseph forgives, and why the idea and institution are born specifically within Judaism.

The answer is that within Judaism a new form of morality was born. Judaism is (primarily) an ethic of guilt, as opposed to most other systems, which are ethics of shame. One of the fundamental differences between them is that shame attaches to the person, while guilt attaches to the act. In shame cultures when a person does wrong he or she is, as it were, stained, marked, defiled. In guilt cultures what is wrong is not the doer but the deed, not the sinner but the sin. The person retains his or her fundamental worth ("the soul you gave me is pure," as we say in our prayers). It is the act that has somehow to be put right. That is why in guilt cultures there are processes of repentance, atonement, and forgiveness.

That is the explanation for Joseph's behaviour from the moment the brothers appear before him in Egypt for the first time to the point where, in *Parashat Vayigash*, he announces his identity and forgives his brothers. It is a textbook case of putting the brothers through a course of atonement, the first in literature. Joseph is thus teaching them, and the Torah is teaching us, what it is to *earn* forgiveness.

3. Frans de Waal, *Peacemaking among Primates* (Cambridge, MA: Harvard University Press, 1989).

Recall what happens: First he accuses the brothers of a crime they have not committed. He says they are spies. He has them imprisoned for three days. Then, holding Simeon as a hostage, he tells them that they must now go back home and bring back their youngest brother Benjamin. In other words, he is forcing them to re-enact that earlier occasion when they came back to their father with one of the brothers, Joseph, missing. Note what happens next:

> They said to one another, "Surely we deserve to be punished [*ashemim*] because of our brother. We saw how distressed he was when he pleaded with us for his life, but we would not listen; that is why this distress has come on us...." They did not realise that Joseph could understand them, since he was using an interpreter. (Gen. 42:21–23)

This is the first stage of repentance. They *admit they have done wrong*.

Next, after the second meeting, Joseph has his special silver cup planted in Benjamin's sack. It is found and the brothers are brought back. They are told that Benjamin must stay as a slave.

> "What can we say to my lord?" Judah replied. "What can we say? How can we prove our innocence? God has uncovered your servants' guilt. We are now my lord's slaves – we ourselves and the one who was found to have the cup." (Gen. 44:16)

This is the second stage of repentance. They *confess*. In fact, they do more; they admit collective responsibility. This is important. When the brothers sold Joseph into slavery it was Judah who proposed the crime (Gen. 37:26–27) but they were all (except Reuben) complicit in it.

Finally, at the climax of the story Judah himself says, "So now let me remain as your slave in place of the lad. Let the lad go back with his brothers!" (Gen. 42:33). Judah, who sold Joseph as a slave, is now willing to become a slave so that his brother Benjamin can go free. This is what the sages and Rambam define as *complete repentance*, namely when circumstances repeat themselves and you have an opportunity to commit the same crime again, but you refrain from doing so because *you have changed*.

Now Joseph can forgive, because his brothers, led by Judah, have gone through all three stages of repentance: (1) admission of guilt, (2) confession, and (3) behavioural change.

Forgiveness only exists in a culture in which repentance exists. Repentance presupposes that we are free and morally responsible agents who are capable of change, specifically the change that comes about when we recognise that something we have done is wrong, that we are responsible for it and must never do it again. The possibility of that kind of moral transformation simply did not exist in ancient Greece or any other pagan culture. Greece was a shame-and-honour culture that turned on the twin concepts of character and fate.[4] Judaism was a repentance-and-forgiveness culture whose central concepts were will and choice. The idea of forgiveness was then adopted by Christianity, making the Judaeo-Christian ethic the primary vehicle of forgiveness in history.

Repentance and forgiveness are not just two ideas among many. They transformed the human situation. For the first time, repentance established the possibility that we are not condemned endlessly to repeat the past. When I repent I show I can change. The future is not predestined. I can make it different from what it might have been. Forgiveness liberates us from the past. *Forgiveness breaks the irreversibility of reaction and revenge.* It is the undoing of what has been done.[5]

Humanity changed the day Joseph forgave his brothers. When we forgive and are worthy of being forgiven, we are no longer prisoners of our past. The moral life is one that makes room for forgiveness.

4. See Bernard Williams, *Shame and Necessity* (Berkeley: University of California Press, 1993).
5. Hannah Arendt makes this point in *The Human Condition* (Chicago: University of Chicago Press, 1958), 241.

Vayeḥi

When Is One Permitted to Tell a Lie?

After the death of Jacob, as we saw, Joseph's brothers were afraid. Years earlier, when he had revealed his true identity to them, Joseph appeared to have forgiven them for selling him as a slave. Yet the brothers were not wholly reassured. Maybe Joseph did not mean what he said. Perhaps he still harboured resentment. Maybe the only reason he had not yet taken revenge was respect for Jacob. There was a convention in those days that there was to be no settling of scores between siblings in the lifetime of the father. We know this from an earlier episode: after Jacob took his brother's blessing, Esau said, "The days of mourning for my father are near; then I will kill my brother Jacob" (Gen. 27:41).

So the brothers come before Joseph and say:

> Your father left these instructions before he died: "This is what you are to say to Joseph: 'I ask you to forgive your brothers for the sins and the wrongs they committed in treating you so badly.'" Now please forgive the sins of the servants of the God

of your father. When their message came to him, Joseph wept. (Gen. 50:16–17)

The text makes it as plain as possible that the story they told Joseph was a lie. If Jacob had really said those words he would have said them to Joseph himself, not to the brothers. The time to have done so was on his deathbed in the previous chapter. The brothers' tale, as we noted in the previous chapter, was a "white lie." Its primary aim was not to deceive but to ease a potentially explosive situation. Perhaps that is why Joseph wept, understanding that his brothers still thought him capable of revenge.

The sages derived a principle from this text. *Mutar leshanot mipnei hashalom*, "It is permitted to tell an untruth (literally, "to change" the facts) for the sake of peace" (Yevamot 65b). A white lie is permitted in Jewish law.

This is not the only place where the sages invoked this principle. They even attributed it to God Himself.[1] When the angels came to visit Abraham to tell him and Sarah that they were about to have a child, "Sarah laughed to herself as she thought, 'After I am worn out and my lord is old, will I now have this pleasure?'" God then asked Abraham, "Why did Sarah laugh and say, 'Will I really have a child, now that I am old?'" (Gen. 18:12–13).

God did not mention that Sarah believed that not only was she too old to have a child – so was Abraham (this turned out to be quite untrue: Abraham had six more children after Sarah's death). The sages inferred that God did not mention it because He did not want there to be bad feelings between husband and wife. Here too the sages said: it is permitted to change for the sake of peace.

It is clear that the sages needed both episodes to establish the principle. Had we only known about the case of Sarah, we could not infer that we are permitted to tell a white lie. God did not tell a white lie about Sarah. He merely did not tell Abraham the whole truth. Had we only known about the case of Joseph's brothers, we could not have inferred that what they did was permitted. Perhaps it was forbidden, and

---

1. *Midrash Sekhel Tov, Toledot,* 27:19.

that is why Joseph wept. The fact that God Himself had done something similar is what led the sages to say that the brothers were justified.

What is at stake here is an important feature of the moral life, despite the fact that we seem to be speaking of no more than social niceties: tact. The late Sir Isaiah Berlin pointed out that not all values coexist in a kind of platonic harmony. His favourite example was freedom and equality: You can have a free economy but the result will be inequality. You can have economic equality – communism – but the result will be a loss of freedom. In the world as currently configured, moral conflict is unavoidable.[2]

This was an important fact, though one about which Judaism seems never to have been in doubt. There was, for example, a powerful moment in Tanakh when King David's son Absalom mounted a coup d'état against his father. David was forced to flee. Eventually there was a battle between Absalom's troops and David's. Absalom, who was handsome and had fine hair, was caught by it when it became entangled in the branches of a tree. Left hanging there, Joab, captain of David's army, killed him.

When David heard the news he was overcome with grief: "The king was shaken. He went up to the room over the gateway and wept. As he went, he said: 'O my son Absalom! My son, my son Absalom! If only I had died instead of you – O Absalom, my son, my son!'" (II Sam. 18:33). Joab was brutal in his words to the king: "Today you have humiliated all your men, who have just saved your life. … You love those who hate you and hate those who love you. … Now go out and encourage your men" (II Sam. 19:6–8). David's grief at the loss of his son conflicted with his responsibilities as head of state and his loyalty to the troops who saved his life. Which should have come first: his duties as a father or as a king?

The existence of conflicting values means that the kind of morality we adopt and society we create depend not only on the values we embrace but also on the way we prioritise them. Prioritising equality over freedom creates one kind of society – Soviet Communism for example. Prioritising

---

2. Isaiah Berlin, "Two Concepts of Liberty," in *Four Essays on Liberty* (London: Oxford University Press, 1969). See also the important work by Stuart Hampshire, *Morality and Conflict* (Cambridge, MA: Harvard University Press, 1983).

freedom over equality leads to market economics. People in both societies may value the same things but they rank them differently in the scale of values, and thus prioritise how they choose when the two conflict.

This is what is at stake in the stories of Sarah and Joseph's brothers. Truth and peace are both values, but which do we choose when they conflict? Not everyone among the rabbinic sages agreed.

There is, for example, a famous argument between the schools of Hillel and Shammai as to what to say about the bride at a wedding (Ketubbot 16b). The custom was to say that "the bride is beautiful and graceful." Members of the School of Shammai, however, were not prepared to say so if, in their eyes, the bride was not beautiful and graceful. For them the supreme value was the Torah's insistence on truth: "Keep far from falsehood" (Ex. 23:7). The School of Hillel did not accept this. Who was to judge whether the bride was beautiful and graceful? Surely the bridegroom himself. So praise of the bride was not an objective statement that could be tested empirically. It was simply endorsing the bridegroom's choice. It was a way of celebrating the couple's happiness.

Courtesies are often like this. Telling someone how much you like the gift they have brought, even if you do not, or saying to someone, "How lovely to see you" when you were hoping to avoid them, is more like good manners than an attempt to deceive. We all know this, and thus no harm is done, as it would be if we were to tell a lie when substantive interests were at stake.

More fundamental and philosophical is an important midrash about a conversation between God and the angels as to whether human beings should be created at all:

> R. Shimon said: When God was about to create Adam, the ministering angels split into contending groups. Some said, "Let him be created." Others said, "Let him not be created." That is why it is written: "Mercy and truth collided, righteousness and peace clashed" (Ps. 85:11).
>
> Mercy said, "Let him be created, because he will do merciful deeds."
>
> Truth said, "Let him not be created, for he will be full of falsehood."

Righteousness said, "Let him be created, for he will do righteous deeds."

Peace said, "Let him not be created, for he will never cease quarrelling."

What did the Holy One, Blessed Be He do? He took truth and threw it to the ground.

The angels said, "Sovereign of the universe, why do You do thus to Your own seal, truth? Let truth arise from the ground."

Thus it is written, "Let truth spring up from the earth" (Ps. 85:12).[3]

This is a challenging text. What exactly were the angels saying? What does it mean to say that God "took truth and threw it to the ground"? And what happened to the claim made by the angel of peace that humans "will never cease quarrelling"?

I interpret it as meaning that humans are destined to conflict so long as contending groups each claim to have a monopoly on truth. The only way they will learn to live at peace is by realising that they, finite as all humans are, will never in this life achieve truth as it is in heaven. For us, truth is always partial, fragmentary, the view from somewhere and not, as philosophers sometimes say, "the view from nowhere."[4]

This deep insight is, I believe, the reason why the Torah is multi-perspectival, why Tanakh contains so many different kinds of voices, why Mishna and Talmud are structured around argument, and why Midrash is built on the premise that there are "seventy faces" to Torah. No other civilisation I know has had so subtle and complex an understanding of the nature of truth.

Nor has any other so valued peace. Judaism is not and never was pacifist. National self-defence sometimes requires war. But Isaiah and Micah were the first visionaries of a world in which "nation shall not lift up sword against nation" (Is. 2:4; Mic. 4:3). Isaiah is the poet laureate of peace.

3. Genesis Rabba 8:5.
4. Thomas Nagel, *The View From Nowhere* (New York: Oxford University Press, 1986). The only person to have achieved a non-anthropocentric, God's-eye-view of creation was Job in chapters 38–41 of the book that bears his name.

Given the choice, when it came to interpersonal relations the sages valued peace over truth, not least because truth can flourish in peace while it is often the first casualty in war. So the brothers were not wrong to tell Joseph a white lie for the sake of peace within the family. It reminded them all of the deeper truth that not only their human father, now dead, but also their heavenly Father, eternally alive, wants the people of the covenant to be at peace. For how can Jews be at peace with the world if they are not at peace with themselves?

Exodus
שמות

Shemot

On Not Obeying Immoral Orders

The opening chapters of Exodus plunge us into the midst of epic events. Almost at a stroke the Israelites are transformed from protected minority to slaves. Moses passes from prince of Egypt to Midianite shepherd to leader of the Israelites through a history-changing encounter at the burning bush. Yet it is one small episode that deserves to be seen as a turning point in the history of humanity. Its heroines are two remarkable women, Shifra and Puah.

We do not know who they were. The Torah gives us no further information about them than that they were midwives, instructed by Pharaoh: "When you are helping the Hebrew women during childbirth on the delivery stool, if you see that the baby is a boy, kill him; but if it is a girl, let her live" (Ex. 1:16). The Hebrew description of the two women as *hameyaldot haIvriyot* is ambiguous. It could mean "the Hebrew midwives"; so most translations and commentaries read it. But it could equally mean, "the midwives to the Hebrews," in which case they may have been Egyptian. That is how Josephus,[1] Abrabanel, and Samuel David Luzzatto understand it, arguing that it is simply implausible to suppose that Hebrew women would have been party to an act of genocide against their own people.

What we do know, however, is that they refused to carry out the order: "The midwives, however, feared God and did not do what the king of Egypt had told them to do; they let the boys live" (Ex. 1:17). This is the *first recorded instance in history of civil disobedience*: refusing to obey an order, given by the most powerful man in the most powerful empire of the ancient world, simply because it was immoral, unethical, inhuman.

The Torah suggests that they did so without fuss or drama. Summoned by Pharaoh to explain their behaviour, they simply replied: "Hebrew women are not like Egyptian women; they are vigorous and give birth before the midwives arrive" (Ex. 1:19). To this, Pharaoh had no reply. The matter-of-factness of the entire incident reminds us of one of the most salient findings about the courage of those who saved Jewish lives during the Holocaust. They had little in common except for the fact that they saw nothing remarkable in what they did.[2] Often the mark of real moral heroes is that they do not see themselves as moral heroes. They do what they do because that is what a human being is supposed to do. That is probably the meaning of the statement that they "feared God." It is the Torah's generic description of those who have a moral sense.[3]

It took more than three thousand years for what the midwives did to become enshrined in international law. In 1946 the Nazi war criminals on trial at Nuremberg all offered the defence that they were merely obeying orders, given by a duly constituted and democratically elected government. Under the doctrine of national sovereignty every government has the right to issue its own laws and order its own affairs. It took a new legal concept, namely a crime against humanity, to establish the guilt of the architects and administrators of genocide.

1. *Antiquities of the Jews*, 2.9.2.
2. See James Q. Wilson, *The Moral Sense* (New York: Free Press, 1993), 35–39, and the literature cited there.
3. See, for example, Gen. 20:11.

The Nuremberg principle gave legal substance to what the midwives instinctively understood: that there are orders that should not be obeyed because they are immoral. Moral law transcends and may override the law of the state. As the Talmud puts it: "If there is a conflict between the words of the master [God] and the words of a disciple [a human being], the words of the master must prevail" (Kiddushin 42b).

The Nuremberg trials were not the first occasion in which the story of the midwives had a significant impact on history. Throughout the Middle Ages the Church, knowing that knowledge is power and therefore best kept in the hands of the priesthood, had forbidden vernacular translations of the Bible. In the course of the sixteenth century, three developments changed this irrevocably. First was the Reformation, with its maxim *Sola scriptura*, "By Scripture alone," placing the Bible centre-stage in religious life. Second was the invention, in the mid-fifteenth century, of printing. Lutherans were convinced that this was divine providence. God had sent the printing press so that the doctrines of the Reformed church could be spread worldwide. Third was the fact that some people, regardless of the ban, had translated the Bible anyway. John Wycliffe and his followers had done so in the fourteenth century, but the most influential was William Tyndale, whose translation of the New Testament, begun in 1525, became the first printed Bible in English. He paid for this with his life. When Mary I took the Church of England back to Catholicism, many English Protestants fled to Calvin's Geneva, where they produced a new translation, based on Tyndale, called the Geneva Bible. Produced in a small, affordable edition, it was smuggled into England in large numbers.

Able to read the Bible by themselves for the first time, people soon discovered that it was, as far as monarchy is concerned, a highly seditious document. It tells of how God told Samuel that in seeking to appoint a king, the Israelites were rejecting Him as their only sovereign. It describes graphically how the prophets were unafraid to challenge kings, which they did with the authority of God Himself. And it tells the story of the midwives who refused to carry out Pharaoh's order. On this, in a marginal note, the Geneva Bible endorses their refusal, criticising only the fact that in explaining their behaviour they told a lie. The note says, "Their disobedience herein was lawful, but their dissembling evil." King

James understood clearly the dire implication of that one sentence. It meant that a king could be disobeyed on the authority of God Himself, a clear and categorical refutation of the idea of the divine right of kings.[4]

Eventually, unable to stop the spread of Bibles in translation, King James decided to commission his own version, which appeared in 1611. But by then the damage had been done and the seeds of what became the English Revolution had been planted. Throughout the seventeenth century, by far the most influential force in English politics was the Hebrew Bible as understood by the Puritans, and it was the Pilgrim Fathers who took this faith with them on their journey to what would eventually become the United States of America.

A century and a half later, it was the work of another English radical, Thomas Paine, that made a decisive impact on the American Revolution. His pamphlet *Common Sense* was published in America in January 1776 and became an immediate bestseller, selling 100,000 copies almost immediately. Its impact was huge, and because of it he became known as "the father of the American Revolution." Despite the fact that Paine was an atheist, the opening pages of *Common Sense*, justifying rebellion against a tyrannical king, are entirely based on citations from the Hebrew Bible. In the same spirit, that summer Benjamin Franklin drew as his design for the Great Seal of America a picture of the Egyptians (i.e., the English) drowning in the Red Sea, with the caption, "Rebellion to tyrants is obedience to God." Thomas Jefferson was so struck by the sentence that he recommended it be used on the Great Seal of Virginia and later incorporated it in his personal seal.

The story of the midwives belongs to a larger vision implicit throughout the Torah and Tanakh as a whole: that right is sovereign over might, and that even God Himself can be called to account in the name of justice, as He expressly mandates Abraham to do. Sovereignty ultimately belongs to God, so any human act or order that transgresses the will of God is by that fact alone ultra vires. These revolutionary ideas are intrinsic to the biblical vision of politics and the use of power.

---

4. See Christopher Hill, *The English Bible and the Seventeenth-Century Revolution* (London: Allen Lane, 1993).

In the end, though, it was the courage of two remarkable women that created the precedent later taken up by the American writer Thoreau in his classic essay *Civil Disobedience* (1849) that in turn inspired Gandhi and Martin Luther King in the twentieth century.[5] Their story also ends with a lovely touch. The text says: "So God was kind to the midwives and the people increased and became even more numerous. And because the midwives feared God, He gave them houses" (Ex. 1:20–21).

Luzzatto interprets this last phrase to mean that He gave them families of their own. Often, he writes, midwives are women who are unable to have children. In this case, God blessed Shifra and Puah by giving them children, as He had done for Sarah, Rebecca, and Rachel.

This too is a not unimportant point. The closest Greek literature comes to the idea of civil disobedience is the story of Antigone who insisted on giving her brother Polynices a burial despite the fact that King Creon had refused to permit it, regarding him as a traitor to Thebes. Sophocles' *Antigone* is a tragedy: the heroine must die because of her loyalty to her brother and her disobedience to the king. The Hebrew Bible, however, is not a tragedy. In fact biblical Hebrew has no word meaning "tragedy" in the Greek sense. Good is rewarded, not punished, because the universe, God's work of art, is a world in which moral behaviour is blessed and evil, briefly in the ascendant, is ultimately defeated.

Shifra and Puah are two of the great heroines of world literature, the first to teach humanity the moral limits of power.

---

5.   Henry David Thoreau, *Civil Disobedience* (Boston: David R. Godine, 1969).

Va'era

Free Will

The question is ancient. If God hardened Pharaoh's heart, then it was God who made Pharaoh refuse to let the Israelites go, not Pharaoh himself. How can this be just? How could it be right to punish Pharaoh and his people for a decision – a series of decisions – that were not made freely by Pharaoh himself? Punishment presupposes guilt. Guilt presupposes responsibility. Responsibility presupposes freedom. We do not blame weights for falling or the sun for shining. Natural forces are not choices made by reflecting on alternatives. Homo sapiens alone is free. Take away that freedom and you take away our humanity. How then can it say, as it does in *Parashat Va'era*, that God hardened[1] Pharaoh's heart (Ex. 7:3)?

All the commentators are exercised by this question. Rambam and others note a striking feature of the narrative: for the first five plagues we read that Pharaoh himself hardened his heart. Only later, during the

---

1. Three different verbs are used in the narrative to indicate hardening of the heart: K-SH-H, Ḥ-Z-K, and K-B-D. They have different nuances: the first means "harden," the second, "strengthen," and the third, "make heavy."

last five plagues, do we read about God doing so. The last five plagues were therefore a punishment for the first five refusals, freely made by Pharaoh himself.[2]

A second approach, in precisely the opposite direction, is that during the last five plagues God intervened not to *harden* but to *strengthen* Pharaoh's heart. He acted to ensure that Pharaoh kept his freedom and did not lose it. Such was the impact of the plagues that in the normal course of events a national leader would have no choice but to give in to a superior force. As Pharaoh's own advisers said before the eighth plague, "Do you not yet realise that Egypt is destroyed?" (Ex. 10:7). To give in at that point would have been action under duress, not a genuine change of heart. Such is the approach of Joseph Albo[3] and Ovadiah Sforno (on Ex. 7:3).

A third approach calls into question the very meaning of the phrase, "God hardened Pharaoh's heart." In a profound sense, God, author of history, is behind every event, every act, every gust of wind that blows, every drop of rain that falls. Normally, however, we do not attribute human action to God. We are what we are because that is how we have chosen to be, even if this was written long before in the divine script for humankind. What do we attribute to an act of God? Something that is unusual, falling so far outside the norms of human behaviour that we find it hard to explain in any other way than to say that surely this happened for a purpose.

God Himself says about Pharaoh's obstinacy that it allowed Him to demonstrate to all humanity that even the greatest empire is powerless against the hand of Heaven (Ex. 7:5; 14:18). Pharaoh acted freely, but his last refusals were so strange that it was obvious to everyone that God had anticipated this. It was predictable, part of the script. God had disclosed this to Abraham centuries earlier when He told him in a fearful vision that his descendants would be strangers in a land not theirs (Gen. 15:13–14).

These are all interesting and plausible interpretations. It seems to me, though, that the Torah is telling a deeper story, one that never loses

2. Rambam, *Mishneh Torah, Hilkhot Teshuva* 6:3.
3. Albo, *Sefer HaIkkarim*, IV, 25.

its relevance. Philosophers and scientists have tended to think in terms of abstractions and universals. Some have concluded that we have free will, others that we do not. There is no conceptual space in between.

In life, however, that is not the way freedom works at all. Consider addiction: the first few times you smoke a cigarette or drink alcohol or take drugs, you do so freely. You know the risks but you ignore them. As time goes on, your dependency increases until the craving is so intense that you are almost powerless to resist it. At that point you may have to go into rehabilitation. You no longer, on your own, have the ability to stop. As the Talmud says, "A prisoner cannot release himself from prison" (Berakhot 5b).

Addiction is a physical phenomenon. But there are moral equivalents. For example, suppose on one significant occasion, you tell a lie. People now believe something about you that is not true. As they question you about it, or it comes up in conversation, you find yourself having to tell more lies to support the first. "Oh what a tangled web we weave," Sir Walter Scott famously said, "when first we practise to deceive."

That is as far as individuals are concerned. When it comes to organisations, the risk is even greater. Let us say that a senior member of staff has made a costly mistake that, if exposed, threatens the entire future of the company. He will make an attempt to cover it up. To do so he must enlist the help of others, who become his co-conspirators. As the circle of deception widens, it becomes part of the corporate culture, making it ever more difficult for honest people within the organisation to resist or protest. It then needs the rare courage of a whistle-blower to expose and halt the deception. There have been many such stories in recent years.[4]

Within nations, especially non-democratic ones, the risk is higher still. In commercial enterprises, losses can be quantified. Someone somewhere knows how much has been lost, how many debts have been concealed and where. In politics, there may be no such objective test. It is easy to claim that a policy is working and explain away apparent counter-indicators. A narrative emerges and becomes the received

---

4. On Enron, see Bethany McLean and Peter Elkind, *The Smartest Guys in the Room: The Amazing Rise and Scandalous Fall of Enron* (New York: Portfolio, 2003).

wisdom. Hans Christian Andersen's *The Emperor's New Clothes* is the classic parable of this phenomenon. A child sees the truth and in inno-cence blurts it out, breaking the conspiracy of silence on the part of the king's counsellors.

We lose our freedom gradually, often without noticing it. That is what the Torah has been implying almost from the beginning. The classic statement of free will appears in the story of Cain and Abel. See-ing that Cain is angry that his offering has not found favour, God says to him: "If you do what is right, will you not be accepted? But if you do not do what is right, sin is crouching at your door; it desires to have you, but you must rule over it" (Gen. 4:7). The maintenance of free will, especially in a state of high emotion like anger, needs willpower. As we noted in our study of *Parashat Noaḥ*, what Daniel Goleman calls an "*amygdala hijack*" can occur, in which instinctive reaction takes the place of reflective decision and we do things that are harmful to us as well as to others.[5] That is the emotional threat to freedom.

Then there is a social threat. After the Holocaust, a number of path-breaking experiments were undertaken to judge the power of conformism and obedience to authority. Solomon Asch conducted a series of experiments in which eight people were gathered in a room and were shown a line; they were then asked which of three others was the same length. Unknown to the eighth person, the seven others were associates of the experimenter and were following his instructions. On a number of occasions the seven gave an answer that was clearly false, yet in 75 per cent of cases the eighth was willing to give an answer, in confor-mity with the group, which he knew to be false.

Yale psychologist Stanley Milgram showed that ordinary indi-viduals were willing to inflict what appeared to be devastatingly painful electric shocks on someone in an adjacent room when instructed to do so by an authority figure, the experimenter.[6] The Stanford Prison Experi-ment, conducted by Philip Zimbardo, divided participants into the roles of prisoners and guards. Within days the "guards" were acting cruelly

5.   Daniel Goleman, *Emotional Intelligence* (New York: Bantam, 1995).
6.   Stanley Milgram, *Obedience to Authority: An Experimental View* (New York: Harper & Row, 1974).

and in some cases abusively towards the prisoners and the experiment, planned to last a fortnight, had to be called off after six days.[7]

The power of conformism, as these experiments showed, is immense. That, I believe, is why Abraham was told to leave his land, his birthplace, and his father's house. These are the three factors – culture, community, and early childhood – that circumscribe our freedom. Jews through the ages have been *in* but not *of* society. To be a Jew means keeping a calibrated distance from the age and its idols. Freedom needs time to make reflective decisions and distance so as not to be lulled into conformity.

Most tragically, there is the moral threat. We sometimes forget, or do not even know, that the conditions of slavery the Israelites experienced in Egypt were often enough felt by Egyptians themselves over history. The great pyramid of Giza, built more than a thousand years before the Exodus, before even the birth of Abraham, reduced much of Egypt to a slave labour colony for twenty years.[8] When life becomes cheap and people are seen as a means, not an end, when the worst excesses are excused in the name of tradition and rulers have absolute power, then conscience is eroded and freedom lost because the culture has created insulated space in which the cry of the oppressed can no longer be heard.

That is what the Torah means when it says that God hardened Pharaoh's heart. Enslaving others, Pharaoh himself became enslaved. He became a prisoner of the values he himself had espoused. Freedom in the deepest sense, the freedom to do the right and the good, is not a given. We acquire it, or lose it, gradually. In the end tyrants bring about their own destruction, whereas those with willpower, courage, and the willingness to go against the consensus acquire a monumental freedom. That is what Judaism is: an invitation to freedom by resisting the idols and siren calls of the age.

---

7. Philip G. Zimbardo, *The Lucifer Effect: Understanding How Good People Turn Evil* (New York: Random House, 2007).
8. Toby Wilkinson, *The Rise and Fall of Ancient Egypt* (London: Bloomsbury, 2010), 72–91. It has been calculated, based on a ten-hour working day, that one giant block of stone weighing more than one ton would have to be transported into place every two minutes of every day for twenty years.

Bo

Telling the Story

Go to Washington and take a tour of the memorials and you will make a fascinating discovery. You can begin at the Lincoln Memorial, with its giant statue of the man who braved civil war and presided over the ending of slavery. On one side you will see the Gettysburg Address, that masterpiece of brevity with its invocation of "a new birth of freedom." On the other is the great Second Inaugural with its message of healing: "With malice toward none, with charity for all, with firmness in the right as God gives us to see the right...."

Walk down to the Potomac Basin and you see the Martin Luther King Memorial with its sixteen quotes from the great fighter for civil rights, among them his 1963 statement, "Darkness cannot drive out darkness, only light can do that. Hate cannot drive out hate, only love can do that." And giving its name to the monument as a whole, a sentence from the "I Have a Dream" speech: "Out of the Mountain of Despair, a Stone of Hope."

Continue along the tree-lined avenue bordering the water and you arrive at the Roosevelt Memorial, constructed as a series of six spaces, one for each decade of his public career, each with a passage from one

Exodus

of the defining speeches of the time – most famously, "We have nothing to fear but fear itself."

Lastly, bordering the Basin at its southern edge is a Greek temple dedicated to the author of the American Declaration of Independence, Thomas Jefferson. Around the dome are the words he wrote to Benjamin Rush: "I have sworn upon the altar of God eternal hostility against every form of tyranny over the mind of man." Defining the circular space are four panels, each with lengthy quotations from Jefferson's writings, one from the Declaration itself, another beginning, "Almighty God hath created the mind free," and a third, "God who gave us life gave us liberty. Can the liberties of a nation be secure when we have removed a conviction that these liberties are the gift of God?"

Each of these four monuments is built around texts and each tells a story.

Now compare the monuments in London, most conspicuously those in Parliament Square. The memorial to David Lloyd George contains three words: David Lloyd George. The one to Nelson Mandela has two, and the Churchill memorial just one: Churchill. Winston Churchill was a man of words – in his early life a journalist, later a historian, author of almost fifty books. He won the Nobel Prize not for peace but for literature. He delivered as many speeches and coined as many unforgettable sentences as Jefferson or Lincoln, Roosevelt or Martin Luther King, but none of his utterances is engraved on the plinth beneath his statue. He is memorialised only by his name.

The difference between the American and British monuments is unmistakable, and the reason is that Britain and the United States have quite different political and moral cultures. England is, or was until recently, a tradition-based society. In such societies, things are as they are because that is how they were "since time immemorial." It is unnecessary to ask why. Those who belong know. Those who need to ask show thereby that they do not belong.

American society is different because from the Pilgrim Fathers onwards it was based on the concept of covenant as set out in Tanakh, especially in Exodus and Deuteronomy. The early settlers were Puritans, in the Calvinist tradition, the closest Christianity came to basing its politics on the Hebrew Bible. Covenantal societies are not based on tradition. The Puritans, like the Israelites three thousand years earlier, were revolutionaries, attempting to create a new type of society, one unlike Egypt or, in the case of America, England. Michael Walzer called his book on the politics of the seventeenth-century Puritans *The Revolution of the Saints.*[1] They were trying to overthrow the tradition that gave absolute power to kings and maintained established hierarchies of class.

Covenantal societies always represent a conscious new beginning by a group of people dedicated to an ideal. The story of the founders, the journey they made, the obstacles they had to overcome, and the vision that drove them are essential elements of a covenantal culture. Retelling the story, handing it on to one's children, and dedicating oneself to continuing the work that earlier generations began are fundamental to the ethos of such a society. A covenanted nation is not simply there because it is there. It is there to fulfil a moral vision. That is what led G. K. Chesterton to call the United States a nation "with the soul of a church,"[2] the only one in the world "founded on a creed"[3] (Chesterton's anti-Semitism prevented him from crediting the true source of America's political philosophy, the Hebrew Bible).

The history of storytelling as an essential part of moral education begins in *Parashat Bo.* It is quite extraordinary how, on the brink of the Exodus, Moses turns to the future and to the duty of parents to educate their children about the story that was shortly to unfold. In fact, he does so three times: "When your children ask you, 'What is this service to you?' you shall answer, 'It is the Passover service to God. He passed over the houses of the Israelites in Egypt when He struck the Egyptians, sparing our homes'" (Ex. 12:25–27); "On that day, you shall tell your child, 'It is because of this that God acted for me when I left Egypt'" (13:8); "Your child may later ask you, 'What is this?' You shall answer him, 'With a show of power, God brought us out of Egypt, the place of slavery'" (13:14).

1. *The Revolution of the Saints: A Study in the Origins of Radical Politics* (Cambridge, MA: Harvard University Press, 1965).
2. *What I Saw in America* (New York: Dodd, Mead and Company, 1922), 10.
3. Ibid., 7.

This is truly extraordinary. The Israelites have not yet emerged into the dazzling light of freedom. They are still slaves. Yet already Moses is directing their minds to the far horizon of the future and giving them the responsibility of passing on their story to succeeding generations. It is as if Moses were saying: Forget where you came from and why, and you will eventually lose your identity, your continuity, and raison d'être. You will come to think of yourself as the mere member of a nation among nations, one ethnicity among many. Forget the story of freedom and you will eventually lose freedom itself.

Rarely indeed have philosophers written on the importance of storytelling for the moral life. Yet that is how we become the people we are. The great exception among modern philosophers has been Alasdair MacIntyre, who wrote, in his classic *After Virtue,* "I can only answer the question 'What am I to do?' if I can answer the prior question 'Of what story or stories do I find myself a part?'" Deprive children of stories, says MacIntyre, and you leave them "anxious stutterers in their actions as in their words."[4]

No one understood this more clearly than Moses because he knew that without a specific identity it is almost impossible not to lapse into whatever is the current idolatry of the age – rationalism, idealism, nationalism, fascism, communism, postmodernism, relativism, individualism, hedonism, or consumerism, to name only the most recent. The alternative, a society based on tradition alone, crumbles as soon as respect for tradition dies, which it always does at some stage or another.

Identity, which is always particular, is based on story, the narrative that links me to the past, guides me in the present, and places on me responsibility for the future. And no story, at least in the West, was more influential than that of the Exodus, the memory that the supreme power intervened in history to liberate the supremely powerless. This was paired with the covenant that followed, whereby the Israelites bound themselves to God in a promise to create a society that would be the opposite of Egypt, where individuals were respected as the image of God, where one day in seven all hierarchies of power were suspended, and

---

4. *After Virtue: A Study in Moral Theory* (Notre Dame, IN: University of Notre Dame Press, 2007), 216.

where dignity and justice were accessible to all. We never quite reached that ideal state but we never ceased to travel towards it and believed it was there at journey's end.

"The Jews have always had stories for the rest of us," said the BBC's political correspondent, Andrew Marr.[5] God created man, Elie Wiesel once wrote, because God loves stories.[6] What other cultures have done through systems, Jews have done through stories. And in Judaism, the stories are not engraved in stone on memorials, magnificent though they are. They are told at home, around the table, from parents to children, as the gift of the past to the future. That is how storytelling in Judaism was devolved, domesticated, and democratised.

Only the most basic elements of morality are universal: "thin" abstractions like justice or liberty that tend to mean different things to different people in different places and times. But if we want our children and our society to be moral, we need a collective story that tells us where we came from and what our task is in the world. The story of the Exodus, especially as told on Passover at the Seder table, is always the same yet ever-changing, an almost infinite set of variations on a single set of themes that we all internalise in ways that are unique to us, yet we all share as members of the same historically extended community.

There are stories that ennoble, and others that stultify, leaving us prisoners of ancient grievances or impossible ambitions. The Jewish story is in its way the oldest of all, yet ever young, and we are each a part of it. It tells us who we are and who our ancestors hoped we would be. Storytelling is the great vehicle of moral education. It was the Torah's insight that a people who told their children the story of freedom and its responsibilities would stay free for as long as humankind lives and breathes and hopes.

5. Andrew Marr, *The Observer,* Sunday, May 14, 2000.
6. *The Gates of the Forest* (New York: Holt, Rinehart, and Winston), preface.

Beshallaḥ

The Face of Evil

After 9/11, when the horror and trauma had subsided, Americans found themselves asking what had happened and why. Was it a disaster? A tragedy? A crime? An act of war? It did not seem to fit the pre-existing paradigms. And why had it happened? The question most often asked about Al Qaeda was, "Why do they hate us?"

In the wake of those events, American thinker Lee Harris wrote two books, *Civilization and Its Enemies* and *The Suicide of Reason*,[1] that were among the most thought-provoking responses of the decade. The reason for the questions and the failure to find answers, said Harris, was that we in the West had *forgotten the concept of an enemy*. Liberal democratic politics and market economics create a certain kind of society, a specific way of thinking, and a characteristic type of personality. At their heart is the concept of *the rational actor*, the person who judges acts by their consequences and chooses the maximal option. He or she believes that for every problem there is a solution, for every conflict a

---

1. Lee Harris, *Civilization and Its Enemies: The Next Stage of History* (New York: Free Press, 2004); *The Suicide of Reason* (New York: Basic Books, 2008).

resolution. The way to achieve it is to sit down, negotiate, and do on balance what is best for all.

In such a world there are no enemies, merely conflicts of interest. An enemy, says Harris, is simply "a friend we hadn't done enough for yet." In the real world, however, not everyone is a liberal democrat. An enemy is "someone who is willing to die in order to kill you. And while it is true that the enemy always hates us for a reason, it is his reason and not ours." He sees a different world from ours, and in that world we are the enemy. Why do they hate us? Answers Harris: "They hate us *because* we are their enemy."[2]

Whatever the rights and wrongs of Harris's specifics, the general point is true and profound. We can become mind-blind, thinking that the way we – our society, our culture, our civilisation – see things is the only way, or at least that it is the way everyone would choose if given the chance. Only a complete failure to understand the history of ideas can explain this error, and it is a dangerous one. When Montezuma, ruler of the Aztecs, met Cortés, leader of the Spanish expedition in 1520, he assumed that he was meeting a civilised man from a civilised nation. That mistake cost him his life and within a year there was no Aztec civilisation any more. Not everyone sees the world the way we do, and, as Richard Weaver once said: "The trouble with humanity is that it forgets to read the minutes of the last meeting."[3]

This explains the significance of the unusual command at the end of *Parashat Beshallah*. The Israelites had escaped the seemingly inexorable danger of the chariots of the Egyptian army, the military high-tech of its day. Miraculously, the sea divided and the Israelites crossed; the Egyptians, their chariot wheels caught in the mud, were unable either to advance or retreat and were caught by the returning tide.

The Israelites sang a song and finally seemed to be free, when something untoward and unexpected happened. They were attacked by a new enemy, the Amalekites, a nomadic group living in the desert. Moses instructed Joshua to lead the people in battle. They fought and won. But the Torah makes it clear that this was no ordinary battle:

2. Harris, *Civilization*, xii–xiii.
3. *Ideas Have Consequences* (Chicago: University of Chicago Press, 1948), 176.

Then the Lord said to Moses, "Write this on a scroll as something to be remembered and make sure that Joshua hears it, because I will completely blot out the name of Amalek from under heaven." Moses built an altar and called it The Lord Is My Banner. He said, "The hand is on the Lord's throne. The Lord will be at war with Amalek for all generations." (Ex. 17:14–16)

This is a very strange statement, and it stands in marked contrast to the way the Torah speaks about the Egyptians. The Amalekites attacked Israel just once during Moses' lifetime. The Egyptians oppressed the Israelites over an extended period, oppressing and enslaving them and starting a slow genocide by killing every male Israelite child. The whole thrust of the narrative would suggest that if any nation would become the symbol of evil, it would be Egypt.

But the opposite turns out to be true. In Deuteronomy the Torah states, "*Do not abhor an Egyptian*, because you were a stranger in his land" (Deut. 23:8). Shortly thereafter, Moses repeats the command about the Amalekites, adding a significant detail:

Remember what the Amalekites did to you along the way when you came out of Egypt. When you were *weary and worn out*, they met you on your journey and attacked all who were *lagging behind*; they had no fear of God.... You shall blot out the name of Amalek from under heaven. Do not forget! (Deut. 25:17–19)

We are commanded not to hate Egypt, but never to forget Amalek. Why the difference? The simplest answer is to recall the rabbis' statement in *Pirkei Avot*: "If love depends on a specific cause, when the cause ends, so does the love. If love does not depend on a specific cause, then it never ends" (Mishna Avot 5:16). The same applies to hate. When hate depends on a specific cause, it ends once the cause disappears. Causeless, baseless hate lasts forever.

The Egyptians oppressed the Israelites because, in Pharaoh's words, "The Israelites are becoming too numerous and strong for us" (Ex. 1:9). Their hate, in other words, came from fear. It was not irrational. The Egyptians had been attacked and conquered before by a foreign group known as the Hyksos, and the memory of that period was still acute and painful. The Amalekites, however, were not being threatened by the Israelites. They attacked a people who was "weary and worn out," specifically those who were "lagging behind." In short: *The Egyptians feared the Israelites because they were strong. The Amalekites attacked the Israelites because they were weak.*

In today's terminology, the Egyptians were rational actors; the Amalekites were not. With rational actors there can be negotiated peace. People engaged in conflict eventually realise that they are not only destroying their enemies, they are destroying themselves. That is what Pharaoh's advisers said to him after seven plagues: "Do you not yet realise that Egypt is destroyed?" (Ex. 10:7). There comes a point at which rational actors understand that the pursuit of self-interest has become self-destructive, and they learn to cooperate.

It is not so, however, with non-rational actors. Emil Fackenheim, one of the great post-Holocaust theologians, noted that towards the end of the Second World War, the Germans diverted trains carrying supplies to their own army, in order to transport Jews to the extermination camps. So driven were they by hate that they were prepared to put their own victory at risk in order to carry out the systematic murder of the Jews of Europe. This was, he said, evil for evil's sake.[4]

The Amalekites function in Jewish memory as "the enemy" in Lee Harris's sense. Jewish law, however, specifies two completely different forms of action in relation to the Amalekites. First is the physical command to wage war against them. That is what Samuel told Saul to do, a command he failed fully to fulfil. Does this command still apply today?

The unequivocal answer given by Rabbi Nachum Rabinovitch is "No."[5] Rambam ruled that the command to destroy the Amalekites only applied if they refused to make peace and accept the seven Noahide laws. He further stated that the command was no longer applicable since Sennacherib, the Assyrian, had transported and resettled the

4. Emil L. Fackenheim and Michael L. Morgan, *The Jewish Thought of Emil Fackenheim: A Reader* (Detroit: Wayne State University Press, 1987), 126.
5. Rabbi N. L. Rabinovitch, *Shu"t Melumdei Milḥama* (Maale Adumim: Maaliyot, 1993), 22–25.

nations he conquered so that it was no longer possible to identify the ethnicity of any of the original nations against whom the Israelites were commanded to fight. He also said, in *The Guide for the Perplexed*, that the command only applies to people of specific biological descent. It is not to be applied in general to enemies or haters of the Jewish people. So the command to wage war against the Amalekites no longer applies.

However, there is a quite different command, to "remember" and "not forget" Amalek, which we fulfil annually by reading the passage about the Amalekites as it appears in Deuteronomy. This we do on the Shabbat before Purim, *Shabbat Zakhor*; the connection with Purim is that Haman the Agagite is assumed to be a descendant of Agag, king of the Amalekites. Here Amalek has become a symbol rather than a reality.

By dividing the response in this way, Judaism marks a clear distinction between an ancient enemy who no longer exists and the evil that enemy embodied, which can break out again at any time in any place. It is easy at times of peace to forget the evil that lies just beneath the surface of the human heart. Never was this truer than in the past three centuries. The birth of Enlightenment, toleration, emancipation, liberalism, and human rights persuaded many – Jews among them – that collective evil was as extinct as the Amalekites. Evil was then, not now. That age eventually begat nationalism, fascism, communism, two world wars, some of the most brutal tyrannies ever known, and the worst crime of man against man.

Today, the great danger is terror. Here the words of Princeton political philosopher Michael Walzer are particularly apt:

> Wherever we see terrorism, we should look for tyranny and oppression.... The terrorists aim to rule, and murder is their method. They have their own internal police, death squads, disappearances. They begin by killing or intimidating those comrades who stand in their way, and they proceed to do the same, if they can, among the people they claim to represent. If terrorists are successful, they rule tyrannically, and their people bear, without consent, the costs of the terrorists' rule.[6]

6. Michael Walzer, *Arguing About War* (New Haven, CT: Yale University Press, 2004), 64–65.

Evil never dies, and – like liberty – it demands constant vigilance. We are commanded to remember, not for the sake of the past but for the sake of the future, and not for revenge but the opposite: a world free of revenge and other forms of violence.

Lee Harris began *Civilization and Its Enemies* with the words, "The subject of this book is forgetfulness,"[7] and ends with a question: "Can the West overcome the forgetfulness that is the nemesis of every successful civilization?"[8] That is why we are commanded to remember and never forget Amalek, not because the historic people still exists, but because a society of rational actors can sometimes believe that the world is full of rational actors with whom one can negotiate peace. It is not always so.

Rarely was a biblical message so relevant to the future of the West and of freedom itself. Peace is possible, implies Moses, even with an Egypt that enslaved and tried to destroy us. But peace is not possible with those who attack people they see as weak and who deny their own people the freedom for which they claim to be fighting. Freedom depends on our ability to remember and, whenever necessary, confront "the eternal gang of ruthless men,"[9] the face of Amalek throughout history. Sometimes there may be no alternative but to fight evil and defeat it. This may be the only path to peace.

7. Harris, *Civilization*, xi.
8. Ibid., 218.
9. Ibid., 216.

Yitro

The Structure of the Good Society

In the House of Lords there is a special chamber used, among other things, as the place where new peers are robed before their introduction into the House. When my predecessor Lord Jakobovits was introduced, the official robing him commented that he was the first rabbi to be honoured in the Upper House. Lord Jakobovits replied, "No, I am the second." "Who was the first?" asked the surprised official. Lord Jakobovits pointed to the large mural that decorates the chamber and gave it its name. It is known as the Moses Room because of the painting that dominates the room. It shows Moses bringing the Ten Commandments down from Mount Sinai. So Moses was the first rabbi to adorn the House of Lords.

The Ten Commandments that appear in *Parashat Yitro* have long held a special place not only in Judaism but also within the broader configuration of values we call the Judaeo-Christian ethic. In the United States they were often to be found adorning American law courts, though their presence has been challenged, in some states successfully, on the grounds that they breach the First Amendment and the separation of church and state. They remain the supreme expression of the higher law to which all human law is bound.

Within Judaism, too, they have always held a special place. In Second Temple times they were recited in the daily prayers as part of the *Shema*, which then had four paragraphs rather than three (Mishna Tamid 5:1; Berakhot 12a). It was only when sectarians began to claim that only these and not the other 603 commandments came directly from God that the recitation was brought to an end.[1]

The text retained its hold on the Jewish mind nonetheless. Even though it was removed from daily communal prayers, it was preserved in the siddur as a private meditation to be said after the formal service has been concluded. In most congregations, people stand when they are read as part of the Torah reading, despite the fact that Rambam explicitly ruled against that.[2]

Yet their uniqueness is not straightforward. As moral principles, they were mostly not new. Almost all societies have had laws against murder, robbery, and false testimony. There is some originality in the fact that they are apodictic, that is, simple statements of "You shall not...," as opposed to the casuistic form, "If...then." But they are only ten among a much larger body of 613 commandments. Nor are they even described by the Torah itself as "ten commandments." The Torah calls them the *aseret hadevarim*, that is, "ten utterances." Hence the Greek translation, *Decalogue*, meaning "ten words."

What makes them special is that they are simple and easy to memorise. That is because in Judaism, law is not intended for judges alone. The covenant at Sinai, in keeping with the profound egalitarianism at the heart of the Torah, was made not as other covenants were in the ancient world, between kings. The Sinai covenant was made by God

---

1. We do not know who the sectarians were; they may have included early Christians. The argument was that only these were directly heard by the Israelites from God – the others were heard only through Moses (see Rashi to Berakhot 12a).
2. Rambam, *Teshuvot HaRambam* (Responsa of the Rambam), Blau Edition (Jerusalem: Mekitzei Nirdamim, 1960), no. 263.

with the entire people. Hence the need for a simple statement of basic principles that everyone can remember and recite.

More than this, they establish for all time the parameters – the corporate culture, we could almost call it – of Jewish existence. To understand how, it is worth reflecting on their basic structure. There was a fundamental disagreement between Rambam and Ramban on the status of the first sentence: "I am the Lord your God, who brought you out of Egypt, out of the land of slavery" (Ex. 20:2). Rambam, in line with the Talmud, held that this is in itself a command: to believe in God. Ramban held that it was not a command at all. It was a prologue or preamble to the commandments.[3] Modern research on ancient Near Eastern covenant formulae tends to support Ramban.

The other fundamental question is how to divide them. Most depictions of the Ten Commandments divide them into two, because of the "two tablets of stone" (Deut. 4:13) on which they were engraved. Roughly speaking, the first five are about the relationship between humans and God, the second five about the relationship between humans themselves. There is, however, another way of thinking about numerical structures in the Torah.

The seven days of creation, for example, are structured as two sets of three followed by an all-embracing seventh. During the first three days God separated domains: light and dark, upper and lower waters, and sea and dry land. During the second three days He filled each with the appropriate objects and life forms: sun and moon, birds and fish, animals and man. The seventh day was set apart from the others as holy.

Likewise the ten plagues consist of three cycles of three followed by a stand-alone tenth. In each cycle of three, the first two were forewarned while the third struck without warning. In the first of each series, Pharaoh was warned in the morning (Ex. 7:16; 8:17; 9:13), in the second Moses was told to "come in before Pharaoh" (7:26; 9:1; 10:1) in the palace, and so on. The tenth plague, unlike the rest, was announced at the very outset (Ex. 4:23). It was less a plague than a punishment.

Similarly, it seems to me that the commandments are structured in three groups of three, with a tenth that is set apart from the rest. Thus

3. Rambam, *Sefer HaMitzvot*, positive command 1; Ramban, glosses ad loc.

understood, we can see how they form the basic structure, the depth grammar, of Israel as a society bound by covenant to God as "a kingdom of priests and a holy nation" (Ex. 19:6).

The first three – no other gods besides Me, no graven images, and no taking of God's name in vain – define the Jewish people as "one nation under God." God is our ultimate sovereign. Therefore all other earthly rule is subject to the overarching imperatives linking Israel to God. Divine sovereignty transcends all other loyalties (no other gods besides Me). God is a living force, not an abstract power (no graven images). And sovereignty presupposes reverence (do not take My name in vain).

The first three commandments, through which the people declare their obedience and loyalty to God above all else, establish the single most important principle of a free society, namely *the moral limits of power*. Without this, the danger even in democracy is the tyranny of the majority, against which the best defence is the sovereignty of God.

The second three commands – Shabbat, honouring parents, and the prohibition of murder – are all about the principle of *the createdness of life*. They establish limits to the idea of autonomy, namely that we are free to do whatever we like so long as it does not harm others. Shabbat is the day dedicated to seeing God as creator and the universe as His creation. Hence, one day in seven, all human hierarchies are suspended and everyone – master, slave, employer, employee, even domestic animals – is free.

Honouring parents acknowledges our human createdness. It tells us that not everything that matters is the result of our choice – chiefly, the fact that we exist at all. Other people's choices matter, not just our own. "Thou shall not murder" restates the central principle of the universal Noahide covenant that murder is not just a crime against man but a sin against God, in whose image we are. So commandments four to six form the basic jurisprudential principles of Jewish life. They tell us to remember where we came from if we are to be mindful of how to live.

The third three – against adultery, theft, and bearing false witness – establish the basic institutions on which society depends. Marriage is sacred because it is the human bond closest in approximation to the covenant between us and God. Not only is marriage the human institution par excellence that depends on loyalty and fidelity, it is also the matrix of a free society. Alexis de Tocqueville put it best: "As long as family feeling is kept alive, the opponent of oppression is *never alone*."[4]

The prohibition against theft establishes the integrity of property. Whereas Jefferson defined as inalienable rights those of "life, liberty, and the pursuit of happiness," John Locke, closer in spirit to the Hebrew Bible, saw them as "life, liberty, or possession."[5] Tyrants abuse the property rights of the people, and the assault of slavery against human dignity is that it deprives me of the ownership of the wealth I create.

The prohibition of false testimony is the precondition of justice. A just society needs more than a structure of laws, courts, and enforcement agencies. As Judge Learned Hand said, "Liberty lies in the hearts of men and women; when it dies there, no constitution, no law, no court can save it; no constitution, no law, no court can even do much to help it."[6] There is no freedom without justice, but there is no justice without each of us accepting individual and collective responsibility for "telling the truth, the whole truth, and nothing but the truth."

Finally comes the stand-alone prohibition against envying your neighbour's house, wife, slave, maid, ox, donkey, or anything else belonging to him or her. This seems odd if we think of the "ten words" as commands, but not if we think of them as the basic principles of a free society. The greatest challenge of any society is how to contain the universal, inevitable phenomenon of envy, the desire to have what belongs to someone else. Envy lies at the heart of violence.[7] It was envy that led Cain to murder Abel, made Abraham and Isaac fear for their lives because they were married to beautiful women, led Joseph's brothers to hate him and sell him into slavery. It is envy that leads to adultery, theft, and false testimony; it was envy of their neighbours that led the Israelites time and again to abandon God in favour of the pagan practices of the time.

---

4. Alexis de Tocqueville, *Democracy in America*, abridged with an introduction by Thomas Bender (New York: Vintage Books, 1954), I:340.
5. *The Two Treatises of Civil Government* (Cambridge: Cambridge University Press, 1988), 136.
6. Learned Hand, "The Spirit of Liberty," "'I Am an American' Day" ceremony (Central Park, New York City, May 21, 1944).
7. The best book on the subject is Helmut Schoeck's *Envy: A Theory of Social Behaviour* (New York: Harcourt, Brace & World, 1969).

Envy is the failure to understand the principle of creation as set out in Genesis 1, that everything has its place in the scheme of things. Each of us has our own task and our own blessings, and we are each loved and cherished by God. Live by these truths and there is order. Abandon them and there is chaos. Nothing is more pointless and destructive than letting someone else's happiness diminish your own, which is what envy is and does. The antidote to envy is, as Ben Zoma famously said, "to rejoice in what we have" (Mishna Avot 4:1) and not to worry about what we do not yet have. Consumer societies are built on the creation and intensification of envy, which is why they lead to people having more and enjoying it less.

Thirty-three centuries after they were first given, the Ten Commandments remain the simplest, shortest guide to creation and maintenance of a good society. Many alternatives have been tried, and most have ended in tears. The wise aphorism remains true: when all else fails, read the instructions.

Mishpatim

Healing the Heart of Darkness

Jobbik, otherwise known as the Movement for a Better Hungary, is an ultra-nationalist Hungarian political party that has been described as fascist, neo-Nazi, racist, and anti-Semitic. It has accused Jews of being part of a "cabal of western economic interests" attempting to control the world, the libel otherwise known as the Protocols of the Elders of Zion, a fiction created by members of the Czarist secret service in Paris in the late 1890s and revealed as a forgery by *The Times* in 1921.[1] On one occasion the Jobbik party asked for a list of all the Jews in the Hungarian government. Disturbingly, in the Hungarian parliamentary elections in April 2014, the party secured over 20 per cent of the votes, making it the third largest party.

1. Marcin Goettig and Christian Lowe, "Special Report: From Hungary, far-right party spreads ideology, tactics," Reuters, http://www.reuters.com/article/us-europe-farright-special-report-idUSBREA380IU20140409#PUagU6ZvCiQtZgD8.99 (accessed December 22, 2015).

Until 2012, one of the party's leading members was a politician in his late twenties, Csanad Szegedi. Szegedi was a rising star in the movement, widely spoken of as its future leader. Until one day in 2012. That was the day Szegedi discovered he was a Jew.

Some of Jobbik's members had wanted to stop Szegedi's progress and spent time investigating his background to see whether they could find anything that would do him damage. What they found was that his maternal grandmother was a Jewish survivor of Auschwitz. So was his maternal grandfather. Half of Szegedi's family was killed during the Holocaust.

Szegedi's opponents started spreading rumours about his Jewish ancestry on the internet. Soon Szegedi himself discovered what was being said and decided to check whether the claims were true. They were. After Auschwitz, his grandparents, once Orthodox Jews, decided to hide their identity completely. When his mother was fourteen, her father told her the secret but ordered her not to reveal it to anyone. Szegedi now knew the truth about himself.

Szegedi decided to resign from the party and find out more about Judaism. He went to a local Chabad rabbi, Slomó Köves, who at first thought he was joking. Nonetheless he arranged for Szegedi to attend classes on Judaism and to come to the synagogue. At first, Szegedi says, people were shocked. He was treated by some as "a leper." But he persisted. Today he attends synagogue, keeps Shabbat, has learned Hebrew, and calls himself Dovid; in 2013, he underwent circumcision.

When he first admitted the truth about his Jewish ancestry, one of his friends in the Jobbik party said, "The best thing would be if we shoot you so you can be buried as a pure Hungarian." Another urged him to make a public apology. It was this comment, he says, that made him leave the party. "I thought, wait a minute, I am supposed to apologise for the fact that my family was killed at Auschwitz?"[2]

As the realisation that he was a Jew began to change his life, it also transformed his understanding of the world. Today, he says, his focus

2. Ofer Aderet, "Former Anti-Semitic Hungarian Leader Now Keeps Shabbat," *Haaretz*, October 21, 2013.

as a politician is to defend human rights for everyone. "I am aware of my responsibility and I know I will have to make it right in the future."[3]

Szegedi's story is not just a curiosity. It takes us to the very heart of the strange, fraught nature of our existence as moral beings. What makes us human is the fact that we are rational, reflective, capable of thinking things through. We feel empathy and sympathy, and this begins early. Even new-born babies cry when they hear another child cry. We have mirror neurons in the brain that make us wince when we see someone else in pain. Homo sapiens is the moral animal.

Yet much of human history has been a story of violence, oppression, injustice, corruption, aggression, and war. Nor, historically, has it made a significant difference whether the actors in this story have been barbarians or citizens of a high civilisation. The Greeks of antiquity, masters of art, architecture, drama, poetry, philosophy, and science, wasted themselves on the internecine Peloponnesian War between Athens and Sparta in the last quarter of the fifth century BCE. They never fully recovered. It was the end of the golden age of Greece. Fin de siècle Paris and Vienna in the 1890s were the leading centres of European civilisation. Yet they were also the world's leaders in anti-Semitism – Paris with the Dreyfus Affair; Vienna with its anti-Semitic mayor, Karl Lueger, whom Hitler later cited as his inspiration.

When we are good we are little lower than the angels. When we are bad we are lower than the beasts. What makes us moral? And what, despite it all, makes humanity capable of being so inhumane?

Plato thought that virtue was knowledge. If we know something is wrong, we will not do it. All vice is the result of ignorance. Teach people the true, the good, and the beautiful and they will behave well. David Hume and Adam Smith, two intellectual giants of the Scottish Enlightenment, thought that morality came from emotion. Hume said the most remarkable feature of human nature is the "propensity we have to sympathise with others."[4] Adam Smith began his *Theory of Moral*

---

3. Dale Hurd, "Crisis of Conscience: Anti-Semite Learns He's a Jew," Christian Broadcasting Network, December 6, 2013, http://www.cbn.com/cbnnews/world/2013/August/Crisis-of-Conscience-Anti-Semite-Learns-Hes-a-Jew/.
4. *Of Pride and Humility*, part I., section XI, T 2.1.11.2.

Sentiments with the words, "How selfish soever man may be supposed, there are evidently some principles in his nature, which interest him in the fortune of others, and render their happiness necessary to him, though he derives nothing from it except the pleasure of seeing it."[5] Immanuel Kant, the supreme rationalist, believed that rationality itself was the source of morality. A moral principle is one you are willing to prescribe for everyone. Therefore, for example, lying cannot be moral because you do not wish others to lie to you.

All three views have some truth to them, and we can find similar sentiments in the rabbinic literature. In the spirit of Plato, the sages spoke of the *tinok shenishba*, someone who does wrong because he or she was not educated to know what is right.[6] They said that the angels of mercy and righteousness argued for the creation of man because we naturally do such acts: we feel for others, as Hume and Smith argued. Kant's principle is presupposed by the rabbinic ruling that you may not take someone else's life to save your own because "What makes you think that your blood is redder than his?" Kantian rationality is similar to what the sages called *sevara*, "reason."

But these insights only serve to deepen the question. If knowledge, emotion, and reason lead us to be moral, why is that that humans hate, harm, and kill? A full answer would take longer than a lifetime, but the short answer is simple. We are tribal animals. We form ourselves into groups. Morality is both cause and consequence of this fact. Towards people with whom we are or feel ourselves to be related we are capable of altruism. But towards strangers we feel fear, and that fear is capable of turning us into monsters.

Morality, in Jonathan Haidt's phrase, binds and blinds.[7] It binds us to others in a bond of reciprocal altruism. But it also blinds us to the humanity of those who stand outside that bond. It unites and divides. It divides because it unites. Morality turns the "I" of self-interest into the

5. *Theory of Moral Sentiments* (CreateSpace, 2013), 9.
6. See Shabbat 68b; Rambam, *Mishneh Torah, Hilkhot Mamrim* 3:3. This certainly applies to ritual laws; whether it applies to moral ones also may be a moot point.
7. Jonathan Haidt, *The Righteous Mind: Why Good People Are Divided by Politics and Religion* (New York: Pantheon Books, 2012).

"we" of the common good. But the very act of creating an "us" simultaneously creates a "them," the people not like us. Even the most universal of religions, founded on principles of love and compassion, have often seen those outside the faith as Satan, the infidel, the antichrist, the child of darkness, the unredeemed. They have committed unspeakable acts of brutality in the name of God.

Neither Platonic knowledge nor Adam Smith's moral sense nor Kantian reason has cured the heart of darkness in the human condition. That is why two sentences blaze through *Parashat Mishpatim* like the sun emerging from behind thick clouds:

> You must not mistreat or oppress the stranger in any way. Remember, *you yourselves were once strangers* in the land of Egypt. (Ex. 22:21)

> You must not oppress strangers. *You know what it feels like* to be a stranger, for you yourselves were once strangers in the land of Egypt. (Ex. 23:9)

The great crimes of humanity have been committed against the stranger, the outsider, the one-not-like-us. Recognising the humanity of the stranger has been the historic weak point in most cultures. The Greeks saw non-Greeks as barbarians. Germans called Jews vermin, lice, a cancer in the body of the nation. In Rwanda, Hutus called Tutsis *inyenzi*, cockroaches.

Dehumanise the other and all the moral forces in the world will not save us from evil. Knowledge is silenced, emotion anaesthetised, and reason perverted. The Nazis convinced themselves (and others) that in exterminating the Jews they were performing a moral service for the Aryan race.[8] Suicide bombers are convinced that they are acting for the greater glory of God.[9] There is such a thing as altruistic evil.

---

8. See Claudia Koonz, *The Nazi Conscience* (Cambridge, MA: Belknap, 2003).
9. See Scott Atran, *Talking to the Enemy: Faith, Brotherhood, and the (Un)Making of Terrorists* (New York: Ecco, 2010). The classic text is Eric Hoffer, *The True Believer: Thoughts on the Nature of Mass Movements* (New York: Harper & Row, 1951).

That is what makes these two commands so significant. The Torah emphasises the point time and again: the rabbis said that the command to love the stranger appears thirty-six times in the Torah. Jewish law is here confronting directly the fact that care for the stranger is not something for which we can rely on our normal moral resources of knowledge, empathy, and rationality. Usually we can, but under situations of high stress, when we feel our group threatened, we cannot. *The very inclinations that bring out the best in us – our genetic inclination to make sacrifices for the sake of kith and kin – can also bring out the worst in us* when we fear the stranger. We are tribal animals and we are easily threatened by the members of another tribe.

Note that these commands are given shortly after the Exodus. Implicit in them is a very radical idea indeed. Care for the stranger is why the Israelites had to experience exile and slavery before they could enter the Promised Land and build their own society and state. You will not succeed in caring for the stranger, implies God, until you yourselves know in your very bones and sinews what it feels like to be a stranger. And lest you forget, I have already commanded you to remind yourselves and your children of the taste of affliction and bitterness every year on Passover. Those who forget what it feels like to be a stranger eventually come to oppress strangers, and if the children of Abraham oppress strangers, why did I make them My covenantal partners?

Empathy, sympathy, knowledge, and rationality are usually enough to let us live at peace with others. But not in hard times. Serbs, Croats, and Muslims lived peaceably together in Bosnia for years. So did Hutus and Tutsis in Rwanda. The problem arises at times of change and disruption when people are anxious and afraid. That is why exceptional defences are necessary, which is why the Torah speaks of memory and history – things that go to the very heart of our identity. We have to remember that we were once on the other side of the equation. We were once strangers – the oppressed, the victims. Remembering the Jewish past forces us to undergo role reversal. In the midst of freedom we have to remind ourselves of what it feels like to be a slave.

What happened to Csanad, now Dovid, Szegedi was exactly that: role reversal. He was a hater who discovered that he belonged among the hated. *What cured him of anti-Semitism was his role-reversing discovery that he was a Jew.* That, for him, was a life-changing discovery. The Torah tells us that the experience of our ancestors in Egypt was meant to be life-changing as well. Having lived and suffered as strangers, we became the people commanded to care for strangers.

The best way of curing anti-Semitism is to get people to experience what it feels like to be a Jew. The best way of curing hostility to strangers is to remember that we, too – from someone else's perspective – are strangers. Memory and role-reversal are the most powerful resources we have to cure the darkness that can sometimes occlude the human soul.

Teruma

The Labour of Gratitude

There is an important principle in Judaism, a source of hope and also one of the structuring principles of the Torah. It is the principle that *God creates the cure before the disease* (Megilla 13b). Bad things may happen but God has already given us the remedy if we know where to look for it. So for instance in *Parashat Ḥukkat*, we read of the deaths of Miriam and Aaron and how Moses was told that he would die in the desert without entering the Promised Land. This is a terrifying encounter with mortality. Yet before we read any of this, we first hear the law of the Red Heifer, the rite of purification after contact with death. The Torah has placed it here to assure us in advance that we can be purified after any bereavement. Human mortality does not ultimately bar us from being in the presence of divine immortality.

This is the key to understanding *Parashat Teruma*. Though not all commentators agree, its real significance is that it is God's answer in advance to the sin of the Golden Calf. In strict chronological terms it is out of place here. It (and *Tetzaveh*) should have appeared after *Ki Tissa*, which tells the story of the Calf. It is set here *before* the sin to tell us that the cure existed before the disease, the *tikkun* before the *kilkul*, the mending before the fracture, the rectification before the sin.

So to understand *Teruma* and the phenomenon of the *Mishkan*, the Sanctuary and all that it entailed, we have first to understand what went wrong at the time of the Golden Calf. Here the Torah is very subtle and gives us, in *Ki Tissa*, a narrative that can be understood at three quite different levels.

The first and most obvious is that the sin of the Golden Calf was due to a failure of leadership on the part of Aaron. This is the overwhelming impression we receive on first reading Exodus 32. We sense that Aaron should have resisted the people's clamour. He should have told them to be patient. He should have shown leadership. He did not. When Moses comes down the mountain and asks him what he has done, Aaron replies:

> Do not be angry, my lord. You know how prone these people are to evil. They said to me, "Make an oracle to lead us, since we do not know what happened to Moses, the man who took us out of Egypt." So I told them, "Whoever has any gold jewellery, take it off." Then they gave me the gold, and I threw it into the fire, and out came this calf! (Ex. 32:22–24)

This is a failure of responsibility. It is also a spectacular act of denial ("I threw it into the fire, and out came this calf!").[1] So the first reading of the story is of Aaron's failure.

But only the first. A deeper reading suggests that it is about Moses. It was his absence from the camp that created the crisis in the first place. "The people began to realise that Moses was taking a long time to come down from the mountain. They gathered around Aaron and said to him, 'Make us an oracle to lead us. We have no idea what happened to Moses, the man who brought us out of Egypt'" (Ex. 32:1).

---

1. In Deuteronomy 9:20, Moses discloses a fact which has been kept from us until that point: "God also expressed great anger towards Aaron, threatening to destroy him, so, at that time, I also prayed for Aaron."

God told Moses what was happening and said: "Go down, because your people, whom you brought up out of Egypt, have wrought ruin" (Ex. 32:7). The undertone is clear. "Go down," suggests that God was telling Moses that his place was with the people at the foot of the mountain, not with God at the top. "*Your* people" implies that God was telling Moses that the people were his problem, not God's. He was about to disown them.

Moses urgently prayed to God for forgiveness, then descended. What follows is a whirlwind of action. Moses descends, sees what has happened, breaks the tablets, burns the Calf, mixes its ashes with water and makes the people drink it, and then summons help in punishing the wrongdoers. He has become the leader in the midst of the people, restoring order where a moment before there was chaos. In this reading the central figure is Moses. He was the strongest of strong leaders. The result, though, was that when he was not there, the people panicked. That is the downside of strong leadership.

But there then follows a chapter, Exodus 33, that is one of the hardest in the Torah to understand. It begins with God announcing that, though He would send an "angel" or "messenger" to accompany the people on the rest of their journey, He Himself would not be in their midst "because you are a stiff-necked people and I might destroy you on the way." This deeply distresses the people (Ex. 33:1–6).

In verses 12–23, Moses challenges God on this verdict. He wants God's presence to go with the people. He asks, "Let me know Your ways" (Ex. 33:13) and "Pray let me see Your glory" (33:18). This is hard to understand. The entire exchange between Moses and God, one of the most intense in the Torah, is no longer about sin and forgiveness. It seems almost to be a metaphysical inquiry into the nature of God. What is its connection with the Golden Calf?

It is what happens *between* these two episodes that is the most puzzling of all. The text says that Moses "took his tent and pitched it for himself outside the camp, far from the camp" (Ex. 33:7). This must surely have been *precisely the wrong thing to do.* If, as God and the text have implied, the problem was the *distance* of Moses as a leader, the single most important thing for him to do now would be to stay in the people's midst, not position himself outside the camp. Moreover, the Torah has just told us that God had said He would not be in the midst of the people – and this caused the people distress. Moses' decision to do likewise would surely have doubled their distress. Something deep is happening here.

It seems to me that in Exodus 33, Moses is undertaking the most courageous act of his life. He is saying to God: "It is not *my* distance that is the problem. It is Your distance. The people are terrified of You. They have witnessed Your overwhelming power. They have seen You bring the greatest empire the world has ever known to its knees. They have seen You turn sea into dry land, send down food from heaven, and bring water from a rock. When they heard Your voice at Mount Sinai, they came to me to beg me to be an intermediary. They said, 'You speak to us and we will hearken, but let not God speak to us lest we die' (Ex. 20:16). They made a Calf not because they wanted to worship an idol, but because they wanted some symbol of Your presence that was not terrifying. They need You to be close. They need to sense You not in the sky or the summit of the mountain but in the midst of the camp. And even if they cannot see Your face, for no one can do that, at least let them see some visible sign of Your glory."

That, it seems to me, is Moses' request to which *Parashat Teruma* is the answer. "Let them make for Me a Sanctuary that I may dwell in their midst" (Ex. 25:8). This is the first time in the Torah that we hear the verb SH-KH-N, meaning "to dwell," in relation to God. As a noun it means literally "a neighbour." From this is derived the key word in post-biblical Judaism, *Shekhina*, meaning God's immanence as opposed to His transcendence, God-as-One-who-is-close, the daring idea of God as a near neighbour.

In terms of the theology of the Torah, the very idea of a *Mishkan*, a Sanctuary or Temple, a physical "home" for "God's glory," is deeply paradoxical. God is beyond space. As King Solomon said at the inauguration of the First Temple, "Behold, the heavens and the heavens of the heavens cannot encompass You, how much less this house?" (I Kings 8:27). Or as Isaiah said in God's name: "The heavens are My throne and the earth My footstool. What house shall you build for Me, where can My resting place be?" (Is. 66:1).

The answer, as the Jewish mystics emphasised, is that God does not live in a building but rather in the hearts of the builders:

"Let them make for Me a Sanctuary and I will dwell among them" (Ex. 25:8) – "among *them*," not "in it." How, though, does this happen? What human act causes the Divine Presence to live within the camp, the community? The answer is the name of this *parasha*, *Teruma*, meaning, a gift, a contribution.

"The Lord spoke to Moses, saying, 'Tell the Israelites to bring Me an offering. You are to receive the offering for Me from everyone whose heart moves them to give'" (Ex. 25:1–2). This would prove to be the turning point in Jewish history.

Until that moment the Israelites had been recipients of God's miracles and deliverances. He had taken them from slavery to freedom and performed miracles for them. There was only one thing God had not yet done, namely, *give the Israelites the chance to give back something to God*. The very idea sounds absurd. How can we, God's creations, give back to the God who made us? All we have is His. As David said, at the gathering he convened at the end of his life to initiate the building of the Temple:

> Wealth and honour come from You; You are the ruler of all things. . . . Who am I, and who are my people, that we should be able to give as generously as this? Everything comes from You, and we have given You only what comes from Your hand. (I Chr. 29:12, 14)

That ultimately is the logic of the *Mishkan*. God's greatest gift to us is the ability to give to Him. From a Judaic perspective the idea is fraught with risk. The idea that God might be in need of gifts is close to paganism and heresy. Yet, knowing the risk, God allowed Himself to be persuaded by Moses to cause His spirit to rest within the camp and allow the Israelites to give something back to God.

At the heart of the idea of the Sanctuary is what Lewis Hyde beautifully described as the labour of gratitude. His classic study, *The Gift*,[2] looks at the role of the giving and receiving of gifts, for example, at critical moments of transition. He quotes the Talmudic story of R. Akiva

---

2. Lewis Hyde, *The Gift: How the Creative Spirit Transforms the World* (Edinburgh: Canongate, 2006).

whose daughter was about to get married, but who had been told that she would not survive to the end of the day. The next morning R. Akiva visited his daughter and saw that she was still alive. Unknown to both of them, when she hung up her hat after the wedding, its pin pierced a serpent that would otherwise have bitten and killed her. R. Akiva wanted to know what his daughter had done that merited this divine intervention. She answered, "A poor man came to the door yesterday. Everyone was so busy with the wedding preparations that they did not have time to deal with him. So I took the portion that had been intended for me and gave it to him." It was this act of generosity that was the cause of her miraculous deliverance (Shabbat 156b).

The construction of the Sanctuary was fundamentally important because it gave the Israelites the chance to give back to God. Later decisors of Jewish law recognised that giving is an integral part of human dignity when they made the remarkable ruling that even a poor person completely dependent on charity is still obliged to give charity.[3] To be in a situation where you can only receive, not give, is to lack human dignity.

The *Mishkan* became the home of the Divine Presence because God specified that it be built only out of voluntary contributions. Giving creates a gracious society by enabling each of us to make our contribution to the public good. That is why the building of the Sanctuary was the cure for the sin of the Golden Calf. A people that only received but could not give was trapped in dependency and lack of self-respect. God allowed the people to come close to Him, and He to them, by giving them the chance to give.

That is why a society based on rights, not responsibilities, based on what we claim from – not what we give to – others, will always eventually go wrong. It is why the most important gift a parent can give a child is the chance to give back. The etymology of the word *teruma* hints at this. It means, not simply a contribution, but literally something "raised up." When we give, it is not just our contribution but we who are raised up. We survive by what we are given, but we achieve dignity by what we give.

---

3. Rambam, *Mishneh Torah, Hilkhot Shekalim* 1:1; *Hilkhot Matnot Aniyim* 7:5.

Tetzaveh

The Ethic of Holiness

With *Parashat Tetzaveh*, something new enters Judaism: *Torat Kohanim*, the world and mindset of the priest. Rapidly it became a central dimension of Judaism. It dominates the next book of the Torah, Leviticus. Until this point, though, priests in the Torah had a marginal presence.

For the first time in this *parasha* we encounter the idea of a hereditary elite within the Jewish people – Aaron and his male descendants – whose task was to minister in the Sanctuary. For the first time we find the Torah speaking about *robes of office*, those of the priests and the high priest worn while officiating in the sacred place. For the first time too we encounter the phrase, used about the robes: *lekhavod uletiferet*, "for glory and beauty" (Ex. 28:2). Until this point, *kavod* in the sense of glory or honour was attributed only to God. As for *tiferet*, this is the first time it appears in the Torah. It opens up a whole dimension of Judaism – namely, the aesthetic.

All these phenomena are related to the *Mishkan*, the Sanctuary, the subject of the preceding chapters. They emerge from the project of making a "home" for the infinite God within finite space. The question I want to ask here, though, is: Do they have anything to do with *morality?* With the kind of lives the Israelites were called on to live and their relationships to one another? If so, what is their connection to morality? And why does the priesthood appear specifically at this point in the story?

It is common to divide the religious life in Judaism into two dimensions. There was the priesthood and the Sanctuary, and there were the prophets and the people. The priests focused on the relationship between the people and God, *mitzvot bein adam laMakom*. Prophets focused on the relationship between the people and one another, *mitzvot bein adam leḥavero*. The priests supervised ritual and the prophets spoke about ethics. One group was concerned with holiness, the other with virtue. You do not need to be holy to be good. You need to be good to be holy, but that is an entrance requirement, not what being holy is about. Pharaoh's daughter, who rescued Moses when he was a baby, was good but not holy. These are two separate ideas.

In this essay I want to challenge that conception. The priesthood and the Sanctuary made a moral difference, not just a spiritual one. Understanding how they did so is important not only to our understanding of history but also to how we lead our lives today. We can see this by looking at some important recent experimental work in the field of moral psychology.

Our starting point is American psychologist Jonathan Haidt and his book, *The Righteous Mind*.[1] Haidt makes the point that in contemporary secular societies our *range* of moral sensibilities has become very narrow. He calls such societies WEIRD – **W**estern, **e**ducated, **i**ndustrialised, **r**ich, and **d**emocratic. They tend to see more traditional cultures as rigid, hidebound, and repressive. People from those traditional cultures tend to see Westerners as strange in abandoning much of the richness of the moral life.

To take a non-moral example: A century ago in most British and American (non-Jewish) families, dining was a formal occasion. The family ate together and would not begin until everyone was at the table. They would begin with grace, thanking God for the food they

1. *The Righteous Mind: Why Good People Are Divided by Politics and Religion* (New York: Pantheon Books, 2012).

were about to eat. There was an order in which people were served or served themselves. Conversation around the table was governed by conventions. There were things you might discuss and other subjects that were deemed unsuitable.

Today that has changed completely. Many British homes do not have a dining table. A recent survey showed that half of all meals in Britain are eaten alone. The members of the family come in at different times, take a meal from the freezer, heat it in the microwave, and eat it watching a television or computer screen. This is not dining but serial grazing.

Haidt became interested in the fact that his American students reduced morality to two principles, one relating to harm, the other to fairness. On harm they thought like John Stuart Mill, who said that "the only purpose for which power can be rightfully exercised over any member of a civilised community, against his will, is to prevent harm to others."[2] For Mill this was a political principle but it has become a moral one: if it does not harm others, we are morally entitled to do what we want.

The other principle is fairness. We do not all have the same idea of what is fair and what is not, but we all care about basic rules of justice: what is right for some should be right for all, do as you would be done to, do not bend the rules to your advantage, and so on. Often the first moral sentence a young child utters is, "That's not fair." John Rawls formulated the best-known modern statement of fairness: "Each person is to have an equal right to the most extensive basic liberty compatible with a similar liberty for others."[3]

Those are the ways WEIRD people think. If it is fair and does no harm, it is morally permissible. However – and this is Haidt's fundamental point – there are at least three other dimensions of the moral life as understood in non-WEIRD cultures throughout the world.

One is *loyalty* and its opposite, betrayal. Loyalty means that I am prepared to make sacrifices for the sake of my family, my team, my co-religionists and my fellow citizens, the groups that help make me the person I am. I take their interests seriously – not just my own.

---

2. *On Liberty and Other Writings*, ed. Stefan Collini (New York: Cambridge University Press, 1989), 13.
3. *A Theory of Justice* (Cambridge, MA: Belknap Press, 2005), 60.

Another is *respect for authority* and its opposite, subversion. Without this no institution is possible – perhaps no culture, either. The Talmud illustrates this with a famous story about a would-be proselyte who came to Hillel and said, "Convert me to Judaism on condition that I accept only the Written Torah, not the Oral Torah." Hillel began to teach him Hebrew. The first day he taught him *aleph-beit-gimmel*. The next day he taught him *gimmel-beit-aleph*. The man protested, "Yesterday you taught me the opposite." Hillel replied, "You see, you have to rely on me even to learn the *aleph-beit*. Rely on me also about the Oral Torah" (Shabbat 31a). Schools, armies, courts, professional associations, and even sports depend on respect for authority.

The third arises from the need to ring-fence certain values we regard as non-negotiable. They are not mine to do with as I wish. These are the things we call *sacred*, sacrosanct, not to be treated lightly or defiled.

Why are loyalty, respect, and the sacred not included in the way liberal elites think in the West? The most fundamental answer is that WEIRD societies define themselves as groups of autonomous individuals seeking to pursue their own interests with minimal interference from others. Each of us is a self-determining individual with our own wants, needs, and desires. Society should let us pursue those desires as far as possible without interfering in our or other people's lives. To this end, we have developed principles of rights, liberty, and justice that allow us to coexist peacefully. If an act is unfair or causes someone to suffer, we are prepared to condemn it morally, but not otherwise.

Loyalty, respect, and sanctity do not naturally thrive in secular societies based on market economics and liberal democratic politics. The market erodes loyalty. It invites us not to stay with the product we have used until now but to switch to one that is better, cheaper, faster, newer. Loyalty is the first victim of market capitalism's "creative destruction."

Respect for figures of authority – politicians, bankers, journalists, heads of corporations – has been falling for many decades. We are living through a loss of trust and the death of deference. Even the patient Hillel might have found it hard to deal with someone brought up on the 1979 Pink Floyd creed: "We don't need no education, we don't need no thought control."

As for the sacred, that too has been lost. Marriage is no longer seen as a holy commitment, a covenant. At best it is viewed as a contract. Life itself is in danger of losing its sanctity with the spread of abortion on demand at the beginning and "assisted dying" at the end.

What makes loyalty, respect, and sanctity key moral values is that they *create a moral community* as opposed to a group of autonomous individuals. Loyalty bonds the individual to the group. Respect creates structures of authority that allow people to function effectively as teams. Sanctity binds people together in a shared moral universe. The sacred is where we enter the realm of that-which-is-greater-than-the-self. The very act of gathering as a congregation can lift us into a sense of transcendence in which we merge our identity with that of the group.

Once we understand this distinction we can see how the moral universe of the Israelites changed over time. Abraham was chosen by God "so that he will instruct his children and his household after him that they may keep the way of the Lord by doing what is right and just" (*tzedaka umishpat;* Gen. 18:19). What his servant looked for when choosing a wife for Isaac was kindness, *ḥesed.* These are the key prophetic virtues. As Jeremiah said in God's name:

> Let not the wise boast of their wisdom, or the strong of their strength, or the rich of their wealth but let one who boasts, boast about this: that they have the understanding to know Me, that I am the Lord, who exercises kindness, justice, and righteousness [*ḥesed mishpat utzedaka*] on earth, for in these I delight. (Jer. 9:22–23).

Kindness is the equivalent of care, which is the opposite of harm. Justice and righteousness are specific forms of fairness. In other words, the prophetic virtues are close to those that prevail today in the liberal democracies of the West. That is a measure of the impact of the Hebrew Bible on the West, but that is another story for another time. The point is that kindness and fairness are about relationships between individuals. Until Sinai, the Israelites *were* just individuals, albeit part of the same extended family that had undergone Exodus and exile together.

After the Revelation at Mount Sinai the Israelites were a covenanted people. They had a sovereign: God. They had a written constitution: the Torah. They had agreed to become "a kingdom of priests and a holy nation" (Ex. 19:6). Yet at the Golden Calf they showed that they had not yet understood what it is to be a nation. They were a mob. The Torah says, "Moses saw that the people were *running wild* and that Aaron had let them *get out of control* and so become a laughing stock to their enemies" (32:25). That was the crisis to which the Sanctuary and the priesthood were the answer. They turned Jews into a nation.

The service of the Sanctuary performed by the priests in their robes worn *lekhavod*, "for honour," established the principle of *respect*. The *Mishkan* itself embodied the principle of *the sacred*. Set in the middle of the camp, the Sanctuary and its service turned the Israelites into a circle at whose centre was God. And even though, after the destruction of the Second Temple, there was no more Sanctuary or functioning priesthood, Jews found substitutes that performed the same function. What *Torat Kohanim* brought into Judaism was the choreography of holiness and respect that helped Jews walk and dance together as a nation.

Two further research findings are relevant here. Richard Sosis analysed a series of voluntary communities set up by various groups in the course of the nineteenth century, some religious, some secular. He discovered that the religious communes had an average lifespan of *more than four times longer* than their secular counterparts. There is something about the religious dimension that turns out to be important, even essential, in sustaining community.[4]

We now also know on the basis of considerable neuro-scientific evidence that we make our choices based on emotion rather than reason. People whose emotional centres (specifically the ventromedial prefrontal cortex) have been damaged can analyse alternatives in great detail, but they cannot make good decisions. One interesting experiment revealed that academic books on ethics were more often stolen or never returned to libraries than books on other branches of philosophy.[5]

4. "Religion and Intragroup Cooperation: Preliminary Results of a Comparative Analysis of Utopian Communities," *Cross Cultural Research* 34, no. 1 (2003): 11–39.
5. Haidt, *The Righteous Mind*, 89.

Expertise in moral reasoning, in other words, does not necessarily make us more moral. Reason is often something we use to rationalise choices made on the basis of emotion.

That explains the presence of the aesthetic dimension of the service of the Sanctuary. It had beauty, gravitas, and majesty. In the time of the Temple it had music. There were choirs of Levites singing psalms. Beauty speaks to emotion and emotion to the soul, lifting us in ways reason cannot do to heights of love and awe, taking us above the narrow confines of the self into the circle at whose centre is God.

The Sanctuary and priesthood introduced into Jewish life the ethic of *kedusha*, holiness, which strengthened the values of loyalty, respect, and the sacred by creating an environment of *reverence*, the humility felt by the people once they had these symbols of the Divine Presence in their midst. As Rambam wrote in a famous passage in *The Guide for the Perplexed* (III:51), we do not act when in the presence of a king as we do when we are merely in the company of friends or family. In the Sanctuary people sensed they were in the presence of the King.

Reverence gives power to ritual, ceremony, social conventions, and civilities. It helps transform autonomous individuals into a collectively responsible group. You cannot sustain a national identity or even a marriage without loyalty. You cannot socialise successive generations without respect for figures of authority. You cannot defend the non-negotiable value of human dignity without a sense of the sacred. That is why the prophetic ethic of justice and compassion had to be supplemented with the priestly ethic of holiness.

Ki Tissa

Can There Be Compassion Without Justice?

At the height of the drama of the Golden Calf, a vivid and enigmatic scene takes place. Moses has secured forgiveness for the people. But now, on Mount Sinai yet again, he does more. He asks God to be with the people. He asks Him to "teach me Your ways" and "show me Your glory" (Ex. 33:13, 18). God replies: "I will cause all My goodness to pass in front of you, and I will proclaim My name, the Lord, in your presence.... I will have mercy on whom I will have mercy, and I will have compassion on whom I will have compassion. But," He says, "you cannot see My face, for no one may see Me and live" (Ex. 33:19–20).

God then places Moses in a cleft in the rock face, telling him he will be able to "see My back" but not His face, and Moses hears God say these words:

> The Lord, the Lord, the compassionate and gracious God, slow to anger, abounding in love and faithfulness, maintaining love to

thousands, and forgiving wickedness, rebellion, and sin. Yet He does not leave the guilty unpunished. (Ex. 34:6–7)

This passage became known as the "Thirteen Attributes of Mercy."
The sages understood this episode as the moment in which God taught Moses, and through him future generations, how to pray when atoning for sin (Rosh HaShana 17b). Moses himself used these words with slight variations during the next crisis, that of the spies. Eventually they became the basis of the special prayers known as *Seliḥot*, prayers of penitence. It was as if God were binding Himself to forgive the penitent in each generation by this self-definition.[1] God is compassionate and lives in love and forgiveness. This is an essential element of Jewish faith.

But there is a caveat. God adds: *"Yet He does not leave the guilty unpunished."* There is a further clause about visiting the sins of the parents on the children which demands separate attention and is not our subject here. The caveat tells us that there is forgiveness but also punishment. There is compassion but also justice.

Why so? Why must there be justice as well as compassion, punishment as well as forgiveness? The sages said that "when God created the universe He did so under the attribute of justice, but then saw it could not survive. What did He do? He added compassion to justice and created the world" (Rashi, Gen. 1:1). This statement prompts the same question: Why did God not abandon justice altogether? Why is forgiveness alone not enough?

Some fascinating recent research in diverse fields from moral philosophy to evolutionary psychology, and from game theory to environmental ethics, provides us with an extraordinary and unexpected answer.

The best point of entry is Garrett Hardin's famous paper written in 1968 about "the tragedy of the commons."[2] He asks us to imagine an asset with no specific owner: pasture land that belongs to everyone

1. The Talmud in Rosh HaShana 17b says that God made a covenant on the basis of these words, binding Himself to forgive those who, in penitence, appealed to these attributes. Hence their centrality in the prayers leading up to Rosh HaShana and Yom Kippur and on Yom Kippur itself.
2. Garrett Hardin, "The Tragedy of the Commons," *Science* 162, no. 3859 (December 13, 1968): 1243–1248.

(the commons), for example, or the sea and the fish it contains. The asset provides a livelihood to many people, the local farmers or fishermen. But eventually it attracts too many people. There is over-pasturing or over-fishing, and the resource is depleted. The pasture is at risk of becoming wasteland. The fish are in danger of extinction.[3]

What then happens? The common good demands that everyone from here on must practise restraint. They must limit the number of animals they graze or the amount of fish they catch. But some individuals are tempted not to do so. They continue to over-pasture or overfish. The gain to them is great and the loss to others is small, since it is divided by many. Self-interest takes precedence over the common good, and if enough people act on these feelings the result is disaster.

This is the tragedy of the commons, and it explains how environmental catastrophes and other disasters occur. The problem is the *free rider*, the person who pursues his or her self-interest without bearing his or her share of the cost of the common good. Because of the importance of this type of situation to many contemporary problems, they have been intensively studied by mathematical biologists like Anatol Rapoport and Martin Nowak and behavioural economists like Daniel Kahneman and the late Amos Tversky.[4]

One of the things researchers have done is to create experimental situations that simulate this sort of problem. Here is one example: Four players are given $8 each. They are told they can choose to invest as much or as little as they want in a common fund. The experimenter

---

3. Long before Garrett Hardin there was an old hasidic story about the village where the people decided to each donate an amount of wine to fill a vat to present to the king on his forthcoming visit to the village. Secretly at night over the next few weeks, each of the villagers took some wine, arguing to themselves that such a small amount would not be noticed. Each added an equal amount of water to the vat so that it stayed full. The king arrived and the villagers presented him with the vat; he drank from it and said, "It is just plain water." I guess many folk traditions have similar stories. This is, in essence, the tragedy of the commons.

4. See Robert Axelrod, *The Evolution of Cooperation* (New York: Basic, 1984); Matt Ridley, *The Origins of Virtue* (New York: Penguin, 1998); Daniel Kahneman, *Thinking, Fast and Slow* (New York: Farrar, Straus, and Giroux, 2011); Martin Nowak and Roger Highfield, *Super Cooperators: Evolution, Altruism and Human Behaviour or Why We Need Each Other to Succeed* (Edinburgh: Canongate, 2011).

collects the contributions, adds them up, adds 50% (the gain the farmer or fisherman would have made by using the commons), and distributes the sum equally to all four players. So if each contributes the full $8 to the fund, they each receive $12 at the end. But if one player contributes nothing, the fund will total $24, which with 50% added becomes $36. Distributed equally, it means that each will receive $9. Three will thus have gained $1, while the fourth, the free rider, will have gained $9.

This, though, is not a stable situation. As the game is played repeatedly, the participants begin to realise there is a free rider among them even if the experiment is structured so that they do not know who it is. One of two things then tends to happen. Either everyone stops contributing to the fund (i.e., the common good) or they agree, if given the choice, to punish the free rider. Often people are keen to punish, even if it means that they will lose thereby, a phenomenon sometimes called "altruistic punishment."

Some have linked participants to MRI machines to see which parts of the brain are activated by such games. Interestingly, altruistic punishment is linked to pleasure centres in the brain. As Kahneman puts it: "It appears that maintaining the social order and the rules of fairness in this fashion is its own reward. Altruistic punishment could well be the glue that holds societies together."[5] This, though, is hardly a happy situation. Punishment is bad news for everyone. The offender suffers, but so do the punishers, who have to spend time or money they might otherwise use in improving the collective outcome. And in cross-cultural studies, it turns out that people from countries where there is widespread free-riding punish most severely. People are most punitive in the societies that have the most corruption and the least public-spiritedness. Punishment, in other words, is the solution of last resort.

This brings us to religion. A whole series of experiments has shed light on the role of religious practice in such circumstances. Tests have been carried out in which participants have the opportunity to cheat and gain by so doing. If, without any connection being made to the experiment at hand, participants have been primed to think religious thoughts – by being shown words relating to God, for example, or being

5. Kahneman, *Thinking, Fast and Slow*, 308.

reminded of the Ten Commandments – they cheat significantly less.[6] What is particularly fascinating about such tests is that outcomes show no relationship to the underlying beliefs of the participants. What makes the difference is not *believing* in God, but rather *being reminded* of God before the test. This may well be why daily prayer and other regular rituals are so important. What affects us at moments of temptation is not so much background belief but the act of bringing that belief into awareness.

Of much greater significance have been the experiments designed to test the impact of different ways of thinking about God. Do we think primarily in terms of divine forgiveness, or of divine justice and punishment? Some strands within the great faiths emphasise one, others the other. There are hellfire preachers and those who speak in the still, small voice of love. Which is the more effective?

Needless to say, when the experimental subjects are atheists or agnostics, there is no difference. They are not affected either way. Among believers, though, the difference is significant. *Those who believe in a punitive God cheat and steal less than those who believe in a forgiving God.* Experiments were then performed to see how believers relate to free riders in common-good situations like those described above. Were they willing to forgive? Or did they punish the free riders even at a cost to themselves? Here the results were revelatory. *People who believe in a punitive God punish people less than those who believe in a forgiving God.*[7] Those who believe that, as the Torah says, God "does not leave the guilty unpunished" are more willing to leave punishment to God. *Those who focus on divine forgiveness are more likely to practise human retribution or revenge.*

The same applies to societies as a whole. Here the experimenters used terms not entirely germane to Judaism: they compared countries in terms of percentages of the population who believed in heaven and hell.

Nations with the highest levels of belief in hell and the lowest levels of belief in heaven had the lowest crime rates. In contrast,

6. Ara Norenzayan, *Big Gods: How Religion Transformed Cooperation and Conflict* (Princeton, NJ: Princeton University Press, 2013), 34–35.
7. Ibid., 44–47.

nations that privileged heaven over hell were champions of crime. These patterns persisted across nearly all major religious faiths, including various Christian, Hindu and syncretic religions that are a blend of several belief systems.[8]

This was so surprising a finding that people asked: In that case, why are there religions that de-emphasise divine punishment? Azim Shariff offered the following explanation: "Because though Hell might be better at getting people to be good, Heaven is much better at making them feel good."[9] So, if a religion is intent on making converts, "it's much easier to sell a religion that promises a divine paradise than one that threatens believers with fire and brimstone."[10]

It is now clear why, at the very moment He is declaring His compassion, grace, and forgiveness, God insists that He does not leave the guilty unpunished. *A world without divine justice would be one where there is more resentment, punishment, and crime – and less public-spiritedness and forgiveness, even among religious believers.* The more we believe that God punishes the guilty, the more forgiving we become. The less we believe that God punishes the guilty, the more resentful and punitive we become. This is a totally counterintuitive truth, yet one that finally allows us to see the profound wisdom of the Torah in helping us create a humane and compassionate society.

8. Ibid., 46.
9. Cited in ibid.
10. Ibid.

Vayak'hel

The Spirit of Community

What do you do when your people has just made a Golden Calf, run riot, and lost its sense of ethical and spiritual direction? How do you restore moral order – not just then in the days of Moses, but even now? The answer lies in the first word of this *parasha*: "*Vayak'hel*." But to understand it we have to retrace two journeys that were among the most fateful in the modern world.

The story begins in the year 1831 when two young men, both in their twenties – one from England, the other from France – set out on voyages of discovery that would change them, and eventually our understanding of the world. The Englishman was Charles Darwin. The Frenchman was Alexis de Tocqueville. Darwin's journey aboard the *Beagle* ultimately took him to the Galapagos Islands where he began to think about the origin and evolution of species. Tocqueville's journey was to investigate a phenomenon that became the title of his book: *Democracy in America*.

Although the two men were studying completely different things, the one zoology and biology, the other politics and sociology, as we will see, they came to strikingly similar conclusions – the same conclusion God taught Moses after the episode of the Golden Calf.

Darwin, as we know, made a series of discoveries that led him to the theory known as natural selection. Species compete for scarce resources and only the best adapted survive. The same, he believed, was true of humans. But this left him with a serious problem: If evolution is the struggle to survive, if the strong win and the weak go to the wall, then everywhere ruthlessness should prevail. But this is not the case. All societies value altruism. People esteem those who make sacrifices for the sake of others. This, in Darwinian terms, does not seem to make sense at all, and he knew it.

The bravest, most sacrificial people, he wrote in *The Descent of Man*, "would on average perish in larger number than other men." A noble man "would often leave no offspring to inherit his noble nature." It seems scarcely possible, he wrote, that virtue "could be increased through natural selection, that is, by survival of the fittest."[1]

It was Darwin's greatness that he saw the answer, even though it contradicted his general thesis: natural selection operates at the level of the individual. It is as individual men and women that we pass on our genes to the next generation. But civilisation works at the level of the group. As he put it,

> a tribe including many members who, from possessing in a high degree the spirit of patriotism, fidelity, obedience, courage, and sympathy, were always ready to give aid to each other and to sacrifice themselves for the common good, would be victorious over most other tribes; and this would be natural selection.

How to get from the individual to the group was, he said, "at present much too difficult to be solved."[2]

The conclusion was clear even though biologists to this day still argue about the mechanisms involved.[3] We survive as groups. One man

1. Charles Darwin, *The Descent of Man* (Princeton, NJ: Princeton University Press, 1981), 158–84.
2. Ibid., 166.
3. This is the argument between E. O. Wilson and Richard Dawkins. See Edward O. Wilson, *The Social Conquest of Earth* (New York: Liveright, 2012), and the review by Richard Dawkins, "The Descent of Edward Wilson," *Prospect Magazine*,

versus one lion: lion wins. Ten men against one lion: the lion may lose. Homo sapiens, in terms of strength and speed, is a poor player when ranked against the outliers in the animal kingdom. But human beings have unique skills when it comes to creating and sustaining groups. We have language. We can communicate. We have culture. We can pass on our discoveries to future generations. Humans form larger and more flexible groups than any other species, while at the same time leaving room for individuality. We are not ants in a colony or bees in a hive. Humans are the community-creating animal.

Meanwhile in America, Alexis de Tocqueville, like Darwin, faced a major intellectual problem he felt driven to solve. His problem, as a Frenchman, was to try to understand the role of religion in democratic America. He knew that the United States had voted to separate religion from power by way of the First Amendment, the separation of church and state. So religion in America had no power. He assumed that it had no influence either. What he discovered was precisely the opposite. "There is no country in the world where the Christian religion retains a greater influence over the souls of men than in America."[4]

This did not make sense to him at all, and he asked Americans to explain it to him. They all gave him essentially the same answer. Religion in America (we are speaking of the early 1830s, remember) does not get involved in politics. He asked clergymen why not. Again they were unanimous in their answer. Politics is divisive. Therefore if religion were to become involved in politics, it too would be divisive. That is why religion stayed away from party political issues.

Tocqueville paid close attention to what religion actually did in America, and he came to some fascinating conclusions. It strengthened marriage, and he believed that strong marriages were essential to free societies. He wrote: "As long as family feeling is kept alive, the opponent of oppression is never alone."[5]

May 24, 2012, http://www.prospectmagazine.co.uk/science-and-technology/edward-wilson-social-conquest-earth-evolutionary-errors-origin-species.

4. Alexis de Tocqueville, *Democracy in America*, abridged with an introduction by Thomas Bender (New York: Vintage Books, 1954), I:314.

5. Ibid., I:340.

Exodus

It also led people to form communities around places of worship. It encouraged people in those communities to act together for the sake of the common good. The great danger in a democracy, said Tocqueville, is individualism. People come to care about themselves, not about others. As for the others, the danger is that people will leave their welfare to the government, a process that ends in the loss of liberty as the state takes on more and more of the responsibility for society as a whole.

What protects Americans against these twin dangers, he said, is the fact that, encouraged by their religious convictions, they form associations, charities, voluntary associations – what in Judaism we call ḥevrot. At first bewildered, and then charmed, Tocqueville noted how quickly Americans formed local groups to deal with the problems in their lives. He called this the "art of association," and said about it that it was "the apprenticeship of liberty."

All of this was the opposite of what he knew of France, where religion in the form of the Catholic Church had much power but little influence. In France, he said, "I had almost always seen the spirit of religion and the spirit of freedom marching in opposite directions. But in America I found they were intimately united and that they reigned in common over the same country."[6]

So religion safeguarded the "habits of the heart" essential to maintaining democratic freedom. It sanctified marriage and the home. It guarded public morals. It led people to work together in localities to solve problems themselves rather than leaving them to the government. If Darwin discovered that man is the community-creating animal, Tocqueville discovered that religion in America is the community-building institution.

It still is. Harvard sociologist Robert Putnam became famous in the 1990s for his discovery that more Americans than ever are going tenpin bowling, but fewer are joining bowling clubs and leagues. He took this as a metaphor for a society that has become individualistic rather than community-minded. He called it *Bowling Alone*.[7] It was a phrase

6. Ibid., I:319.
7. Robert D. Putnam, *Bowling Alone: The Collapse and Revival of American Community* (New York: Simon & Schuster, 2000).

that summed up the loss of "social capital," that is, the extent of social networks through which people help one another.

Years later, after extensive research, Putnam revised his thesis. A powerful store of social capital still exists and it is to be found in places of worship. Survey data showed that frequent church- or synagogue-goers are more likely to give money to charity, regardless of whether the charity is religious or secular. They are also more likely to do voluntary work for a charity, give money to a homeless person, spend time with someone who is feeling depressed, offer a seat to a stranger, or help someone find a job. On almost every measure, they are demonstrably more altruistic than non-worshippers.

Their altruism goes beyond this. Frequent worshippers are also significantly more active citizens. They are more likely to belong to community organisations, neighbourhood and civic groups, and professional associations. They get involved, turn up, and lead. The margin of difference between them and the more secular is large.

Tested on attitudes, religiosity as measured by church or synagogue attendance is the best predictor of altruism and empathy – better than education, age, income, gender, or race. Perhaps the most interesting of Putnam's findings was that these attributes were related not to people's religious *beliefs* but to the frequency with which they attend a place of worship.[8]

Religion creates community, community creates altruism, and altruism turns us away from self and towards the common good. Putnam goes so far as to speculate that an atheist who went regularly to synagogue (perhaps because of a spouse) would be more likely to volunteer or give to charity than a religious believer who prays alone. There is something about the tenor of relationships within a community that makes it the best tutorial in citizenship and good neighbourliness.

What Moses had to do after the Golden Calf was *Vayak'hel* – turn the Israelites into a *kehilla*, a community. He did this in the obvious sense of restoring order. When Moses came down the mountain and saw the Calf, the Torah says the people were *parua*, meaning "wild," "disorderly,"

8. Robert D. Putnam and David E. Campbell, *American Grace: How Religion Divides and Unites Us* (New York: Simon & Schuster, 2010).

"chaotic," "unruly," "tumultuous." He "saw that the people were running wild and that Aaron had let them get out of control and so become a laughing stock to their enemies" (Ex. 32:25). They were not a community but a crowd. He did it in a more fundamental sense as we see in the rest of the *parasha*. He began by reminding the people of the laws of Shabbat. Then he instructed them to build the *Mishkan*, the Sanctuary, as a symbolic home for God.

Why these two commands rather than any others? Because Shabbat and the *Mishkan* are the two most powerful ways of building community. The best way of turning a diverse, disconnected group into a team is to get them to build something together.[9] Hence the *Mishkan*. The best way of strengthening relationships is to set aside dedicated time when we focus not on the pursuit of individual self-interest but on the things we share, by praying together, studying Torah together, and celebrating together – in other words, Shabbat. Shabbat and the *Mishkan* were the two great community-building experiences of the Israelites in the desert.

More than this: in Judaism, community is essential to the spiritual life. Our holiest prayers require a *minyan*. When we celebrate or mourn we do so as a community. Even when we confess, we do so together. Rambam rules:

> One who separates himself from the community, even if he does not commit a transgression but merely holds himself aloof from the congregation of Israel, does not fulfil the commandments together with his people, shows himself indifferent to their distress, and does not observe their fast days but goes on his own way like one of the nations who does not belong to the Jewish people – such a person has no share in the World to Come.[10]

That is not how religion has always been seen. Plotinus called the religious quest "the flight of the alone to the Alone."[11] A. N. Whitehead

9. See Jonathan Sacks, *The Home We Build Together* (London: Continuum, 2007).
10. Rambam, *Mishneh Torah, Hilkhot Teshuva* 3:11.
11. Andrew Louth, trans., *The Origins of the Christian Mystical Tradition from Plato to Denys* (Oxford: Oxford University Press, 2007), 50.

said religion is what an individual does with his solitariness.[12] Jean-Paul Sartre notoriously said: "Hell is other people." In Judaism, it is *as a community* that we come before God. For us the key relationship is not I-Thou, but We-Thou.

Vayak'hel is thus no ordinary episode in the history of Israel. It marks the essential insight to emerge from the crisis of the Golden Calf. We find God in community. We develop virtue, strength of character, and a commitment to the common good in community. Community is local. It is society with a human face. It is not government. It is not the people we pay to look after the welfare of others. It is the work we do ourselves, together.

Community is the antidote to individualism on the one hand and overreliance on the state on the other. Darwin understood its importance to human flourishing. Tocqueville saw its role in protecting democratic freedom. Robert Putnam has documented its value in sustaining social capital and the common good. And it began in this *parasha*, when Moses turned an unruly mob into a *kehilla*, a community.

12. A. N. Whitehead, *Religion in the Making* (New York: Macmillan, 1926), 16.

Pekudei

Integrity in Public Life

There is a verse so familiar that we do not often stop to reflect on what it means. It is the line from the first paragraph of the *Shema*: "You shall love the Lord your God with all your heart, with all your soul, and with all your *meod*" (Deut. 6:5). That last word is usually translated as "strength" or "might." But Rashi, following the Midrash and *Targum*, translates it as "with all your wealth."

If so, the verse seems to be unintelligible, at least in the order in which it is written. "With all your soul" was understood by the sages to mean, "with your life" if need be (Berakhot 61b). There are times, thankfully very rare indeed, when we are commanded to give up life itself rather than commit a sin or a crime. If that is the case then it should go without saying that we should love God with all our wealth, meaning, even if it demands great financial sacrifice. Yet Rashi and the sages say that this phrase applies to those "to whom wealth means more than life itself."

Of course, life is more important than wealth. Yet the sages also knew that, in their words, *adam bahul al mammono* – people do strange, hasty, ill-considered, and irrational things when money is at stake (Shabbat 117b). Financial gain can be a huge temptation, leading us to acts that harm others and ultimately ourselves. So when it comes to financial matters, especially when public funds are involved, there must be no room for temptation, no space for doubt as to whether it has been used for the purpose for which it was donated. There must be scrupulous auditing and transparency. Without this there is moral hazard: the maximum of temptation combined with the maximum of opportunity.

Hence the *parasha* of *Pekudei*, with its detailed account of how the donations to the building of the *Mishkan* were used: "These are the amounts of the materials used for the tabernacle, the tabernacle of the Testimony, which were recorded at Moses' command by the Levites under the direction of Itamar son of Aaron, the priest" (Ex. 38:21). The passage goes on to list the exact amounts of gold, silver, and bronze collected, and the purposes to which it was put.

Why did Moses do this? A midrash suggests an answer:

> "They gazed after Moses" (Ex. 33:8) – People criticised Moses. They used to say to one another, "Look at that neck. Look at those legs. Moses is eating and drinking what belongs to us. All that he has belongs to us." The other would reply: "A man who is in charge of the work of the Sanctuary – what do you expect? That he should not get rich?" As soon as he heard this, Moses replied, "By your life, as soon as the Sanctuary is complete, I will make a full reckoning with you."[1]

Moses issued a detailed reckoning to avoid coming under suspicion that he had personally appropriated some of the donated money. Note the emphasis that the accounting was undertaken not by Moses himself but "by the Levites under the direction of Itamar," in other words, by independent auditors.

There is no hint of these accusations in the text itself, but the midrash may be based on the remark Moses made during the Korah rebellion, "I have not taken so much as a donkey from them, nor have I wronged any of them" (Num. 16:15). Accusations of corruption and

---

1.   *Tanḥuma* (Buber), *Pekudei* 4.

personal enrichment have often been levelled against leaders, with or without justification. We might think that since God sees all we do, this is enough to safeguard against wrongdoing. Yet Judaism does not say this. The Talmud records a scene at the deathbed of R. Yoḥanan b. Zakkai, as the master lay surrounded by his disciples:

> They said to him, "Our master, bless us." He said to them, "May it be God's will that the fear of heaven shall be as much upon you as the fear of flesh and blood." His disciples asked, "Is that all?" He replied, "Would that you obtained no less than such fear! You can see for yourselves the truth of what I say: when a man is about to commit a transgression, he says, I hope no man will see me." (Berakhot 28b)

When humans commit a sin they worry that other people might see them. They forget that God certainly sees them. Temptation befuddles the brain, and no one should believe he is immune to it.

A later passage in Tanakh seems to indicate that Moses' account was not strictly necessary. The book of Kings relates an episode in which, during the reign of King Yehoash, money was raised for the restoration of the Temple: "They did not require an accounting from those to whom they gave the money to pay the workers, because they acted with complete honesty" (II Kings 12:16). Moses, a man of complete honesty, may thus have acted "beyond the strict requirement of the law."[2]

It is precisely the fact that Moses did not *need* to do what he did that gives the passage its force. There must be transparency and accountability when it comes to public funds even if the people involved have impeccable reputations. People in positions of trust must be, and be *seen to be*, individuals of moral integrity. Yitro, Moses' father-in-law, had already said this when he told Moses to appoint subordinates to help him in the task of leading the people. They should be, he said, "Men who fear God, trustworthy men who hate dishonest gain" (Ex. 18:21).

---

2. A key concept in Jewish law (see, e.g., Berakhot 7a, 45b; Bava Kamma 99b), meaning supererogation, doing more, in a positive sense, than the law requires.

Without a reputation for honesty and incorruptibility, judges cannot ensure that justice is seen to be done. This general principle was derived by the sages from the episode in the book of Numbers when the Reubenites and Gadites expressed their wish to settle on the far side of the Jordan where the land provided good grazing ground for their cattle (Num. 32:1–33). Moses told them that if they did so, they would demoralise the rest of the nation. They would give the impression that they were unwilling to cross the Jordan and fight with their brothers in their battles to conquer the land.

The Reubenites and Gadites made it clear that they were willing to be in the front line of the troops and would not return to the far side of the Jordan until the land had been fully conquered. Moses accepted the proposal, saying that if they kept their word, they would be "clear [*viheyitem nekiyim*] before the Lord and before Israel" (Num. 32:22). This phrase entered Jewish law as the principle that "one must acquit oneself before one's fellow human beings as well as before God" (Mishna Shekalim 3:2). It is not enough to do right. We must be *seen to do right*, especially when there is room for rumour and suspicion.

There are several instances in the early rabbinic literature of applications of this rule. So, for example, when people came to take coins for sacrifices from the Temple's Shekel Chamber, where the money was kept:

> They did not enter the chamber wearing either a bordered cloak or shoes or sandals or *tefillin* or an amulet, lest if he became poor people might say that he became poor because of an iniquity committed in the chamber, or if he became rich people might say that he became rich from the appropriation in the chamber. For it is a person's duty to be free of blame before men as before God, as it is said, "and be clear before the Lord and before Israel" (Num. 32:22), and it also says: "So shall thou find favour and good understanding in the sight of God and man" (Prov. 3:4). (Mishna Shekalim 3:2)

Those who entered the chamber were forbidden to wear any item of clothing in which they could hide stolen coins. Similarly, when charity overseers had funds left over, they were not permitted to change copper for silver coins of their own money; they had to make the exchange with a third party. Overseers in charge of a soup kitchen were not allowed to purchase surplus food when there were no poor people to whom to distribute it. Surpluses had to be sold to others so as not to arouse suspicion that the charity overseers were profiting from public funds (Pesaḥim 13a).

The *Shulḥan Arukh* rules that charity collection must always be done by a minimum of two individuals so that each can see what the other is doing.[3] There is a difference of opinion between Rabbi Joseph Karo and Rabbi Moses Isserles on the need to provide detailed accounts. Rabbi Joseph Karo rules on the basis on the passage in II Kings – "They did not require an accounting from those to whom they gave the money to pay the workers, because they acted with complete honesty" (12:15) – that no formal accounting is required from people of unimpeachable honesty. Rabbi Moses Isserles however says that it is right to do so because of the principle, "Be clear before the Lord and before Israel."[4]

Trust is of the essence in public life. A nation that suspects its leaders of corruption cannot function effectively as a free, just, and open society. It is the mark of a good society that public leadership is seen as a form of service rather than a means to power, which is all too easily abused. Tanakh is a sustained tutorial in the importance of high standards in public life. The prophets were the world's first social critics, mandated by God to speak truth to power and to challenge corrupt leaders. Elijah's challenge to King Ahab and the protests of Amos, Hosea, Isaiah, and Jeremiah against the unethical practices of their day are classic texts in this tradition, establishing for all time the ideals of equity, justice, honesty, and integrity. A free society is built on moral foundations, and those must be unshakable.

Moses' personal example, in giving an accounting of the funds that had been collected for the first collective project of the Jewish people, set a vital precedent for all time.

3.   *Shulḥan Arukh, Yoreh De'ah* 257:1.
4.   Ibid., 257:2.

Leviticus
ויקרא

Vayikra

What Do We Sacrifice?

The laws of sacrifices that dominate the early chapters of the book of Leviticus are among the hardest in the Torah to relate to in the present. It has been almost two thousand years since the Temple was destroyed and the sacrificial system came to an end. But Jewish thinkers, especially the more mystical among them, strove to understand the inner significance of the sacrifices and the statement they made about the relationship between humanity and God. They were thus able to rescue their spirit even if their physical enactment was no longer possible.

Among the simplest yet most profound was the comment made by Rabbi Shneur Zalman of Liadi, the first Rebbe of Lubavitch. He noticed a grammatical oddity about the second line of this *parasha*:

> Speak to the Children of Israel and say to them: "*When one of you offers a sacrifice* to the Lord, the sacrifice must be taken from the cattle, sheep, or goats." (Lev. 1:2)

Or so the verse *would* read if it were constructed according to the normal rules of grammar. However, in Hebrew, the word order of the sentence is strange and unexpected. We would expect to read: *adam mikem ki yakriv*, "when one of you offers a sacrifice." Instead, what it says is *adam ki yakriv mikem*, "when one offers a sacrifice *of you*." The essence of sacrifice, said Rabbi Shneur Zalman, is that we offer ourselves. We bring to God our faculties, our energies, our thoughts and emotions. The physical form of sacrifice – an animal offered on the altar – is only an external manifestation of an inner act. The real sacrifice is *mikem*, "of you." We give God something of ourselves.[1]

What exactly is it that we give God when we offer a sacrifice? The Jewish mystics, among them Rabbi Shneur Zalman, spoke about two souls that each of us has – the animal soul (*nefesh habehemit*) and the Godly soul. On the one hand we are physical beings. We are part of nature. We have physical needs: food, drink, shelter. We are born, we live, we die. As Ecclesiastes puts it:

> Man's fate is like that of the animals; the same fate awaits them both: as one dies, so dies the other. Both have the same breath; man has no advantage over the animal. Everything is a mere fleeting breath. (3:19)

Yet we are not simply animals. We have within us immortal longings. We can think, speak, and communicate. We can, by acts of speaking and listening, reach out to others. We are the one life form known to us in the universe that can ask the question "why?" We can formulate ideas and be moved by high ideals. We are not governed by biological drives alone. Psalm 8 is a hymn of wonder on this theme:

> When I consider Your heavens,
> the work of Your fingers,
> the moon and the stars,
> which You have set in place,
> what is man that You are mindful of him,

---

1. Rabbi Shneur Zalman of Liadi, *Likkutei Torah* (Brooklyn, NY: Kehot, 1984), *Vayikra* 2aff.

the son of man that You care for him?
Yet You made him a little lower than the angels
and crowned him with glory and honour.
You made him ruler over the works of Your hands;
You put everything under his feet. (Ps. 8:4–7)

Physically, we are almost nothing; spiritually, we are brushed by the wings of eternity. We have a Godly soul. The nature of sacrifice, understood psychologically, is thus clear. What we offer God is (not just an animal but) the *nefesh habehemit*, the animal soul within us.

How does this work out in detail? A hint is given by the three types of animal mentioned in the verse: *behema* (animal), *bakar* (cattle), and *tzon* (flock). Each represents a separate animal-like feature of the human personality.

Behema represents the animal instinct itself. The word refers to domesticated animals. It does not imply the savage instincts of the predator. What it means is something more tame. Animals spend their time searching for food. Their lives are bounded by the struggle to survive. To sacrifice the animal within us is to be moved by something more than mere survival.

Wittgenstein, when asked what was the task of philosophy, answered, "To show the fly the way out of the fly-bottle."[2] The fly, trapped in the bottle, bangs its head against the glass, trying to find a way out. The one thing it fails to do is to look up. The Godly soul within us is the force that makes us look up, beyond the physical world, beyond mere survival, in search of meaning, purpose, goal.

The Hebrew word *bakar*, cattle, reminds us of the word *boker*, "dawn," literally to "break through," as the first rays of sunlight break through the darkness of night. Cattle, stampeding, break through barriers. Unless constrained by fences, cattle are no respecters of boundaries. To sacrifice the *bakar* is to learn to recognise and respect boundaries – between holy and profane, pure and impure, permitted and forbidden. Barriers of the mind can sometimes be stronger than walls.

---

2. Ludwig Wittgenstein, *Philosophical Investigations* (New York: Macmillan, 1953), 309.

Finally, the word *tzon*, flocks, represents the herd instinct – the powerful drive to move in a given direction because others are doing likewise.[3] The great figures of Judaism – Abraham, Moses, the prophets – were distinguished precisely by their ability to stand apart from the herd; to be different, to challenge the idols of the age, to refuse to capitulate to the intellectual fashions of the moment. That, ultimately, is the meaning of holiness in Judaism. *Kadosh*, the holy, is something set apart, different, separate, distinctive. Jews were the only minority in history consistently to refuse to assimilate to the dominant culture or convert to the dominant faith.

The noun *korban*, "sacrifice," and the verb *lehakriv*, "to offer something as a sacrifice," actually mean "that which is brought close" and "the act of bringing close." The key element is not so much giving something up (the usual meaning of sacrifice), but rather bringing something close to God. *Lehakriv* is to bring the animal element within us to be transformed through the divine fire that once burned on the altar, and still burns at the heart of prayer if we truly seek closeness to God.

By one of the ironies of history, this ancient idea has become suddenly contemporary. Darwinism, the decoding of the human genome, and scientific materialism (the idea that the material is all there is) have led to the widespread conclusion that we are animals, nothing more, nothing less. We share 98 per cent of our genes with the primates. We are, as Desmond Morris used to put it, "the naked ape."[4] On this view, Homo sapiens exists by mere accident. We are the result of a random series of genetic mutations and just happened to be more adapted to survival than other species. The *nefesh habehemit*, the animal soul, is all there is.

The refutation of this idea – and it is surely among the most reductive ever to be held by intelligent minds – lies in the very act of sacrifice itself as the mystics understood it. We can redirect our animal instincts.

---

3. The classic works on crowd behaviour and the herd instinct are Charles Mackay, *Extraordinary Popular Delusions and the Madness of Crowds* (London: Richard Bentley, 1841); Gustave le Bon, *The Crowd: A Study of the Popular Mind* (London: T. F. Unwin, 1897); Wilfred Trotter, *Instincts of the Herd in Peace and War* (London: T. F. Unwin, 1916); and Elias Canetti, *Crowds and Power* (New York: Viking Press, 1962).
4. Desmond Morris, *The Naked Ape* (New York: Dell Publishing, 1984).

We can rise above mere survival. We are capable of honouring boundaries. We can step outside our environment. As Harvard neuroscientist Steven Pinker put it: "Nature does not dictate what we should accept or how we should live," adding, "and if my genes don't like it they can go jump in the lake."[5] Or as Katharine Hepburn majestically said to Humphrey Bogart in *The African Queen*, "Nature, Mr Allnut, is what we were put on earth to rise above."

We can transcend the *behema*, the *bakar*, and the *tzon*. No animal is capable of self-transformation, but we are. Poetry, music, love, wonder – the things that have no survival value but which speak to our deepest sense of being – all tell us that we are not mere animals, assemblages of selfish genes. By bringing that which is animal within us close to God, we allow the material to be suffused with the spiritual and we become something else: no longer slaves of nature but servants of the living God.

5. Steven Pinker, *How the Mind Works* (New York: W.W. Norton, 1997), 54.

Tzav

Violence and the Sacred

Why sacrifices? To be sure, they have not been part of the life of Judaism since the destruction of the Second Temple, almost two thousand years ago. But why, if they are a means to an end, did God choose *this* end? This is, of course, one of the deepest questions in Judaism, and there are many answers. Here I want explore just one, first given by the early-fifteenth-century Jewish thinker, Rabbi Joseph Albo, in his *Sefer HaIkkarim.*

Albo's theory took as its starting point not sacrifices but two other questions. The first: Why after the Flood did God permit human beings to eat meat? (Gen. 9:3–5). Initially, neither human beings nor animals had been meat eaters (Gen. 1:29–30). What caused God, as it were, to change His mind? The second: What was wrong with the first act of sacrifice, Cain's offering of "some of the fruits of the soil" (Gen. 4:3–5)? God's rejection of that offering led directly to the first murder, when Cain killed Abel. What was at stake in the difference between the offerings Cain and Abel brought to God?

Albo's theory is that killing animals for food is inherently wrong. It involves taking the life of a sentient being to satisfy our needs. Cain knew this. He believed there was a strong kinship between man and the animals. That is why he offered not an animal sacrifice, but a vegetable one (his error, according to Albo, is that he should have brought fruit, not vegetables – the highest, not the lowest, of non-meat produce). Abel, by contrast, believed that there was a qualitative difference between man and the animals. Had God not told the first humans: "Rule over the fish of the sea and the birds of the air and over every living creature that moves in the ground"? That is why he brought an animal sacrifice.

Once Cain saw that Abel's sacrifice had been accepted while his own was not, he reasoned thus: if God, who forbids us to kill animals for food, permits and even favours killing an animal as a sacrifice, and if, as Cain believed, there is no ultimate difference between human beings and animals, then I shall offer the highest living being as a sacrifice to God, namely my brother Abel. *Cain killed Abel as a human sacrifice.*

That is why God permitted meat-eating after the Flood. Before the Flood, the world had been "filled with violence." Perhaps violence is an inherent part of human nature. If humanity were to be allowed to exist at all, God would have to lower His demands. *Let humans kill animals*, He said, *rather than kill human beings* – the one form of life that is not only God's creation but also God's image. Hence the otherwise almost unintelligible sequence of verses after Noah and his family emerge on dry land:

> Then Noah built an altar to the Lord and, taking some of all the clean animals and clean birds, he sacrificed burnt offerings on it. The Lord smelled the pleasing aroma and said in His heart, "Never again will I curse the ground because of man, even though every inclination of his heart is evil from childhood…"
>
> Then God blessed Noah and his sons, saying to them…
>
> "Everything that lives and moves will be food for you. Just as I gave you the green plants, I now give you everything…
>
> Whoever sheds the blood of man, by man shall his blood be shed; for in the image of God has God made man." (Gen. 8:29–9:6)

According to Albo the logic of the passage is clear. Noah offers an animal sacrifice in thanksgiving for having survived the Flood. God sees that human beings need this way of expressing themselves. They are genetically predisposed to violence ("every inclination of his heart is evil from childhood"). If society were to survive, humans would need to be able to direct their violence towards non-human animals, whether as food or sacrificial offerings. The crucial line to be drawn is between human and non-human. The permission to kill animals is accompanied by an absolute prohibition against killing human beings, "for in the image of God has God made man."

It is not that God approves of killing animals, whether for sacrifice or food, but that to forbid this to human beings, given their genetic predisposition to bloodshed, is utopian. It is not for now but for the end of days. Until then, the least bad solution is to let people kill animals rather than murder their fellow humans. Animal sacrifices are a concession to human nature.[1] *Sacrifices are a substitute for violence directed against mankind.*

The contemporary thinker who has done most to revive this understanding is French-American literary critic and philosophical anthropologist René Girard, in such books as *Violence and the Sacred*, *The Scapegoat*, and *Things Hidden Since the Foundation of the World*. The common denominator in sacrifices, he argues, is

> ... internal violence – all the dissensions, rivalries, jealousies, and quarrels within the community that the sacrifices are designed to suppress. The purpose of the sacrifice is to restore harmony to the community, to reinforce the social fabric. Everything else derives from that.[2]

The worst form of violence within and between societies is *vengeance*, "an interminable, infinitely repetitive process." This is in line with Hillel's saying, on seeing a human skull floating on water, "Because you drowned others, they drowned you, and those who drowned you will in the end themselves be drowned" (Mishna Avot 2:7).

---

1. On why God never chooses to *change* human nature, see Rambam, *The Guide for the Perplexed*, III:32.
2. René Girard, *Violence and the Sacred* (Baltimore: Johns Hopkins University Press, 1977), 8.

There is no natural end to the cycle of retaliation and revenge. The Montagues keep killing and being killed by the Capulets. So do the Tattaglias and the Corleones and the other feuding groups in fiction and history. It is a destructive cycle that has devastated whole communities. According to Girard this was the problem that religious ritual was developed to resolve. The primary religious act, he says, is the sacrifice, and the primary sacrifice is the scapegoat. If tribes A and B who have been fighting can sacrifice a member of tribe C, then both will have sated their desire for bloodshed without inviting revenge, especially if tribe C is in no position to retaliate. Sacrifices divert the destructive energy of violent reciprocity.

Why then, if violence is embedded in human nature, are sacrifices a feature of ancient rather than modern societies? Because, argues Girard, there is another and more effective way of ending vengeance:

> Vengeance is a vicious circle whose effect on primitive societies can only be surmised. For us the circle has been broken. We owe our good fortune to one of our social institutions above all: our judicial system, which serves to deflect the menace of vengeance. The system does not suppress vengeance; rather, it effectively limits itself to a single act of reprisal, enacted by a sovereign authority specialising in this particular function. The decisions of the judiciary are invariably presented as the final word on vengeance.[3]

Girard's terminology here is not one to which we can subscribe. Justice is not vengeance. Retribution is not revenge. Revenge is inherently I-Thou, or We-Them. It is personal. Retribution is impersonal. It is no longer the Montagues versus the Capulets, but both under the impartial judgement of the law. But Girard's substantive point is correct and essential. The only effective antidote to violence is the rule of law.

Girard's theory confirms the view of Albo. Sacrifice (as with meat-eating) entered Judaism as a substitute for violence. It also helps us understand the profound insight of the prophets that *sacrifices are not ends in themselves, but part of the Torah's programme to create a world redeemed from the otherwise interminable cycle of revenge. The other part of that programme,*

3. Ibid., 15.

and God's greatest desire, is a world governed by justice. That, we recall, was His first charge to Abraham, to "instruct his children and his household after him to keep the way of the Lord by *doing what is right and just*" (Gen. 18:19).

Have we therefore moved beyond that stage in human history in which animal sacrifices have a point? Has justice become a powerful enough reality that we no longer need religious rituals to divert the violence between human beings? Sadly, the answer is no. The collapse of the Soviet Union, the fall of the Berlin Wall, and the end of the Cold War led some thinkers to argue that we had reached "the end of history." There would be no more ideologically driven wars. Instead the world would turn to the market economy and liberal democracy.[4]

The reality was radically different. There were waves of ethnic conflict and violence in Bosnia, Kosovo, Chechnya, and Rwanda, followed by even bloodier conflicts throughout the Middle East, sub-Saharan Africa, and parts of Asia. In his book *The Warrior's Honour*, Michael Ignatieff offered the following explanation of why this happened:

> The chief moral obstacle in the path of reconciliation is the desire for revenge. Now, revenge is commonly regarded as a low and unworthy emotion, and because it is regarded as such, its deep moral hold on people is rarely understood. But revenge – morally considered – is a desire to keep faith with the dead, to honour their memory by taking up their cause where they left off. Revenge keeps faith between generations…
>
> This cycle of intergenerational recrimination has no logical end…. But it is the very impossibility of intergenerational vengeance that locks communities into the compulsion to repeat…
>
> Reconciliation has no chance against vengeance unless it respects the emotions that sustain vengeance, unless it can replace the respect entailed in vengeance with rituals in which communities once at war learn to mourn their dead together.[5]

---

4. Francis Fukuyama, *The End of History and the Last Man* (New York: Free Press, 1992).
5. Michael Ignatieff, *The Warrior's Honor: Ethnic War and the Modern Conscience* (Toronto: Penguin, 2006), 188–190.

Far from speaking to an age long gone and forgotten, the laws of sacrifice tell us three things as important now as then:

First, violence is still part of human nature, never more dangerous than when combined with an ethic of revenge.

Second, rather than denying its existence, we must find ways of redirecting it so that it does not claim yet more human sacrifices.

Third, the only ultimate alternative to sacrifices, animal or human, is the one first propounded millennia ago by the prophets of ancient Israel, few more powerfully than Amos:

> Even though you bring Me burnt offerings and offerings of grain,
> I will not accept them…
> But let justice roll down like a river,
> And righteousness like a never-failing stream. (Amos 5:23–24)

Shemini

Fire – Holy and Unholy

The shock is immense. For several weeks and many chapters – the longest prelude in the Torah – we have read of the preparations for the moment at which God would bring His presence to rest in the midst of the people. Five *parashot* (*Teruma, Tetzaveh, Ki Tissa, Vayak'hel,* and *Pekudei*) describe the instructions for building the Sanctuary. Two (*Vayikra, Tzav*) detail the sacrificial offerings to be brought there. All is now ready. For seven days the priests (Aaron and his sons) are consecrated into office. Now comes the eighth day, when the service of the Tabernacle will begin.

The entire people have played their part in constructing what will become the visible home of the Divine Presence on earth. With a simple, moving verse the drama reaches its climax: "Moses and Aaron went into the Tent of Meeting and when they came out, they blessed the people. God's glory was then revealed to all the people" (Lev. 9:23).

Just as we think the narrative has reached closure, a terrifying scene takes place:

> Aaron's sons, Nadav and Avihu, took their censers, put fire into them, and added incense; and they offered unauthorised fire

before God, which He had not instructed them to offer. Fire came forth from before God, and it consumed them so that they died before God. Moses then said to Aaron: "This is what God spoke of when He said: 'Among those who approach Me, I will show Myself holy; in the sight of all the people I will be honoured.'" (10:1–3)

Celebration turned to tragedy. The two eldest sons of Aaron die. The sages and commentators offer many explanations. Nadav and Avihu died because: they entered the holy of holies;[1] they were not wearing the requisite clothes;[2] they took fire from the kitchen, not the altar;[3] they did not consult Moses and Aaron;[4] nor did they consult one another.[5] According to some they were guilty of hubris. They were impatient to assume leadership roles themselves;[6] and they did not marry, considering themselves above such things.[7] Yet others see their deaths as delayed punishment for an earlier sin, when at Mount Sinai they "ate and drank" in the presence of God (Ex. 24:9–11).

These interpretations represent close readings of the four places in the Torah which mention the deaths of Nadav and Avihu (Lev. 10:2, 16:1, Num. 3:4, 26:61), as well as the reference to their presence on Mount Sinai. Each is a profound meditation on the dangers of over-enthusiasm in the religious life. However, the simplest explanation is the one explicit in the Torah itself. Nadav and Avihu died because they offered unauthorised – literally, "strange" – fire, meaning "that which was not commanded." To understand the significance of this, we must go back to first principles and remind ourselves of the meaning of *kadosh*, "holy," and thus of *mikdash* as the home of the holy.

The holy is that segment of time and space God has reserved for His presence. *Creation involves concealment.* The word *olam*, universe,

1. *Midrash Tanḥuma* (Buber), *Parashat Aḥarei Mot* 7.
2. Leviticus Rabba 20:9.
3. *Midrash Tanḥuma*, ad loc.
4. *Yalkut Shimoni*, 1:524.
5. *Midrash Tanḥuma*, ad loc.
6. Aggada (Buber), *Vayikra* 10.
7. Leviticus Rabba 20:10.

is semantically linked to the word *ne'elam*, "hidden." To give mankind some of His own creative powers – the use of language to think, communicate, understand, imagine alternative futures, and choose between them – God must do more than create Homo sapiens. He must efface Himself (what the kabbalists called *tzimtzum*) to create space for human action. No single act more profoundly indicates the love and generosity implicit in creation. God as we encounter Him in the Torah is like a parent who knows He must hold back, let go, refrain from intervening, if His children are to become responsible and mature.

But there is a limit. To efface Himself entirely would be equivalent to abandoning the world, deserting His own children. That, God may not and will not do. How then does God leave a trace of His presence on earth?

The biblical answer is not philosophical. A philosophical answer (I am thinking here of the mainstream of Western philosophy, beginning in antiquity with Plato, in modernity with Descartes) would be one that applies universally – i.e., at all times, in all places. But there *is* no answer that applies to all times and places. *That is why philosophy cannot and never will understand the apparent contradiction between divine creation and human free will, or between Divine Presence and the empirical world in which we reflect, choose, and act.*

Jewish thought is counter-philosophical. It insists that truths are embodied precisely *in* particular times and places. There are holy times (the seventh day, seventh month, seventh year, and the end of seven septennial cycles, the Jubilee). There are holy people (the Children of Israel as a whole; within them, the Levites, and within them, the priests). And there is holy space (eventually, Israel; within that, Jerusalem; within that, the Temple; in the desert, they were the Tabernacle, the Holy, and the Holy of Holies).

The holy is that point of time and space in which the presence of God is encountered by *tzimtzum* – self-renunciation – on the part of mankind. *Just as God makes space for man by an act of self-limitation, so man makes space for God by an act of self-limitation.* The holy is where God is experienced as absolute presence. Not accidentally but essentially, this can only take place through the total renunciation of human will and initiative. That is not because God does not value human will and initiative. To the contrary: God has empowered mankind to use them to become His "partners in the work of creation."

However, to be true to God's purposes, there must be times and places at which humanity experiences the reality of the divine. Those times and places require absolute obedience. The most fundamental mistake – the mistake of Nadav and Avihu – is to take the powers that belong to man's encounter with the world, and apply them to man's encounter with the divine. Had Nadav and Avihu used their own initiative to fight evil and injustice they would have been heroes. Because they used their own initiative in the arena of the holy, they erred. They asserted their own presence in the absolute presence of God. That is a contradiction in terms. That is why they died.

We err if we think of God as capricious, jealous, angry: a myth spread by early Christianity in an attempt to define itself as the religion of love, superseding the cruel/harsh/retributive God of the "Old Testament." When the Torah itself uses such language it "speaks in the language of humanity" (Berakhot 31a) – that is to say, in terms people will understand.

In truth, Tanakh is a love story through and through – the passionate love of the creator for His creatures that survives all the disappointments and betrayals of human history. God needs us to encounter Him, not because He needs mankind but because we need Him. If civilisation is to be guided by love, justice, and respect for the integrity of creation, there must be moments in which we leave the "I" behind and encounter the fullness of being in all its glory.

That is the function of the holy – the point at which "I am" is silent in the overwhelming presence of "There is." That is what Nadav and Avihu forgot – that to enter holy space or time requires ontological humility, the total renunciation of human initiative and desire.

The significance of this fact cannot be over-estimated. When we confuse God's will with our will, we turn the holy – the source of life – into something unholy and a source of death. The classic example of this is "holy war," jihad, Crusade – investing imperialism (the desire to rule over other people) with the cloak of sanctity as if conquest and forced conversion were God's will.

The story of Nadav and Avihu reminds us yet again of the warning first spelled out in the days of Cain and Abel. *The first act of worship led to the first murder.* Like nuclear fission, worship generates power, which can be benign but can also be profoundly dangerous.

The episode of Nadav and Avihu is written in three kinds of fire. First there is the fire from heaven:

> Fire came forth from before God and consumed the burnt offering. (Lev. 9:24)

This was the fire of favour, consummating the service of the Sanctuary. Then came the "unauthorised fire" offered by the two sons:

> Aaron's sons Nadav and Avihu took their censers, put fire in them, and added incense; and they offered unauthorised fire before the Lord, which He had not instructed them [to offer]. (Lev. 10:1)

Then there was the counter-fire from heaven:

> Fire came forth from before the Lord, and it consumed them so that they died before the Lord. (Lev. 10:2)

The message is simple and intensely serious: Religion is not what the European Enlightenment thought it would become: mute, marginal, and mild. It is fire – and like fire, it warms but it also burns. And we are the guardians of the flame.

Tazria

The Circumcision of Desire

I t is hard to trace with any precision the moment when a new idea makes its first appearance on the human scene, especially one as amorphous as that of love. But love has a history.[1] There is the contrast we find in Greek, and then Christian, thought between *eros* and *agape*: sexual desire and a highly abstract love for humanity in general.

There is the concept of chivalry that makes its appearance in the age of the Crusades, the code of conduct that prized gallantry and feats of bravery to "win the heart of a lady." There is the romantic love that makes its appearance in the novels of Jane Austen, hedged with the proviso that the young or not-so-young man destined for the heroine must have the right income and country estate, so as to exemplify the "truth universally acknowledged, that a single man in possession of a good fortune, must be in want of a wife."[2] And there is the moment in *Fiddler on the Roof* where, exposed by their children to the new ideas

---

1. See, for example, C. S. Lewis, *The Four Loves* (New York: Harcourt, Brace, 1960); Simon May, *Love: A History* (New Haven, CT: Yale University Press, 2011).
2. The famous first line of Jane Austen's *Pride and Prejudice*.

in pre-revolutionary Russia, Tevye turns to his wife Golde, and the following conversation ensues:

> Tevye: Do you love me?
> Golde: I'm your wife!
> Tevye: I know! But do you love me?
> Golde: Do I love him? For twenty-five years I've lived with him, fought with him, starved with him. Twenty-five years, my bed is his…
> Tevye: Shh!
> Golde: If that's not love, what is?
> Tevye: Then you love me!
> Golde: I suppose I do!

The inner history of humanity is in part the history of the idea of love. And at some stage a new idea makes its appearance in biblical Israel. We can trace it best in a highly suggestive passage in the book of one of the great prophets of the Bible, Hosea.

Hosea lived in the eighth century BCE. The kingdom had been divided since the death of Solomon. The northern kingdom in particular, where Hosea lived, had lapsed after a period of peace and prosperity into lawlessness, idolatry, and chaos. Between 747 and 732 BCE there were no less than five kings, the result of a series of intrigues and bloody struggles for power. The people, too, had become lax: "There is no faithfulness or kindness, and no knowledge of God in the land; there is swearing, lying, killing, stealing, and committing adultery; they break all bounds and murder follows murder" (Hos. 4:1–2).

Like other prophets, Hosea knew that Israel's destiny depended on its sense of mission. Faithful to God, it was able to do extraordinary things: survive in the face of empires and generate a society unique in the ancient world, with the equal dignity of all as fellow citizens under the sovereignty of the Creator of heaven and earth. Faithless, however, it was just one more minor power in the ancient Near East, whose chances of survival against larger political predators were minimal.

What makes the book of Hosea remarkable is the episode with which it begins. God tells the prophet to marry a prostitute, and see what it feels like to have a love betrayed. Only then will Hosea have a glimpse into God's sense of betrayal by the People of Israel. Having liberated them from slavery and brought them into their land, God saw them forget the past, forsake the covenant, and worship strange gods. Yet He cannot abandon them despite the fact that they have abandoned Him. It is a powerful passage, conveying the astonishing assertion that *more than the Jewish people love God, God loves the Jewish people.* The history of Israel is a love story between the faithful God and His often faithless people. Though God is sometimes angry, He cannot but forgive. He will take them on a kind of second honeymoon, and they will renew their marriage vows:

> Therefore I am now going to allure her;
> I will lead her into the desert
> and speak tenderly to her...
> I will betroth you to Me forever;
> I will betroth you in righteousness and justice,
> in love and compassion.
> I will betroth you in faithfulness,
> and you will know the Lord. (Hos. 2:16–22)

It is this last sentence – with its explicit comparison between the covenant and a marriage – that Jewish men say when they put on the hand-*tefillin*, winding its strap around the finger like a wedding ring.

One verse in the midst of this prophecy deserves the closest scrutiny. It contains two complex metaphors that must be unravelled strand by strand:

> "On that day," declares the Lord,
> "you will call Me 'my husband' [*ishi*];
> you will no longer call Me 'my master' [*baali*]." (Hos. 2:18)

This is a double pun. *Baal*, in biblical Hebrew, means "a husband," but in a highly specific sense – namely, "master, owner, possessor, controller." It signalled physical, legal, and economic dominance. It was also the name of the Canaanite god – whose prophets Elijah challenged in the famous confrontation at Mount Carmel. Baal (often portrayed as a bull) was the god of the storm, who defeated Mot, the god of sterility and death. Baal was the rain that impregnated the earth and made it fertile. The religion of Baal is the worship of *god as power*.

Hosea contrasts this kind of relationship with the other Hebrew word for husband, *ish*. Here he is recalling the words of the first man to the first woman:

> This is now bone of my bones
> and flesh of my flesh;
> She shall be called "woman" [*isha*],
> because she was taken from man [*ish*]. (Gen. 2:23)

Here the male-female relationship is predicated on something quite other than power and dominance, ownership and control. Man and woman confront one another in sameness and difference. Each is an image of the other, yet each is separate and distinct. The only relationship able to bind them together without the use of force is marriage as covenant – a bond of mutual loyalty and love in which each makes a pledge to the other to serve one another.

Not only is this a radical way of reconceptualising the relationship between man and woman. It is also, implies Hosea, the way we should think of the relationship between human beings and God. God reaches out to humanity not as power – the storm, the thunder, the rain – but as love, and not an abstract, philosophical love, but a deep and abiding passion that survives all the disappointments and betrayals. Israel may not always behave lovingly towards God, says Hosea, but God loves Israel and will never cease to do so.

How we relate to God affects how we relate to other people. That is Hosea's message – and vice versa: *how we relate to other people affects the way we think of God.* Israel's political chaos in the eighth century BCE was intimately connected to its religious waywardness. A society built on corruption and exploitation is one where might prevails over right. That is not Judaism but idolatry, Baal-worship.

Now we understand why the sign of the covenant is circumcision. For faith to be more than the worship of power, it must affect the most intimate relationship between men and women. In a society founded on covenant, male-female relationships are built on something other and gentler than male dominance, masculine power, sexual desire, and the drive to own, control, and possess. *Baal* must become *ish*. The alpha male must become the caring husband. Sex must be sanctified and tempered by mutual respect. The sexual drive must be circumcised and circumscribed so that it no longer seeks to possess and is instead content to love.

There is thus more than an accidental connection between *monotheism* and *monogamy*. Although biblical law does not command monogamy, it nonetheless depicts it as the normative state from the start of the human story: Adam and Eve, one man, one woman. Whenever in Genesis a patriarch marries more than one woman, there is tension and anguish. The commitment to one God is mirrored in the commitment to one person.

The Hebrew word *emuna*, often translated as "faith," in fact means faithfulness, fidelity, precisely the commitment one undertakes in making a marriage. Conversely, for the prophets there is a connection between idolatry and adultery. That is how God describes Israel to Hosea. God married the Israelites but they, in serving idols, acted the part of a promiscuous woman (Hos. 1–2).

The love of husband and wife – a love at once personal and moral, passionate and responsible – is as close as we come to understanding God's love for us and our ideal love for Him. When Hosea says, "You will know the Lord," he does not mean knowledge in an abstract sense. He means the knowledge of intimacy and relationship, the touch of two selves across the metaphysical abyss that separates one consciousness from another. That is the theme of *Song of Songs*, that deeply human yet deeply mystical expression of *eros*, the love between humanity and God. It is also the meaning of one of the definitive sentences in Judaism: "You shall love the Lord your God with all your heart and with all your soul and with all your strength" (Deut. 6:5).

Judaism from the beginning made a connection between sexuality and violence on the one hand, marital faithfulness and social order on the other. Not by chance is marriage called *kiddushin*, "sanctification." Like covenant itself, marriage is a pledge of loyalty between two parties, each recognising the other's integrity, honouring their differences even as they come together to bring new life into being. Marriage is to society what covenant is to religious faith: a decision to make love – not power, wealth, or *force majeure* – the generative principle of life.

Just as spirituality is the most intimate relationship between us and God, so sex is the most intimate relationship between us and another person. Circumcision is the eternal sign of Jewish faith because it unites the life of the soul with the passions of the body, reminding us that both must be governed by humility, self-restraint, and love.

Brit mila helps transform the male from *baal* to *ish*, from dominant partner to loving husband, just as God tells Hosea that this is what He seeks in His relationship with the people of the covenant. Circumcision turns biology into spirituality. The instinctive male urge to reproduce becomes instead a covenantal act of partnership and mutual affirmation. It was thus as decisive a turn in human civilisation as Abrahamic monotheism itself. Both are about abandoning power as the basis of relationship, and instead aligning ourselves with what Dante called "the love that moves the sun and other stars."[3] Circumcision is the physical expression of the faith that lives in love.

---

3. *The Divine Comedy*, 30:143–45.

Metzora

The Power of Shame

O n December 20, 2013, a young woman named Justine Sacco was waiting in Heathrow airport before boarding a flight to Africa. To while away the time she sent a tweet in questionable taste about the hazards of catching AIDS. There was no immediate response, and she boarded the plane unaware of the storm that was about to break. Eleven hours later, on landing, she discovered that she had become an international cause célèbre. Her tweet and responses to it had gone viral. Over the next eleven days she would be googled more than a million times. She was branded a racist and dismissed from her job. Overnight she had become a pariah.[1]

The new social media have brought about a return to an ancient phenomenon, public shaming. Two recent books – Jon Ronson's *So You've Been Publicly Shamed* and Jennifer Jacquet's *Is Shame Necessary?*[2] – have discussed it. Jacquet believes it is a good thing. It can

---

1. Jon Ronson, *So You've Been Publicly Shamed* (London: Picador, 2015), 63–86.
2. Jennifer Jacquet, *Is Shame Necessary? New Uses for an Old Tool* (London: Allen Lane, 2015).

be a way of getting public corporations to behave more responsibly, for example. Ronson highlights the dangers. It is one thing to be shamed by the community of which you are a part; it is quite another to be shamed by a global network of strangers who know nothing about you or the context in which your act took place. That is more like a lynch mob than the pursuit of justice.

Either way, this gives us a way of understanding the otherwise bewildering phenomenon of *tzaraat*, the condition dealt with at length in *Parashat Tazria* and in *Metzora*. It has been variously translated as leprosy, skin disease, and scaly infection. Yet there are formidable problems in identifying it with any known disease. First, its symptoms do not correspond to Hansen's Disease, otherwise known as leprosy. Second, as described in the Torah, it affects not only human beings but also the walls of houses, furniture, and clothes. There is no known medical condition that has this property.

Besides, the Torah is a book about holiness and correct conduct. It is not a medical text. Even if it were, as David Zvi Hoffmann points out in his commentary, the procedures to be carried out do not correspond to those that would be done if *tzaraat* were a contagious disease.[3] Finally, *tzaraat* as described in the Torah is a condition that brings not sickness but rather impurity, *tum'a*. Health and purity are different things altogether.

The sages decoded the mystery by relating this *parasha* to the instances in the Torah in which someone was actually afflicted by *tzaraat*. One happened when Miriam spoke against her brother Moses (Num. 12:1–15). Another occurred when Moses at the burning bush said to God that the Israelites would not believe in him. His hand briefly turned "as leprous as snow" (Ex. 4:7). The sages regarded *tzaraat* as a punishment for *lashon hara*, evil speech, speaking negatively about or denigrating another person.

This helped them explain why the symptoms of *tzaraat* – mould, discoloration – could affect walls, furniture, clothes, and human skin. These were a sequence of warnings or punishments. First God warned

---

3. Rabbi David Zvi Hoffman, Commentary to *Sefer Vayikra* [Hebrew] (Jerusalem: Mossad Harav Kook, 1972), vol. 1, 253–55.

the offender by sending a sign of decay to the walls of his house. If the offender repented the condition stopped there. If he failed to do so, his furniture was affected, then his clothes, and finally his skin.

How are we to understand this? Why was "evil speech" regarded as so serious an offence that it took these strange phenomena to point to its existence? And why was it punished this way and not another?

It was the anthropologist Ruth Benedict in her book about Japanese culture, *The Chrysanthemum and the Sword*,[4] who popularised a distinction between two kinds of society – *guilt cultures* and *shame cultures* – as we noted in our introduction. Ancient Greece, like Japan, was a shame culture. Judaism and the religions influenced by it (most obviously, Calvinism) were guilt cultures. The differences between them are substantial.

In shame cultures, what matters is the judgement of others. Acting morally means conforming to public roles, rules, and expectations. You do what other people expect you to do. You follow society's conventions. If you fail to do so, society punishes you by subjecting you to shame, ridicule, disapproval, humiliation, and ostracism. In guilt cultures what matters is not what other people think but what the voice of your conscience tells you. Living morally means acting in accordance with internalised moral imperatives: "You shall" and "You shall not." What matters is what you know to be right and wrong.

People in shame cultures are *other-directed*. They care about how they appear in the eyes of others, or as we would say today, about their "image." People in guilt cultures are *inner-directed*. They care about what they know about themselves in moments of absolute honesty. Even if your public image is undamaged, if you know you have done wrong, it will make you feel uneasy. You will wake up at night, troubled. "O coward conscience, how dost thou afflict me!" says Shakespeare's Richard III. "My conscience hath a thousand several tongues / And every tongue brings in a several tale / And every tale condemns me for a villain." Shame is public humiliation. Guilt is inner torment.

The emergence of a guilt culture in Judaism flowed from its understanding of the relationship between God and humankind. In Judaism

4. Boston: Houghton Mifflin, 1946.

we are not actors on a stage with society as the audience and judge. We can fool society; we cannot fool God. All pretence and pride, every mask and persona, the cosmetic cultivation of public image are irrelevant: "The Lord does not look at the things people look at. People look at the outward appearance, but the Lord looks at the heart" (I Sam. 16:7). Shame cultures are collective and conformist. By contrast, Judaism, the archetypal guilt culture, emphasises the individual and his or her relationship with God. What matters is not whether we conform to the culture of the age but whether we do what is good, just, and right.

This makes the law of *tzaraat* fascinating, because according to the sages' interpretation, it constitutes one of the rare instances in the Torah of *punishment by shame rather than guilt*. The appearance of mould or discolouration on the walls of a house was a public signal of private wrongdoing. It was a way of saying to everyone who lived or visited there, "Bad things have been said in this place." Little by little the signals came ever closer to the culprit, appearing next on his bed or chair, then on his clothes, then on his skin, until eventually he found himself diagnosed as defiled:

> When a person has the mark of the defiling disease, his clothing must have a tear in it, he must go without a haircut, and he must cover his head down to his lips. "Unclean! Unclean!" he must call out. As long as he has the mark, he shall remain unclean. Since he is unclean, he must remain alone, and his place shall be outside the camp. (Lev. 13:45–46)

These are quintessential expressions of shame. First is the *stigma*, the public marks of disgrace or dishonour (the torn clothes, the unkempt hair). Then comes the *ostracism*, temporary exclusion from the normal affairs of society. These have nothing to do with illness and everything to do with social disapproval. This is what makes the law of *tzaraat* so hard to understand at first: it is one of the rare appearances of public shame in a non-shame-based culture, a guilt-based culture.[5] It happened,

5. Another example of shame, according to R. Yoḥanan b. Zakkai, was the ceremony in which a slave who did not wish to go free after the completion of six years of

though, not because society had expressed its disapproval but because God was signalling that it should do so.

Why specifically in the case of *lashon hara*, "evil speech"? Because *speech is what holds society together.* Anthropologists have argued that language evolved among humans precisely in order to strengthen the bonds between them so that they could cooperate in larger groupings than any other animal. What sustains cooperation is *trust*. This allows and encourages me to make sacrifices for the group, knowing that others can be relied on to do likewise. This is precisely why *lashon hara* is so destructive. It undermines trust. It makes people suspicious about one another. It weakens the bonds that hold the group together. If unchecked, *lashon hara* will destroy any group it attacks – a family, a team, a community, even a nation. Hence its uniquely malicious character; it uses the power of language to weaken the very thing language was brought into being to create, namely, the trust that sustains the social bond.

That is why the punishment for *lashon hara* was to be temporarily excluded from society by *public exposure* (the signs that appear on walls, furniture, clothes, and skin), *stigmatisation and shame* (the torn clothes, etc.), and *ostracism* (being forced to live outside the camp). It is difficult, perhaps impossible, to punish the malicious gossiper using the normal conventions of law – courts and the establishment of guilt. This can be done in the case of *motzi shem ra*, libel or slander, because these are all cases of *making a false statement. Lashon hara* is more subtle. It is done not by falsehood but by insinuation. There are many ways of harming a person's reputation without actually telling a lie. Someone accused of *lashon hara* can easily say, "I didn't say it, I didn't mean it, and, even if I did, I did not say anything that was untrue." The best way of dealing with people who poison relationships without actually uttering falsehoods is by naming, shaming, and shunning them.

That, according to the sages, is what *tzaraat* miraculously did in ancient times. It no longer exists in the form described in the Torah. But the use of the Internet and social media as instruments of public shaming

service had his ear pierced against a doorpost (Ex. 20:6). See Rashi ad loc. and Kiddushin 22b.

illustrates both the power and the danger of a culture of shame. Only rarely does the Torah invoke it, and in the case of the *metzora* only by an act of God, not society. Yet the moral of the *metzora* remains. Malicious gossip, *lashon hara*, undermines relationships, erodes the social bond, and damages trust. It deserves to be exposed and shamed.

Never speak ill of others, and stay far from those who do.

Aḥarei Mot

The Scapegoat –
Shame and Guilt

T he strangest and most dramatic element of the service on Yom Kippur, set out in *Parashat Aḥarei Mot* (Lev. 16:7–22), was the ritual of the two goats, one offered as a sacrifice, the other sent away into the desert "to Azazel." They were, to all intents and purposes, indistinguishable from one another: they were chosen to be as similar as possible in size and appearance. They were brought before the high priest and lots were drawn, one bearing the words "To the Lord," the other, "To Azazel." The one on which the lot "To the Lord" fell was offered as a sacrifice. Over the other, the high priest confessed the sins of the nation, and it was then taken away into the desert hills outside Jerusalem where it plunged to its death. Tradition tells us that a red thread would be attached to its horns, half of which was removed before the animal was sent away. If the rite had been effective, the red thread would turn to white.

Much is puzzling about the ritual. First, what is the meaning of "to Azazel," to which the second goat was sent? It appears nowhere else in Scripture. Three major theories emerged as to its meaning. According to the sages and Rashi, it means "a steep, rocky, or hard place," in other words, a description of its destination. According to the Torah, the goat was sent "to a desolate area" (*el eretz gezera*, Lev. 16:22). According to the sages, it was taken to a steep ravine where it fell to its death. That, according to the first explanation, is the meaning of Azazel.

The second, suggested cryptically by Ibn Ezra and explicitly by Ramban, is that Azazel was the name of a spirit or demon, one of the fallen angels referred to in Genesis 6:2, similar to the goat-spirit called Pan in Greek mythology, Faunus in Latin. This is a difficult idea, which is why Ibn Ezra alluded to it, as he did in similar cases, by way of a riddle, a puzzle, that only the wise would be able to decipher. He writes: "I will reveal to you part of the secret by hint: when you reach thirty-three you will know it." Ramban reveals the secret. Thirty-three verses later, the Torah commands: "They must no longer offer any of their sacrifices to the goat idols [*se'irim*] after whom they go astray" (Lev. 17:7).

Azazel, on this reading, is the name of a demon or hostile force, sometimes called Satan or Samael. The Israelites were categorically forbidden to worship such a force. Indeed, the belief that there are powers at work in the universe distinct from, or even hostile to, God is incompatible with Judaic monotheism. Nonetheless, some sages did believe that there were negative forces that were part of the heavenly retinue, like Satan, who brought accusations against humans or tempted them into sin. The goat sent into the wilderness to Azazel was a way of conciliating or propitiating such forces so that the prayers of Israel could rise to heaven without, as it were, any dissenting voices. This way of understanding the rite is similar to the saying on the part of the sages that we blow shofar in a double cycle on Rosh HaShana "to confuse Satan" (Rosh HaShana 16b).

The third interpretation, and the simplest, is that Azazel is a compound noun meaning "the goat [*ez*] that was sent away [*azal*]." This led to the addition of a new word to the English language. In 1530, William Tyndale produced the first English translation of the Hebrew Bible, an act then illegal and for which he paid with his life. Seeking to translate Azazel into English, he called it "the escapegoat," i.e., the goat that was sent away and released. In the course of time, the first letter was dropped, and the word "scapegoat" was born.

The real question, though, is: what was the ritual actually about? It was unique. Sin and guilt offerings are familiar features of the Torah and a normal part of the service of the Temple. The service of Yom Kippur was different in one salient respect. In every other case, the sin was confessed over the animal that was sacrificed. On Yom Kippur, the high priest confessed the sins of the people over the animal that was *not* sacrificed, the scapegoat that was sent away, "carrying on it all their iniquities" (Lev. 16:21–22).

The simplest and most compelling answer was given by Rambam in *The Guide for the Perplexed*:

> There is no doubt that sins cannot be carried like a burden, and taken off the shoulder of one being to be laid on that of another being. But these ceremonies are of a symbolic character, and serve to impress people with a certain idea, and to induce them to repent – as if to say, we have freed ourselves of our previous deeds, have cast them behind our backs, and removed them from us as far as possible.[1]

Expiation demands a ritual, some dramatic representation of the removal of sin and the wiping clean of the past. That is clear. Yet Rambam does not explain why Yom Kippur demanded a rite not used on other days of the year when sin or guilt offerings were brought. Why was the first goat, the one on which the lot "To the Lord" fell and which was offered as a sin offering (Lev. 16:9) not sufficient?

The answer lies in the dual character of the day. The Torah states:

> This shall be an eternal law for you: On the tenth day of the seventh month you must fast and not do any work .... This is because on this day you shall have all your sins atoned [*yekhaper*], so that you will be cleansed [*letaher*]. Before God, you will be cleansed of all your sins. (Lev. 16:29–30)

---

1. Rambam, *The Guide for the Perplexed*, III:46.

Two quite distinct processes were involved on Yom Kippur. First there was *kappara*, atonement. This is the normal function of a sin offering. Second, there was *tahara*, purification, something normally done in a different context altogether, namely the removal of *tum'a*, ritual defilement, which could arise from a number of different causes, among them contact with a dead body, skin disease, or nocturnal discharge. Atonement has to do with guilt. Purification has to do with contamination or pollution. These are usually[2] two separate worlds. On Yom Kippur they were brought together. Why?

As we have already noted, we owe to anthropologists like Ruth Benedict the distinction between shame cultures and guilt cultures.[3] Shame is a social phenomenon. It is what we feel when our wrongdoing is exposed to others. It may even be something we feel when we merely imagine other people knowing or seeing what we have done. Shame is the feeling of being found out, and our first instinct is to hide. That is what Adam and Eve did in the Garden of Eden after they had eaten the forbidden fruit. They were ashamed of their nakedness and they hid.

Guilt is a personal phenomenon. It has nothing to do with what others might say if they knew what we have done, and everything to do with what we say to ourselves. Guilt is the voice of conscience, and it is inescapable. You may be able to avoid shame by hiding or not being found out, but you cannot avoid guilt. Guilt is self-knowledge.

There is another difference, which explains why Judaism is overwhelmingly a guilt rather than a shame culture. Shame attaches to the person. Guilt attaches to the act. It is almost impossible to remove shame once you have been publicly disgraced. It is like an indelible stain on your skin. Shakespeare has Macbeth say, after his crime, "Will these hands ne'er be clean?" In shame cultures, wrongdoers tend either to go into exile, where no one knows their past, or to commit suicide. Playwrights have them die.

Guilt makes a clear distinction between the act of wrongdoing and the person of the wrongdoer. The act was wrong, but the agent

---

2. There were exceptions. A leper – or more precisely, someone suffering from the skin disease known in the Torah as *tzaraat* – had to bring a guilt offering [*asham*] in addition to undergoing rites of purification (Lev. 14:12–20).
3. Ruth Benedict, *The Chrysanthemum and the Sword* (Boston: Houghton Mifflin, 1946).

remains, in principle, intact. That is why guilt can be removed, "atoned for," by confession, remorse, and restitution. "Hate not the sinner but the sin," is the basic axiom of a guilt culture.

Normally, sin and guilt offerings, as their names imply, are about guilt. They atone. But Yom Kippur deals not only with our sins as individuals. It also confronts our sins as a community bound by mutual responsibility. It deals, in other words, with the social as well as the personal dimension of wrongdoing. Yom Kippur is about shame as well as guilt. Hence there has to be purification (the removal of the stain) as well as atonement.

The psychology of shame is quite different to that of guilt. We can discharge guilt by achieving forgiveness – and forgiveness can only be granted by the object of our wrongdoing, which is why Yom Kippur only atones for sins against God. Even God cannot – logically, cannot – forgive sins committed against our fellow humans until they themselves have forgiven us.

Shame cannot be removed by forgiveness. The victim of our crime may have forgiven us, but we still feel defiled by the knowledge that our name has been disgraced, our reputation harmed, our standing damaged. We still feel the stigma, the dishonour, the degradation. That is why an immensely powerful and dramatic ceremony had to take place during which people could feel and symbolically see their sins carried away to the desert, to no-man's-land. A similar ceremony took place when a leper was cleansed. The priest took two birds, killed one, and released the other to fly away across the open fields (Lev. 14:4–7). Again, the act was one of *cleansing*, not *atoning*, and had to do with shame, not guilt.

Judaism is a religion of hope, and its great rituals of repentance and atonement are part of that hope. We are not condemned to live endlessly with the mistakes and errors of our past. That is the great difference between a guilt culture and a shame culture. But Judaism also acknowledges the existence of shame. Hence the elaborate ritual of the scapegoat that seemed to carry away the *tum'a*, the defilement that is the mark of shame. It could only be done on Yom Kippur because that was the one day of the year on which everyone shared, at least vicariously, in the process of confession, repentance, atonement, and purification. When a whole society confesses its guilt, individuals can be redeemed from shame.

Kedoshim

From Priest to People

Something fundamental happens at the beginning of *Parashat Kedoshim*, whose story is one of the greatest, if unacknowledged, contributions of Judaism to the world.

Until now Leviticus has been largely about sacrifices, purity, the Sanctuary, and the priesthood. It has been, in short, about a holy place, holy offerings, and the elite and holy people – Aaron and his descendants – who minister there. Suddenly, in chapter 19, the text opens up to embrace the whole of the people and the whole of life: "The Lord said to Moses, 'Speak to *the entire assembly of Israel* and say to them: be holy because I, the Lord your God, am holy'" (Lev. 19:1–2).

This is the first and only time in Leviticus that so inclusive an address is commanded. The sages said that it meant that the contents of the chapter were proclaimed by Moses to a formal gathering of the entire nation (*hak'hel*). It is the people as a whole who are commanded to "be holy," not just an elite, the priests. It is life itself that is to be sanctified, as the chapter goes on to make clear. Holiness is to be made manifest in the way the nation makes its clothes and plants its fields, in the way justice is administered, workers are paid, and business conducted. The vulnerable – the deaf, the blind, the elderly, and the stranger – are to be afforded special protection. The whole society is to be governed by love, without resentments or revenge.

What we witness here, in other words, is the radical *democratisation of holiness*. All ancient societies had priests. We have encountered four instances in the Torah thus far of non-Israelite priests: Melchizedek, Abraham's contemporary, described as a priest of the most high God; Potiphera, Joseph's father-in-law; the Egyptian priests as a whole whose land Joseph did not nationalise; and Yitro, Moses' father-in-law, a Midianite priest. The priesthood was not unique to Israel, and everywhere it was an elite. Here for the first time we find a code of holiness directed to the people as a whole. We are all called on to be holy.

In a strange way, though, this comes as no surprise. The idea, if not the details, had already been hinted at. The most explicit instance comes in the prelude to the great covenant-making ceremony at Mount Sinai when God tells Moses to say to the people, "Now if you obey Me fully and keep My covenant, then out of all nations you will be My treasured possession. Although the whole earth is Mine, you will be for Me *a kingdom of priests and a holy nation*" (Ex. 19:5–6), that is, a kingdom *all* of whose members are to be in some sense priests, and a nation that is in its entirety holy.

The first intimation is much earlier still, in the first chapter of Genesis, with its monumental assertion, "Let us make mankind in our image, in our likeness. … So God created mankind in His own image, in the image of God He created them; male and female He created them" (Gen. 1:26–27). What is revolutionary in this declaration is not that a human being could be in the image of God. That is precisely how kings of Mesopotamian city-states and pharaohs of Egypt were regarded. They were seen as the representatives, the living images, of the gods. That is how they derived their authority. The revolutionary dimension of the statement is that not some, but *all*, humans share this dignity. Regardless of class, colour, culture, or creed, we are all in the image and likeness of God.

Thus was born the cluster of ideas that, though they took many millennia to be realised, led to the distinctive culture of the West: the non-negotiable dignity of the human person, the idea of human rights, and eventually the political and economic expressions of these ideas – liberal democracy on the one hand, and the free market on the other.

The point is not that these ideas were fully formed in the minds of human beings during the period of biblical history. Manifestly this is not so. The concept of human rights is a product of the seventeenth century. Democracy was not fully implemented until the twentieth. But already in Genesis 1 the seed was planted. That is what Jefferson meant when he wrote, "God who gave us life gave us liberty. And can the liberties of a nation be thought secure when we have removed their only firm basis, a conviction in the minds of the people that these liberties are of the Gift of God?"[1]

The irony is that these three texts – Genesis 1, Exodus 19:6, and Leviticus 19 – are all spoken in the priestly voice Judaism calls *Torat Kohanim*. On the face of it, priests were not egalitarian. They all came from a single tribe, the Levites, and from a single family, that of Aaron, within the tribe. To be sure, the Torah tells us that this was not God's original intention. Initially it was to have been the firstborn – those who were saved from the last of the plagues – who were charged with special holiness as the ministers of God. It was only after the sin of the Golden Calf, in which the tribe of Levi did not participate, that the change was made. Even so the priesthood would have been an elite, a role reserved specifically for firstborn males. So deep is the concept of equality written into monotheism that it emerges precisely from the priestly voice – from which we would least expect it.

The reason is this: religion in the ancient world was, not accidentally but essentially, a defence of hierarchy. With the development first of agriculture and then of cities, what emerged were highly stratified societies with a ruler on top, surrounded by a royal court, beneath which was an administrative elite, and at the bottom an illiterate mass that was conscripted from time to time either as an army or as a corvée, a labour force used in the construction of monumental buildings.

What kept the structure in place was an elaborate doctrine of a heavenly hierarchy whose origins were told in myth, whose most

---

1. *Notes on the State of Virginia, Query XVIII.*

familiar natural symbol was the sun, and whose architectural representation was the pyramid or ziggurat, a massive building broad at the base and narrow at the top. The gods had fought and established an order of dominance and submission. To rebel against the earthly hierarchy was to challenge reality itself. This belief was universal in the ancient world. Aristotle thought that some were born to rule, others to be ruled. Plato constructed a myth in his *Republic* in which class divisions existed because the gods had made some people with gold, some with silver, and others with bronze. This was the "noble lie" that had to be told if a society was to protect itself against dissent from within.

Monotheism removes the entire mythological basis of hierarchy. There is no order among the gods because there are no gods, there is only the one God, creator of all. Some form of hierarchy will always exist: armies need commanders, films need directors, and orchestras, conductors. But these hierarchies are functional, not ontological. They are not a matter of birth. So it is all the more impressive to find the most egalitarian sentiments coming from the world of the priest, whose religious role *was* a matter of birth.

The concept of equality we find in the Torah specifically and Judaism generally is not an equality of wealth: Judaism is not communism. Nor is it an equality of power: Judaism is not anarchy. It is fundamentally an equality of dignity. We are all equal citizens in the nation whose sovereign is God. Hence the elaborate political and economic structure set out in Leviticus, organised around the number seven, the sign of the holy. Every seventh day is free time. Every seventh year, the produce of the field belongs to all; Israelite slaves are to be liberated and debts released. Every fiftieth year, the year following the seventh set of seven years, ancestral land was to return to its original owners. Thus the inequalities that are the inevitable result of freedom are mitigated. The logic of all these provisions is the priestly insight that God, creator of all, is the ultimate owner of all: "The land must not be sold permanently, because the land is Mine and you reside in My land as strangers and temporary residents" (Lev. 25:23). God therefore has the right, not just the power, to set limits to inequality. No one should be robbed of dignity by total poverty, endless servitude, or unrelieved indebtedness.

What is truly remarkable however is what happened *after* the biblical era and the destruction of the Second Temple. Faced with the loss of the entire infrastructure of the holy – the Temple, its priests, its sacrifices – Judaism translated the entire system of *avoda*, divine service, into the everyday life of ordinary Jews. In prayer, every Jew became a priest offering a sacrifice. In repentance, each became a high priest, atoning for his or her sins and those of his or her people. Every synagogue, in Israel or elsewhere, became a fragment of the Temple in Jerusalem. Every table became an altar, every act of charity or hospitality a kind of sacrifice.

Torah study, once the speciality of the priesthood, became the right and obligation of everyone. Not everyone could wear the crown of priesthood but everyone could wear the crown of Torah. A *mamzer talmid ḥakham* – a Torah scholar of illegitimate birth – said the sages, was greater than an *am haaretz kohen gadol*, an ignorant high priest. Out of the devastating tragedy of the loss of the Temple, the sages created a religious and social order that came closer to the ideal of the people as "a kingdom of priests and a holy nation" than had ever previously been realised. The seed had been planted long before, in the opening of Leviticus 19, "Speak to *the entire assembly of Israel* and say to them: be holy because I, the Lord your God, am holy."

Holiness belongs to all of us when we turn our lives into the service of God and society into a home for the Divine Presence. That is the moral life as lived by the kingdom of priests: a world where we aspire to come close to God by coming close, in justice and love, to our fellow humans.

Emor

Sanctifying the Name

A president guilty of sexual abuse; a prime minister indicted on charges of corruption and bribery; rabbis in several countries accused of financial impropriety, sexual harassment, and child abuse. That such things happen testifies to a profound malaise in contemporary Jewish life.

More is at stake than simply morality. Morality is universal. Bribery, corruption, and the misuse of power are wrong, and wrong equally, whoever is guilty of them. When, though, the guilty are leaders, something more is involved – the principles introduced in *Parashat Emor* of *kiddush Hashem* and *hillul Hashem*: "Do not profane My holy name, that I may be sanctified in the midst of the Israelites, I the Lord who sanctify you" (Lev. 22:32).

The concepts of *kiddush* and *hillul Hashem* have a history. Though they are timeless and eternal, their unfolding occurred through the course of time. In this *parasha*, according to Ibn Ezra, the verse has a narrow and localised sense. The chapter in which it occurs has been speaking about the special duties of the priesthood and the extreme care they must take in serving God within the Sanctuary. All Israel is holy, but the priests are a holy elite within the nation. It is their task to preserve the purity and glory of the Sanctuary as God's symbolic home in the midst of the nation. So the commands are a special charge to the priests to take exemplary care as guardians of the holy.

Another dimension was disclosed by the prophets, who used the phrase *ḥillul Hashem* to describe immoral conduct that brings dishonour to God's law as a code of justice and compassion. Amos (2:7) speaks of people who "trample on the heads of the poor as on the dust of the ground, and deny justice to the oppressed...and so profane My holy name." Jeremiah invokes *ḥillul Hashem* to describe those who circumvent the law by emancipating their slaves only to recapture and re-enslave them (Jer. 34:16). Malachi, last of the prophets, says of the corrupt priests of his day, "From where the sun rises to where it sets, My name is honoured among the nations...but you profane it" (Mal. 1:11–12).

The sages[1] suggested that Abraham was referring to the same idea when he challenged God on His plan to destroy Sodom and Gomorrah if this meant punishing the righteous as well as the wicked: "Far be it from You [*ḥalila Lekha*] to do such a thing" (Gen. 18:25). God and the people of God must be associated with justice. Failure to do so constitutes a *ḥillul Hashem*.

A third dimension appears in the book of Ezekiel. The Jewish people, or at least a significant part of it, had been forced into exile in Babylon. The nation had suffered defeat. The Temple lay in ruins. For the exiles this was a human tragedy. They had lost their home, freedom, and independence. It was also a spiritual tragedy: "How can we sing the Lord's song in a strange land?" (Ps. 137:4). But Ezekiel saw it as a tragedy for God as well:

> Son of man, when the people of Israel were living in their own land, they defiled it by their conduct and their actions.... I dispersed them among the nations, and they were scattered through the countries; I judged them according to their conduct and their actions. And *wherever they went among the nations they profaned My holy name*, for it was said of them, "These are the Lord's people, and yet they had to leave His land." (Ezek. 36:17–20)

1. Genesis Rabba 49:9.

Exile was a desecration of God's name because the fact that He had punished His people by letting them be conquered was interpreted by the other nations as showing that God was unable to protect them. This recalls Moses' prayer after the Golden Calf:

> "Lord," he said, "why should Your anger burn against Your people, whom You brought out of Egypt with great power and a mighty hand? Why should the Egyptians say, 'It was with evil intent that He brought them out, to kill them in the mountains and to wipe them off the face of the earth'? Turn from Your fierce anger; relent and do not bring disaster on Your people." (Ex. 32:11–12)

This is part of the divine pathos. Having chosen to identify His name with the people of Israel, God is, as it were, caught between the demands of justice on the one hand, and public perception on the other. What looks like retribution to the Israelites looks like weakness to the world. In the eyes of the nations, for whom national gods were identified with power, the exile of Israel could not but be interpreted as the powerlessness of Israel's God. That, says Ezekiel, is a *ḥillul Hashem*, a desecration of God's name.

A fourth sense became clear in the late Second Temple period. Israel had returned to its land and rebuilt the Temple, but they came under attack first from the Seleucid Greeks in the reign of Antiochus IV, and then from the Romans – both of whom attempted to outlaw Jewish practice. For the first time martyrdom became a significant feature in Jewish life. The question arose: under what circumstances were Jews to sacrifice their lives rather than transgress Jewish law?

The sages understood the verse, "You shall keep My decrees and laws which a person shall keep *and live by them*" (Lev. 18:5), to imply "and not die by them" (Yoma 85b). Saving life takes precedence over most of the commands. But there are three exceptions: the prohibitions against murder, forbidden sexual relations, and idolatry, where the sages ruled that it was necessary to die rather than transgress. They also said that "at a time of persecution" one should resist at the cost of death even a demand "to change one's shoelaces," that is, performing any act that could be construed as going over to the enemy, betraying and demoralising those who remained true to the faith (Sanhedrin 74a–b). It was at this time that the phrase *kiddush Hashem* was used to mean the willingness to die as a martyr.

One of the most poignant of all collective responses on the part of the Jewish people was to categorise all the victims of the Holocaust as "those who died *al kiddush Hashem*," that is, for the sake of sanctifying God's name. This was not a foregone conclusion. Martyrdom in the past meant choosing to die for the sake of God. One of the demonic aspects of the Nazi genocide was that Jews were not given the choice. By calling them "martyrs" in retrospect, Jews gave the victims the dignity in death of which they were so brutally robbed in life.[2]

There is a fifth dimension. This is how Rambam sums it up:

> There are other deeds which are also included in the desecration of God's name. When a person of great Torah stature, renowned for his piety, does deeds which, although they are not transgressions, cause people to speak disparagingly of him, this is also a desecration of God's name.... All this depends on the stature of the sage.[3]

People looked up to as role models must act as role models. Piety in relation to God must be accompanied by exemplary behaviour in relation to one's fellow humans. When people associate religiosity with integrity, decency, humility, and compassion, God's name is sanctified. When they come to associate it with contempt for others and for the law, the result is a desecration of God's name.

Common to all five dimensions of meaning is the radical idea, central to Jewish self-definition, that God has risked His reputation in the world, His "name," by choosing to associate it with a single and singular people. God is the God of all humanity. But God has chosen Israel to

2. There was a precedent. In the *Av HaRahamim* prayer, composed after the massacre of Jews during the Crusades, the victims were described as those "who sacrificed their lives *al kedushat Hashem*." Though some of the victims went to their deaths voluntarily, not all of them did.
3. *Mishneh Torah, Hilkhot Yesodei HaTorah* 5:11.

be His "witnesses," His ambassadors, to the world. When we fail in this role, it is as if God's standing in the eyes of the world has been damaged.

For almost two thousand years the Jewish people was without a home, a land, civil rights, security, and the ability to shape its destiny and fate. It was cast in the role of what Max Weber called "a pariah people." By definition, a pariah cannot be a positive role model. That is when *kiddush Hashem* took on its tragic dimension as the willingness to die for one's faith. That is no longer the case. Today, for the first time in history, Jews have both sovereignty and independence in Israel, and freedom and equality elsewhere. *Kiddush Hashem* must therefore be restored to its positive sense of exemplary decency in the moral life.

That is what led the Hittites to call Abraham "a prince of God in our midst" (Gen. 23:6). It is what leads Israel to be admired when it engages in international rescue and relief. The concepts of *kiddush* and *ḥillul Hashem* forge an indissoluble connection between the holy and the good. Lose that and we betray our mission as "a holy nation." The conviction that being a Jew involves the pursuit of justice and the practice of compassion is what led our ancestors to stay loyal to Judaism despite all the pressures to abandon it. It would be the ultimate tragedy if we lost that connection now, at the very moment that we are able to face the world on equal terms.

Long ago, we were called on to show the world that religion and morality go hand in hand. Never was that more needed than in an age riven by religiously motivated violence in some countries, rampant secularity in others. To be a Jew is to be dedicated to the proposition that loving God means loving His image, humankind. There is no greater challenge, nor, in the twenty-first century, is there a more urgent one.

Behar

The Economics of Liberty

The most surprising bestselling book in 2014 was French economist Thomas Piketty's *Capital in the Twenty-First Century*,[1] a dense seven-hundred-page-long treatise on economic theory backed by massive statistical research – not the usual stuff of runaway literary successes.

Much of its appeal was the way it documented the phenomenon that is reshaping societies throughout the world: in the current global economy, inequalities are growing apace. In the United States, between 1979 and 2013, the top 1 per cent saw their incomes grow by more than 240 per cent, while the lowest fifth experienced a rise of only 10 per cent.[2] More striking still is the difference in capital income from assets such as housing, stocks, and bonds, where the top 1 per cent has seen a growth of 300 per cent, and the bottom fifth has suffered a fall of

---

1. Thomas Piketty, *Capital in the Twenty-First Century*, trans. Arthur Goldhammer (Cambridge, MA: Belknap Press of Harvard University Press, 2014).
2. Derek Thompson, "A Giant Statistical Round-Up of the Income Inequality Crisis in 16 Charts," *The Atlantic*, December 12, 2012, http://www.theatlantic.com/business/archive/2012/12/a-giant-statistical-round-up-of-the-income-inequality-crisis-in-16-charts/266074.

60 per cent. In global terms, the combined wealth of the richest eighty-five individuals is equal to the total of the poorest 3.5 billion – half the population of the world.[3]

Picketty's contribution was in showing why this has happened. The market economy, he argues, tends to makes us more and less equal at the same time: more equal because it spreads education, knowledge, and skills more widely than in the past, but less equal because over time, especially in mature economies, the rate of return on capital tends to outpace the rate of growth of income and output. Those who own capital assets grow richer faster than those who rely entirely on income from their labour. The increase in inequality is, he says, "potentially threatening to democratic societies and to the values of social justice on which they are based."[4]

This is the latest chapter in a very old story indeed. As we saw in our discussion of *Parashat Vayeḥi*, Isaiah Berlin made the point that not all values can coexist – in this case, freedom and equality.[5] You can have one or the other but not both: the more economic freedom, the less equality; the more equality, the less freedom. That was the key conflict of the Cold War era – between capitalism and communism. Communism lost the battle. In the 1980s, under Ronald Reagan in America and Margaret Thatcher in Britain, markets were liberalised, and by the end of the decade the Soviet Union had collapsed. But unfettered economic freedom produces its own discontents, and Picketty's book reveals one of several warning signs.

All of this makes the social legislation of *Parashat Behar* a text for our time, because the Torah is profoundly concerned, not just with economics, but with the more fundamental moral and human issues. What kind of society do we seek? What social order best does justice to human dignity and the delicate bonds linking us to one another and to God?

---

3. Graeme Wearden, "Oxfam: 85 Richest People as Wealthy as Poorest Half of the World," *The Guardian*, January 20, 2014, http://www.theguardian.com/business/2014/jan/20/oxfam-85-richest-people-half-of-the-world.
4. Picketty, *Capital in the Twenty-First Century*, 571.
5. Isaiah Berlin, "Two Concepts of Liberty," in *Four Essays on Liberty* (London: Oxford University Press, 1969).

What makes Judaism distinctive is its commitment to *both* freedom *and* equality, while at the same time recognising the tension between them. The opening chapters of Genesis describe the consequences of God's gift to humans of individual freedom. But since we are social animals, we need also collective freedom. Hence the significance of the opening chapters of Numbers, with their characterisation of Egypt as an example of a society that deprives people of liberty, enslaving populations and making the many subject to the will of the few. Time and again the Torah explains its laws as ways of preserving freedom, remembering what it was like, in Egypt, to be deprived of liberty.

The Torah is also committed to the equal dignity of human beings in the image, and under the sovereignty, of God. That quest for equality was not fully realised in the biblical era. There were hierarchies in biblical Israel. Not everyone could be a king; not everyone was a priest. But Judaism had no class system. It had no equivalent of Plato's division of society into men of gold, silver, and bronze, or Aristotle's belief that some are born to rule, others to be ruled. In the community of the covenant envisaged by the Torah, we are all God's children, all precious in His sight, each with a contribution to make to the common good.

The fundamental insight of *Parashat Behar* is precisely that restated by Piketty, namely that economic inequalities have a tendency to increase over time, and the result may be a loss of freedom as well. People can become enslaved by a burden of debt. In biblical times this might have involved selling yourself literally into slavery as the only way of guaranteeing food and shelter. Families might have been forced into selling their land, their ancestral inheritance from the days of Moses. The result would be a society in which, in the course of time, a few would become substantial landowners while many became landless and impoverished.

The Torah's solution, set out in *Behar*, is a periodic restoration of people's fundamental liberties. Every seventh year, debts were to be released and Israelite slaves set free. After seven sabbatical cycles, the Jubilee year was to be a time when, with few exceptions, ancestral land returned to its original owners. The Liberty Bell in Philadelphia is engraved with the famous words of the Jubilee command, in the King James translation: "Proclaim liberty throughout all the land unto all the inhabitants thereof" (Lev. 25:10). So relevant does this vision remain that the international movement for debt relief for Third World countries by the year 2000 was called *Jubilee 2000*, an explicit reference to the principles set out in this *parasha*.

Three things are worth noting about the Torah's social and economic programme. First, it is more concerned with human freedom than with a narrow focus on economic equality. Losing your land or becoming trapped by debt are real constraints on freedom.[6] Fundamental to a Jewish understanding of the moral dimension of economics is the idea of independence, "each person under his own vine and fig tree," as the prophet Micah puts it (Mic. 4:4). We pray in the Grace after Meals, "Do not make us dependent on the gifts or loans of other people…so that we may suffer neither shame nor humiliation." There is something profoundly degrading in losing your independence and being forced to depend on the goodwill of others. Hence the provisions of *Behar* are directed not at equality but at restoring people's capacity to earn their own livelihood as free and independent agents.

Next, it takes this entire system out of the hands of human legislators. It rests on two fundamental ideas about capital and labour. First, the land belongs to God: "The land must not be sold permanently, because the land is Mine and you reside in My land as strangers and temporary residents" (Lev. 25:23). Second, the same applies to people: "Because the Israelites are My servants, whom I brought out of Egypt, they must not be sold as slaves" (Lev. 25:42). This means that personal and economic liberty are not open to political negotiation. They are inalienable, God-given rights.

Third, it tells us that economics is, and must remain, a discipline that rests on moral foundations. What matters to the Torah is not simply technical indices such as the rate of growth or absolute standards of wealth but the quality and texture of relationships: people's independence and sense of dignity, the ways in which the system allows people to recover from misfortune, and the extent to which it allows the members

---

6. This is the argument set out by Nobel Prize-winning economist Amartya Sen in his book, *Development as Freedom* (Oxford: Oxford Paperbacks, 2001).

of a society to live the truth that "when you eat from the labour of your hands you will be happy and it will be well with you" (Ps. 128:2).

In no other intellectual area have Jews been so dominant. They have won 41 per cent of Nobel Prizes in economics.[7] They have developed some of the greatest ideas in the field: David Ricardo's theory of comparative advantage, John von Neumann's game theory (a development of which gained Professor Robert Aumann a Nobel Prize), Milton Friedman's monetary theory, Gary Becker's extension of economic theory to family dynamics, Daniel Kahneman and Amos Tversky's theory of behavioural economics, and many others. Not always but often, the moral dimension has been evident in their work. There is something impressive, even spiritual, in the fact that Jews have sought to create – down here on earth, not up in heaven in an afterlife – systems that seek to maximise human liberty and creativity. And the foundations lie in this *parasha*, whose ancient words are inspiring still.

7. See the Jewish Virtual Library's list of Jewish Nobel laureates: http://www. jewishvirtuallibrary.org/jsource/Judaism/nobels.html.

Beḥukkotai

The Politics of Responsibility

The twenty-sixth chapter of Leviticus sets out with stunning clarity the terms of Jewish life under the covenant. On the one hand, there is an idyllic picture of the blessing of divine favour. If Israel follows God's decrees and keeps His commands, there will be rain, the earth will yield its fruit, there will be peace, the people will flourish, the people will have children, and the Divine Presence will be in their midst. God will make them free. "I broke the bars of your yoke and enabled you to walk with heads held high" (Lev. 26:13).

The other side of the equation, though, is terrifying: the curses that will befall the nation should the Israelites fail to honour their mission as a holy nation:

> But if you will not listen to Me and carry out all these commands … I will bring upon you sudden terror, wasting diseases, and fever that will destroy your sight and drain away your life. You will plant seed in vain, because your enemies will eat it. … If after all this you will

not listen to Me, I will punish you for your sins seven times over. I will break down your stubborn pride and make the sky above you like iron and the ground beneath you like bronze. ... I will turn your cities into ruins and lay waste your sanctuaries, and I will take no delight in the pleasing aroma of your offerings. I will lay waste the land, so that your enemies who live there will be appalled. ... As for those of you who are left, I will make their hearts so fearful in the lands of their enemies that the sound of a windblown leaf will put them to flight. They will run as though fleeing from the sword, and they will fall, even though no one is pursuing them. (Lev. 26:14–36)

Read in its entirety, this passage is more like Holocaust literature than anything else. The repeated phrases – "If after all this ... if despite this ... if despite everything" – come like hammer blows of fate. It is a passage shattering in its impact, all the more so since so much of it came true at various times in Jewish history. Yet the curses end with the most profound promise of ultimate consolation. Despite everything God will not break His covenant with the Jewish people. Collectively they will be eternal. They may suffer, but they will never be destroyed. They will undergo exile but eventually they will return.

Stated with the utmost drama, this is the logic of covenant. Unlike other conceptions of history or politics, covenant sees nothing inevitable or even natural about the fate of a people. Israel will not follow the usual laws of the rise and fall of civilisations. The Jewish people were not to see their national existence in terms of cosmology, written into the structure of the universe, immutable and fixed for all time, as did the ancient Mesopotamians and Egyptians. Nor were they to see their history as cyclical, a matter of growth and decline. Instead, it would be utterly dependent on moral considerations. If Israel stayed true to its mission, it would flourish. If it drifted from its vocation, it would suffer defeat after defeat.

Only one other nation in history has consistently seen its fate in similar terms, namely the United States. The influence of the Hebrew Bible on American history – carried by the Pilgrim Fathers and reiterated in presidential rhetoric ever since – was decisive. Here is how one writer described the faith of Abraham Lincoln:

We are a nation formed by a covenant, by dedication to a set of principles and by an exchange of promises to uphold and advance certain commitments among ourselves and throughout the world. Those principles and commitments are the core of American identity, the soul of the body politic. They make the American nation unique, and uniquely valuable, among and to the other nations. But the other side of the conception contains a warning very like the warnings spoken by the prophets to Israel: if we fail in our promises to each other, and lose the principles of the covenant, then we lose everything, for they are we.[1]

Covenantal politics is moral politics, driving an elemental connection between the fate of a nation and its vocation. This is statehood as a matter not of power but of ethical responsibility.

One might have thought that this kind of politics robbed a nation of its freedom. Spinoza argued just this. "This, then, was the object of the ceremonial law," he wrote, "that men should do nothing of their own free will, but should always act under external authority, and should continually confess by their actions and thoughts that they were not their own masters."[2] However, in this respect, Spinoza was wrong. Covenant theology is emphatically a politics of liberty.

What is happening in Leviticus 26 is the application to a nation as a whole of the proposition God spelled out to individuals at the beginning of human history:

> Then the Lord said to Cain, "Why are you angry? Why is your face downcast? If you do what is right, will you not be accepted? But if you do not do what is right, sin is crouching at your door; it desires to have you, but you must master it." (Gen. 4:6–7)

---

1. John Schaar, *Legitimacy in the Modern State* (New Brunswick, NJ: Transaction Publishers, 1981), 291.
2. Benedict de Spinoza, *A Theologico-Political Treatise and a Political Treatise* (Mineola, NY: Dover, 2004), 76.

The choice – God is saying – is in your hands. You are free to do what you choose. But actions have consequences. You cannot overeat and take no exercise, and at the same time stay healthy. You cannot act selfishly and win the respect of other people. You cannot allow injustices to prevail and sustain a cohesive society. You cannot let rulers use power for their own ends without destroying the basis of a free and gracious social order. There is nothing mystical about these ideas. They are eminently intelligible. But they are also, and inescapably, moral.

I brought you from slavery to freedom – says God – and I empower you to be free. But I cannot and will not abandon you. I will not intervene in your choices, but I will instruct you on what choices you ought to make. I will teach you the constitution of liberty.

The first and most important principle is this: A nation cannot worship itself and survive. Sooner or later, power will corrupt those who wield it. If fortune favours it and it grows rich, it will become self-indulgent and eventually decadent. Its citizens will no longer have the courage to fight for their liberty, and it will fall to another, more Spartan power.

If there are gross inequalities, the people will lack a sense of the common good. If government is high-handed and non-accountable, it will fail to command the loyalty of the people. None of this takes away your freedom. It is simply the landscape within which freedom is to be exercised. You may choose this way or that, but not all paths lead to the same destination.

To stay free, a nation must worship something greater than itself, nothing less than God, together with holding the belief that all human beings are created in His image. Self-worship on a national scale leads to totalitarianism and the extinction of liberty. It took the loss of more than 100 million lives in the twentieth century to remind us of this truth.

In the face of suffering and loss, there are two fundamentally different questions an individual or nation can ask, and they lead to quite different outcomes. The first is, "What did I, or we, do wrong?" The second is, "Who did this to us?" It is not an exaggeration to say that this is the fundamental choice governing the destinies of people.

The latter leads inescapably to what is today known as the *victim culture*. It locates the source of evil outside oneself. Someone else is to blame. It is not I or we who are at fault, but some external cause. The attraction of this logic can be overpowering. It generates sympathy. It calls for, and often evokes, compassion. It is, however, deeply destructive. It leads people to see themselves as objects, not subjects. They are done to, not doers; passive, not active. The results are anger, resentment, rage, and a burning sense of injustice. None of these, however, ever leads to freedom, since by its very logic this mindset abdicates responsibility for the current circumstances in which one finds oneself. Blaming others is the suicide of liberty.

Blaming oneself, by contrast, is difficult. It means living with constant self-criticism. It is not a route to peace of mind. Yet it is profoundly empowering. It implies that, precisely because we accept responsibility for the bad things that have happened, we also have the ability to chart a different course in the future. Within the terms set by the covenant, the outcome depends on us. That is the logical geography of hope, and it rests on the choice Moses was later to define in these words:

> This day I call heaven and earth as witnesses against you that I have set before you life and death, blessings and curses. Now choose life, so that you and your children may live. (Deut. 30:19)

One of the most profound contributions Torah made to the civilisation of the West is this: that the destiny of nations lies not in the externalities of wealth or power, fate or circumstance, but in moral responsibility – the responsibility for creating and sustaining a society that honours the image of God within each of its citizens, rich and poor, powerful or powerless alike.

The politics of responsibility are not easy. The curses of Leviticus 26 are the very reverse of comforting. Yet the profound consolations with which they end are not accidental, nor are they wishful thinking. They are testimony to the power of the human spirit when summoned to the highest vocation. A nation that sees itself as responsible for the evils that befall it is also a nation that has an inextinguishable power of recovery and return.

Numbers
במדבר

Bemidbar

Law as Love

One of the most amusing scenes in Anglo-Jewish history occurred on October 14, 1663. A mere seven years had passed since Oliver Cromwell had found no legal bar to Jews living in England (hence the so-called "return" of 1656). A small synagogue was opened in Creechurch Lane in the City of London, forerunner of Bevis Marks (1701), the oldest still-extant place of Jewish worship in Britain.

The famous diarist Samuel Pepys decided to pay a visit to this new curiosity to see how Jews conducted themselves at prayer. What he saw amazed and scandalised him. As chance or providence had it, the day of his visit turned out to be Simḥat Torah. This is how he described what he saw:

> And anon their Laws that they take out of the press [i.e., the Ark] are carried by several men, four or five several burthens in all, and they do relieve one another; and whether it is that every one desires to have the carrying of it, I cannot tell, thus they carried it round about the room while such a service is singing.... But, Lord! to see the disorder, laughing, sporting, and no attention, but confusion in all their service, more like brutes than people

knowing the true God, would make a man forswear ever seeing them more and indeed I never did see so much, or could have imagined there had been any religion in the whole world so absurdly performed as this.[1]

This was not the kind of behaviour he was used to in a house of worship.

There is something unique about the relationship of Jews to the Torah, the way we stand in its presence as if it were a king, dance with it as if it were a bride, listen to it telling our story and study it as, as we say in our prayers, "our life and the length of our days." There are few more poignant lines of prayer than the one contained in a poem said at *Ne'ila*, at the end of Yom Kippur: *Ein shiur rak haTorah hazot* – "Nothing remains," after the destruction of the Temple and the loss of the land, "but this Torah." A book, a scroll, was all that stood between Jews and despair.

What non-Jews (and sometimes Jews) fail to appreciate is how, in Judaism, Torah represents law as love, and love as law. Torah is not just "revealed legislation."[2] It represents God's faith in our ancestors that He entrusted them with the creation of a society that would become a home for His presence and an example to the world.

One of the keys as to how this worked is contained in *Parashat Bemidbar*, always read before Shavuot, the commemoration of the giving of the Torah. This reminds us how central is the idea of wilderness – the desert, no-man's-land – to Judaism. It is *midbar*, wilderness, that gives this *parasha* and the book as a whole its name. It was in the desert that the Israelites made a covenant with God and received the Torah, their constitution as a nation under the sovereignty of God. It is the desert that provides the setting for four of the five books of the Torah, and it was there that the Israelites experienced their most intimate contact with God, who sent them water from a rock and manna from heaven and surrounded them with clouds of glory.

1. *The Diary of Samuel Pepys*, ed. Richard Le Gallienne (New York: Modern Library Classics, 2003), 106.
2. Moses Mendelssohn, *Jerusalem, or, On Religious Power and Judaism*, trans. Allan Arkush (Hanover, NH: University Press of New England, 1983), 89–90, 126–28.

What story is being told here? The Torah is telling us three things fundamental to Jewish identity. First is the unique phenomenon that in Judaism the law preceded the land. For every other nation in history the reverse was the case. First came the land, then human settlements, first in small groups, then in villages, towns, and cities. Then came forms of order and governance and a legal system: first the land, then the law.

The fact that in Judaism the Torah was given *bemidbar*, in the desert, before the people had even entered the land, meant that Jews and Judaism were uniquely able to survive, their identity intact, even in exile. *Because the law came before the land, even when Jews lost the land they still had the law.* This meant that even in exile, Jews were still a nation. God remained their sovereign. The covenant was still in place. Even without a geography, they had an ongoing history. Even before they entered the land, Jews had been given the ability to survive outside the land.

Second, there is a tantalising connection between *midbar*, "wilderness," and *davar*, "word." Where other nations found the gods in nature – the rain, the earth, fertility, and the seasons of the agricultural year – Jews discovered God in transcendence, beyond nature, a God who could not be *seen* but rather *heard*. In the desert, there is no nature. Instead there is emptiness and silence, a silence in which one can hear the unearthly voice of the One-beyond-the-world. As Edmond Jabès put it: "The word cannot dwell except in the silence of other words. To speak is, accordingly, to lean on a metaphor of the desert."[3]

The historian Eric Voegelin saw this as fundamental to the completely new form of spirituality born in the experience of the Israelites:

> When we undertake the exodus and wander into the world, in order to found a new society elsewhere, we discover the world as the Desert. The flight leads nowhere, until we stop in order to find our bearings beyond the world. When the world has become Desert, man is at last in the solitude in which he can hear thunderingly the voice of the spirit that with its urgent whispering has already driven and rescued him from Sheol [the domain of death]. In the Desert God spoke to the leader and his tribes; in the desert,

3. Edmond Jabès, *Du Désert au Livre* (Paris: Pierre Belford, 1980), 101.

by listening to the voice, by accepting its offer, and by submitting to its command, they had at last reached life and became the people chosen by God.[4]

In the silence of the desert, Israel became the people for whom the primary religious experience was not seeing but listening and hearing: *Shema Yisrael.* The God of Israel revealed Himself in speech. Judaism is a religion of holy words, in which the most sacred object is a book, a scroll, a text.

Third, and most remarkable, is the interpretation the prophets gave to those formative years in which the Israelites, having left Egypt and not yet entered the land, were alone with God. Hosea, predicting a second exodus, says in God's name:

> I will lead her into the wilderness [says God about the Israelites]
> and speak tenderly to her...
> There she will respond as in the days of her youth,
> As in the day she came out of Egypt. (Hos. 14–15)

Jeremiah (2:2) says in God's name: "'I remember the devotion of your youth, how as a bride you loved Me and followed Me through the wilderness, through a land not sown." *Shir HaShirim*, Song of Songs, contains the line, "Who is this coming up from the wilderness leaning on her beloved?" (8:5).

Common to each of these texts is the idea of the desert as a honeymoon in which God and the people, imagined as bridegroom and bride, were alone together, consummating their union in love. To be sure, in the Torah itself we see the Israelites as a recalcitrant, obstinate people complaining and rebelling against God. Yet the prophets in retrospect saw things differently. The wilderness was a kind of *yiḥud*, an alone-togetherness, in which the people and God bonded in love.

Most instructive in this context is the work of anthropologist Arnold van Gennep, who focused attention on the importance of

---

4. Eric Voegelin, *Israel and Revelation* (Baton Rouge: Louisiana State University Press, 1956), 153.

rites of passage.[5] Societies develop rituals to mark the transition from one state to the next – from childhood to adulthood, for example, or from being single to being married – and they involve three stages. The first is *separation*, a symbolic break with the past. The last is *incorporation*, re-entering society with a new identity. Between the two comes the crucial stage of *transition* when, having cast off one identity but not yet donned another, you are remade, reborn, refashioned.

Van Gennep used the term *liminal*, from the Latin word for "threshold," to describe this transitional state when you are in a kind of no-man's-land between the old and the new. That is what the *wilderness* signifies for Israel: liminal space between slavery and freedom, past and future, exile and return, Egypt and the Promised Land. The desert was the space that made transition and transformation possible. There, in no-man's-land, the Israelites, alone with God and with one another, could cast off one identity and assume another. There they could be reborn, no longer slaves to Pharaoh, instead servants of God, summoned to become "a kingdom of priests and a holy nation" (Ex. 19:6).

Seeing the wilderness as the "space between" helps us to see the connection between the Israelites in the days of Moses and the ancestor whose name they bore. For it was Jacob among the patriarchs who had his most intense experiences of God in liminal space, between the place he was leaving and the one he was travelling to, alone and at night. It was there, fleeing from his brother Esau but not yet arrived at the house of Laban, that he saw a vision of a ladder stretching from earth to heaven with angels ascending and descending, and there on his return that he fought with a stranger from night until dawn and was given the name Israel. These episodes can now be seen to be prefigurations of what would later happen to his descendants (*maaseh avot siman levanim*, "the acts of the fathers are a sign of what will later happen to the children"; see Ramban's commentary on Gen. 12:6).

The desert thus became the birthplace of a wholly new relationship between God and humankind, a relationship built on covenant, speech, and love as concretised in the Torah. Distant from the great centres of civilisation, a people found themselves alone with God and

---

5. *The Rites of Passage* (Chicago: University of Chicago, 1960).

there consummated a bond that neither exile nor tragedy could break. That is the moral truth at the beating heart of our faith: that it is not power or politics that link us to God, but love.

Joy in the celebration of that love led King David to "leap and dance" when the Ark was brought into Jerusalem, earning the disapproval of King Saul's daughter Michal (II Sam. 6:16), and many centuries later led the Anglo-Jews of Creechurch Lane to dance on Simḥat Torah, to the disapproval of Samuel Pepys. When love defeats dignity, faith is alive and well.

Naso

Two Versions of the Moral Life

The *parasha* of *Naso* contains the laws relating to the Nazirite – an individual who undertook, usually for a limited period of time, to observe special rules of holiness and abstinence: not to drink wine or other intoxicants (including anything made from grapes), not to have his hair cut, and not to defile himself by contact with the dead.

The Torah does not make a direct evaluation of the Nazirite. On the one hand, it calls him "holy to God" (Num. 6:8). On the other, it rules that when the period comes to an end the Nazirite has to bring a sin offering (Num. 6:13–14), as if he had done something wrong.

This led to a fundamental disagreement between the rabbis in Mishnaic, Talmudic, and medieval times. According to R. Elazar, and later to Ramban, the Nazirite is worthy of praise. He has voluntarily chosen a higher level of holiness. The prophet Amos (2:11) says, "I raised up some of your sons for prophets, and your young men for Nazirites," suggesting that the Nazirite, like the prophet, is a person especially close to God. The reason he had to bring a sin offering was that he was now returning to ordinary life. The sin lay in *ceasing* to be a Nazirite.

R. Eliezer HaKappar and Shmuel held the opposite opinion. The sin lay in *becoming* a Nazirite in the first place, thereby denying himself some of the pleasures of the world God created and declared good. R. Eliezer added: "From this we may infer that if one who denies himself the enjoyment of wine is called a sinner, all the more so one who denies himself the enjoyment of other pleasures of life" (Taanit 11a; Nedarim 10a).

Clearly the argument is not merely textual. It is substantive. It is about asceticism, the life of self-denial. Almost every religion knows the phenomenon of people who, in pursuit of spiritual purity, withdraw from the pleasures and temptations of the world. They live in caves, retreats, hermitages, monasteries. The Qumran sect known to us through the Dead Sea Scrolls may have been such a movement.

In the Middle Ages there were Jews who adopted similar self-denial – among them the Hasidei Ashkenaz, the Pietists of Northern Europe, as well as many Jews in Islamic lands. In retrospect, it is hard not to see in these patterns of behaviour at least some influence from the non-Jewish environment. The Hasidei Ashkenaz, who flourished during the time of the Crusades, lived among self-mortifying Christians. Their southern counterparts may have been familiar with Sufism, the mystical movement in Islam.

The ambivalence of Jews towards the life of self-denial may therefore lie in the suspicion that it entered Judaism from the outside. There were ascetic movements in the first centuries of the Common Era in both the west (Greece) and the east (Iran) that saw the physical world as a place of corruption and strife. They were, in fact, dualists, holding that the true God was not the creator of the universe. The physical world was the work of a lesser, and evil, deity. The two best-known movements to hold this view were Gnosticism in the west and Manichaeism in the east. So at least some of the negative evaluation of the Nazirite may have been driven by a desire to discourage Jews from imitating non-Jewish practices.

What is more puzzling is the position of Rambam, who holds *both* views, positive and negative, in the same book – his law code, the *Mishneh Torah*.

In *Hilkhot Deot*, he adopts the negative position of R. Eliezer HaKappar:

> A person may say, "Desire, honour, and the like are bad paths to follow and remove a person from the world, therefore I will completely separate myself from them and go to the other extreme." As a result, he does not eat meat or drink wine or take a wife or live in a decent house or wear decent clothing.... This too is bad, and it is forbidden to choose this way.[1]

Yet in *Hilkhot Nezirut* he rules in accordance with the positive evaluation of R. Elazar: "Whoever vows to God [to become a Nazirite] by way of holiness, does well and is praiseworthy.... Indeed Scripture considers him the equal of a prophet."[2] How does any writer come to adopt contradictory positions in a single book, let alone a writer as resolutely logical as Rambam?

The answer lies in one of Rambam's most original insights. He holds that there are two quite different ways of living the moral life. He calls them respectively the way of the saint (*hasid*) and the sage (*hakham*).

The sage follows the "golden mean," the "middle way." The moral life is a matter of moderation and balance, charting a course between too much and too little. Courage, for example, lies midway between cowardice and recklessness. Generosity lies between profligacy and miserliness. This is very similar to the vision of the moral life as set out by Aristotle in the *Nicomachean Ethics*.

The saint, by contrast, does not follow the middle way. He or she tends to extremes, fasting rather than simply eating in moderation, embracing poverty rather than acquiring modest wealth, and so on. At various points in his writings, Rambam explains why people might embrace extremes. One reason is repentance and character transformation.[3] So a person might cure himself of pride by practising,

---

1. *Mishneh Torah, Hilkhot Deot* 3:1.
2. *Mishneh Torah, Hilkhot Nezirut* 10:14.
3. See his *Eight Chapters* (the introduction to his commentary on Mishna Avot), ch. 4, and *Mishneh Torah, Hilkhot Deot*, chapters 1, 2, 5, and 6.

for a while, extreme self-abasement. Another is the asymmetry of the human personality. The extremes do not exert an equal pull. Cowardice is more common than recklessness, and miserliness than over-generosity, which is why the *ḥasid* leans in the opposite direction. A third reason is the lure of the surrounding culture. It may be so opposed to religious values that pious people choose to separate themselves from the wider society, "clothing themselves in woollen and hairy garments, dwelling in the mountains and wandering about in the wilderness,"[4] differentiating themselves by their extreme behaviour.

This is a very nuanced presentation. There are times, for Rambam, when self-denial is therapeutic, others when it is factored into Torah law itself, and yet others when it is a response to an excessively hedonistic age. In general, though, Rambam rules that we are *commanded* to follow the middle way, whereas the way of the saint is *lifnim mishurat hadin*, beyond the strict requirement of the law.[5]

Moshe Halbertal, in his recent, impressive study of Rambam,[6] sees him as finessing the fundamental tension between the civic ideal of the Greek political tradition and the spiritual ideal of the religious radical for whom, as the Kotzker Rebbe famously said, "The middle of the road is for horses." To the *ḥasid*, Rambam's sage can look like a "self-satisfied bourgeois."

Essentially, these are *two ways of understanding the moral life itself.* Is the aim of the moral life to achieve personal perfection? Or is it to create a decent, just, and compassionate society? The intuitive answer of most people would be to say: both. That is what makes Rambam so acute a thinker. He realises that you cannot have both. They are in fact different enterprises.

A saint may give all his money away to the poor. But what about the members of the saint's own family? A saint may refuse to fight in battle. But what about the saint's own country? A saint may forgive all crimes committed against him. But what about the rule of law, and

---

4. *Eight Chapters*, ch. 4.
5. *Mishneh Torah, Hilkhot Deot* 1:5.
6. Moshe Halbertal, *Maimonides: Life and Thought* (Princeton, NJ: Princeton University Press, 2014), 154–163.

justice? Saints are supremely virtuous people, considered as individuals. Yet you cannot build a society out of saints alone. Ultimately, saints are not really interested in society. Their concern is the salvation of the soul.

This deep insight is what led Rambam to his seemingly contradictory evaluations of the Nazirite. The Nazirite has chosen, at least for a period, to adopt a life of extreme self-denial. He is a saint, a *ḥasid*. He has adopted the path of personal perfection. That is noble, commendable, and exemplary.

But it is not the way of the sage – and *you need sages if you seek to perfect society*. The sage is not an extremist, because he or she realises that there are other people at stake. There are the members of one's own family and the others within one's own community. There is a country to defend and an economy to sustain. The sage knows he or she cannot leave all these commitments behind to pursue a life of solitary virtue. For we are called on by God to live in the world, not escape from it; to exist in society, not seclusion; to strive to create a balance among the conflicting pressures on us, not to focus on some while neglecting the others.

Hence, while from a personal perspective the Nazirite is a saint, from a societal perspective he is, at least figuratively, a "sinner" who has to bring an atonement offering.

Rambam lived the life he preached. We know from his writings that he longed for seclusion. There were years when he worked day and night to write his *Commentary to the Mishna*, and later the *Mishneh Torah*. Yet he also recognised his responsibilities to his family and to the community. In his famous letter to his would-be translator Ibn Tibbon, he gives him an account of his typical day and week, in which he had to carry a double burden as a world-renowned physician and an internationally sought halakhist and sage. He worked to exhaustion. There were times when he was almost too busy to study from one week to the next. Rambam was a sage who longed to be a saint – but knew he could not be, if he was to honour his responsibilities to his people. That seems to me a profound judgement, and one still relevant to Jewish life today.

Behaalotekha

From Pain to Humility

D avid Brooks, in his new bestseller, *The Road to Character*,[1] draws a sharp distinction between what he calls the résumé virtues – the achievements and skills that bring success – and the eulogy virtues, the ones that are spoken of at funerals. This latter category is comprised of the virtues and strengths that make you the kind of person you are when you are not wearing masks or playing roles, the inner person that friends and family recognise as the real you.

Brooks relates this distinction to the one made by Rabbi Joseph Soloveitchik in his famous essay, *The Lonely Man of Faith*.[2] There he speaks of Adam I – the human person as creator, builder, master of nature imposing his or her will on the world – and Adam II, the covenantal personality, living in obedience to a transcendent truth, guided by a sense of duty and right and the will to serve.

Adam I seeks success. Adam II strives for charity, love, and redemption. Adam I lives by the logic of economics – the pursuit of

1. New York: Random House, 2015.
2. New York: Doubleday, 1992.

self-interest and maximum utility. Adam II lives by the very different logic of morality, where giving matters more than receiving and conquering desire is more important than satisfying it. In the moral universe, success, when it leads to pride, becomes failure. Failure, when it leads to humility, can be success.

In that essay, first published in 1965, Rabbi Soloveitchik wondered whether there was a place for Adam II in the America of his day, so intent was it on celebrating human powers and economic advance. Fifty years on, Brooks echoes that doubt. "We live," he says, "in a society that encourages us to think about how to have a great career but leaves many of us inarticulate about how to cultivate the inner life."[3]

That is a central theme of *Behaalotekha*. Until now we have seen the outer Moses, worker of miracles, mouthpiece of the divine word, unafraid to confront Pharaoh on the one hand, his own people on the other, the man who shattered the tablets engraved by God Himself and who challenged Him to forgive His people, "and if not, blot me out of the book You have written" (Ex. 32:32). This is the public Moses, a figure of heroic strength. In Soloveitchik terminology, it is Moses I.

In *Behaalotekha* we see Moses II, the lonely man of faith. It is a very different picture. In the first scene we see him break down. The people are complaining again about the food. They have manna but no meat. They engage in false nostalgia: "How we remember the fish that we used to eat in Egypt for free! And the cucumbers, melons, leeks, onions, and garlic!" (Num. 11:5). This is one act of ingratitude too many for Moses, who gives voice to deep despair.

> Why did You bring all this trouble to Your servant? Why have I not found favour in Your eyes, that You are placing the burden of this entire people on me! Did I conceive this people or give birth to them, that You tell me to carry them in my lap the way a nurse carries a baby…. I cannot carry this whole nation! The burden is too heavy for me! If this is how You are going to treat me, please kill me now, if I have found favour in Your eyes, because I cannot bear seeing all this misery! (Num. 11:11–15)

3. Brooks, *The Road to Character*, xiii.

Then comes the great transformation. God tells Moses to take seventy elders who will bear the burden with him. God takes the spirit that is on Moses and extends it to the elders. Two of them, Eldad and Medad, among the six chosen from each tribe but left out of the final ballot, begin prophesying within the camp. They too have caught Moses' spirit. Joshua fears that this may lead to a challenge to Moses' leadership and urges Moses to stop them. Moses answers with surpassing generosity, "Are you jealous on my behalf? Would that all God's people were prophets and that He would rest His spirit on each of them" (Num. 11:29). The mere fact that Moses now knows that he is not alone, seeing seventy elders share his spirit, cures him of his depression, and he now exudes a gentle, generous confidence that is moving and unexpected.

In the third act, we finally see where this drama has been tending. Now Moses' own brother and sister, Aaron and Miriam, start disparaging him. The cause of their complaint (the "Ethiopian woman" he had taken as wife) is not clear and there are many interpretations. The point, though, is that for Moses, this is the "Et tu, Brute?" moment. He has been betrayed, or at least slandered, by those closest to him. Yet Moses is unaffected. It is here that the Torah makes its great statement: "Now the man Moses was very humble, more so than any other man on the face of the earth" (Num. 12:3).

This is a novum in history. The idea that a leader's highest virtue is humility must have seemed absurd, almost self-contradictory, in the ancient world. Leaders were proud, magnificent, distinguished by their dress, appearance, and regal manner. They built temples in their own honour. They had triumphant inscriptions engraved for posterity. Their role was not to serve but to be served. Everyone else was expected to be humble, not they. Humility and majesty could not coexist.

In Judaism, this entire configuration was overturned. Leaders were to serve, not to be served. Moses' highest accolade was to be called *eved Hashem*, God's servant. Only one other person, Joshua, his successor, earns this title in Tanakh. The architectural symbolism of the two great empires of the ancient world, the Mesopotamian ziggurat (Tower of Babel) and the pyramids of Egypt, visually represented a hierarchical society, broad at the base, narrow at the top. The Jewish symbol, the menora, was the opposite, broad at the top, narrow at the base, as if to say that in Judaism the leader serves the people, not vice versa. Moses' first response to God's call at the burning bush was one of humility: "Who am I to lead?" (Ex. 3:11). It was precisely this humility that qualified him to lead.

In *Behaalotekha* we track the psychological process by which Moses acquires a yet deeper level of humility. Under the stress of Israel's continued recalcitrance, Moses turns inwards. Listen again to what he says: "Why have You brought all this trouble to Your servant?...Did I conceive all these people? Did I give them birth?...Where can I get meat for all these people?...I cannot carry all these people by myself; the burden is too heavy for me." The key words here are "I," "me," and "myself." Moses has lapsed into the first person singular. He sees the Israelites' behaviour as a challenge to himself, not God. God has to remind him, "Is the Lord's arm too short?" (Num. 11:23). It is not about Moses; it is about what and whom Moses represents.

Moses had been, for too long, alone. It was not that he needed the help of others to provide the people with food. That was something God would do without the need for any human intervention. It was that he needed the company of others to end his almost unbearable isolation.

As soon as Moses sees that the seventy elders share his spirit, his depression disappears. He can say to Joshua, "Are you jealous on my behalf?" And he is undisturbed by the complaint of his own brother and sister, praying to God on Miriam's behalf when she is punished with leprosy. He has recovered his humility.

We now understand what humility is. It is not self-abasement. A statement often attributed to C. S. Lewis puts it best: humility, it states, is not thinking less of yourself; it is thinking of yourself less. True humility means silencing the "I." For genuinely humble people, it is God and other people and principle that matter, not me. As it was once said of a great religious leader, "He was a man who took God so seriously that he didn't have to take himself seriously at all."

"R. Yoḥanan said, 'Wherever you find the greatness of the Holy One, Blessed Be He, there you find His humility'" (Megilla 31a). Greatness is humility, for God and for those who seek to walk in His ways. It is also the greatest single source of strength, for if we do not think about the "I," we cannot be injured by those who criticise or demean us. They are shooting at a target that no longer exists.

What *Behaalotekha* is telling us through these three scenes in Moses' life is that we sometimes achieve humility only after a great psychological crisis. It is only after Moses had suffered a breakdown and prayed to die that we hear the words, "The man Moses was very humble, more so than any other man on the face of the earth." Suffering breaks through the carapace of the self, making us realise that what matters is not self-regard but rather the part we play in a scheme altogether larger than we are. *Lehavdil*, Brooks reminds us that Abraham Lincoln, who suffered from depression, emerged from the crisis of civil war with the sense that "Providence had taken control of his life, that he was a small instrument in a transcendent task."[4]

The right response to existential pain, Brooks says, is not pleasure but holiness, by which he means, "seeing the pain as part of a moral narrative and trying to redeem something bad by turning it into something sacred, some act of sacrificial service that will put oneself in fraternity with the wider community and with eternal moral demands."[5] This, for me, was epitomised by the parents of the three Israeli teenagers killed in the summer of 2014, who responded to their loss by creating a series of awards for those who have done the most to enhance the unity of the Jewish people – turning their pain outwards, and using it to help heal other wounds within the nation.

Crisis, failure, loss, or pain can move us from Adam I to Adam II, from self- to other-directedness, from mastery to service, and from the vulnerability of the "I" to the humility that "reminds you that you are not the centre of the universe," but rather that "you serve a larger order."[6]

Those who have humility are open to things greater than themselves while those who lack it are not. That is why those who lack it make you feel small, while those who have it make you feel enlarged. Their humility inspires greatness in others.

4. Ibid., 93.
5. Ibid.
6. Ibid., 261.

Shelaḥ

Assembling Reminders

Y ou are driving ever so slightly above the speed limit. You see a
police car in your rearview mirror. You slow down. You know perfectly
well that it is wrong to exceed the speed limit whether anyone is watching or not, but being human, the likelihood of being found out and
penalised makes a difference.

Recently, a series of experiments has been conducted by psycho-
logists to test the impact of the sense of being observed on pro-social
behaviour. Chen-Bo Zhong, Vanessa Bohns, and Francesca Gino constructed a test to see whether a feeling of anonymity made a difference.
They randomly assigned to a group of students either sunglasses or
clear eyeglasses, telling them that they were testing reactions to a new
product line. They were also, in an apparently unrelated task, given six
dollars and the chance to share any of it with a stranger. Those wearing
clear glasses gave an average of $2.71 while those wearing dark sunglasses
gave an average of $1.81. The mere fact of wearing sunglasses, and thus
feeling unrecognised and unrecognisable, reduced generosity. In another
experiment, they found that students given the opportunity to cheat on
a test were more likely to do so in a dimly lit room than in a brightly

lit one.[1] The more we think we may be observed, the more generous and moral we become.

Kevin Haley and Dan Fessler tested students on the so-called Dictator Game, in which you are given, say, ten dollars, together with the opportunity to share any or none of it with an anonymous stranger. Beforehand, and without realising it was part of the experiment, some of the students were briefly shown a pair of eyes as a computer screen saver, while others saw a different image. Those exposed to the eyes gave 55 per cent more to the stranger than the others. In another study, researchers placed a coffee maker in a university hallway. Passersby could take coffee and leave money in the box. On some weeks a poster with watchful eyes was hanging on the wall nearby, on others a picture of flowers. On the weeks when the eyes were showing, people left on average 2.76 times as much money as at other times.[2]

Ara Norenzayan, author of the book *Big Gods* from which these studies are taken, concludes that "watched people are nice people."[3] That is part of what makes religion a force for honest and altruistic behaviour: the belief that God sees what we do. It is no coincidence that, as belief in a personal God has waned in the West, surveillance by CCTV and other means has had to be increased. Voltaire once said that whatever his personal views on the matter, he wanted his attorney, tailor, and servants to believe in God because then he would be cheated less.[4]

Less obvious is the experimental finding that what makes the difference to the way we behave is not simply what we believe, but rather the fact of being *reminded* of it. In one test, conducted by Brandon Randolph-Seng and Michael Nielsen, participants were exposed to words flashed for less than one hundred milliseconds, that is, long enough to

1. Chen-Bo Zhong, Vanessa K. Bohns, and Francesca Gino, "Good Lamps Are the Best Police: Darkness Increases Dishonesty and Self-Interested Behavior," *Psychological Science* 21 (2009): 311–314.
2. This and the following paragraphs are based on Ara Norenzayan, *Big Gods: How Religion Transformed Cooperation and Conflict* (Princeton, NJ: Princeton University Press, 2013), 13–54.
3. Ibid., 19.
4. Voltaire, *Political Writings*, ed. David Williams (Cambridge, NY: Cambridge University Press, 1994), 190.

be detected by the brain but not long enough for conscious awareness. They were then given a test in which they had the opportunity to cheat. Those who had been shown words relating to God were significantly less likely to do so than people who had been shown neutral words. The same result was yielded by another test in which, beforehand, some of the participants were asked to recall the Ten Commandments while others were asked to remember the last ten books they had read. Merely being reminded of the Ten Commandments reduced the tendency to cheat.

Another researcher, Deepak Malhotra, surveyed the willingness of Christians to give to online charitable appeals. The response was 300 per cent greater if the appeal was made on a Sunday than on any other day of the week. Clearly the participants did not change their minds about religious belief or the importance of charitable giving between weekdays and Sundays. It was simply that on Sundays they were more likely to have thought about God. A similar test was carried out among Muslims in Morocco, where it was found that people were more likely to give generously to charity if they lived in a place where they could hear the call to prayer from a local minaret.

Norenzayan's conclusion is that "religion is more in the situation than in the person,"[5] or, to put it another way, what makes the difference to our behaviour is less what we believe than the phenomenon of being *reminded*, even subconsciously, of what we believe.

That is precisely the psychology behind the mitzva of *tzitzit* in *Parashat Shelaḥ*:

> This shall be your *tzitzit* and you shall see it and remember all the Lord's commandments and keep them, not straying after your heart and after your eyes, following your own sinful desires. Thus you will be reminded to keep all My commandments, and be holy to your God. (Num. 15:39)

The Talmud (Menaḥot 44a) tells the story of a man who, in a moment of moral weakness, decided to pay a visit to a certain courtesan. He was in the course of removing his clothes when he saw the *tzitzit*

---

5. Norenzayan, *Big Gods*, 39.

and immediately froze. The courtesan asked him what was the matter, and he told her about the *tzitzit*, saying that the four fringes had become accusing witnesses against him for the sin he was about to commit. The woman was so impressed by the power of this simple command that she converted to Judaism.

We sometimes fail to understand the connection between religion and morality. Dostoevsky is reputed to have said that if God did not exist, all would be permitted.[6] This is not the mainstream Jewish view. According to Rabbi Nissim Gaon, the moral imperatives accessible to reason have been binding since the dawn of humanity.[7] We have a moral sense. We know that certain things are wrong. But we also have conflicting desires. We are drawn to do what we know we should not do, and often we yield to temptation. Anyone who has ever tried to lose weight knows exactly what that means. In the moral domain, it is what the Torah means when it speaks of "straying after your heart and after your eyes, following your own sinful desires" (Num. 15:39).

The moral sense, wrote James Q. Wilson, "is not a strong beacon light radiating outwards to illuminate in sharp outline all that it touches." It is, rather, "a small candle flame, casting vague and multiple shadows, flickering and sputtering in the strong winds of power and passion, greed and ideology." He adds: "But brought close to the heart" it "dispels the darkness and warms the soul."[8]

Wittgenstein once said that "the work of the philosopher consists in assembling reminders."[9] In the case of Judaism the purpose of the outward signs – *tzitzit*, *mezuza*, and *tefillin* – is precisely that: to assemble reminders, on our clothes, our homes, our arms and head, that certain things are wrong, and that even if no other human being sees us, God sees us and will call us to account. We now have the empirical evidence that reminders make a significant difference to the way we act.

6. He did not say these precise words, but said something similar in *The Brothers Karamazov* (1880).
7. *Commentary to Berakhot*, introduction.
8. James Q. Wilson, *The Moral Sense* (New York: Free Press, 1993), 251.
9. *Philosophical Investigations*, §127.

"The heart is deceitful above all things and desperately wicked; who shall know it?" said Jeremiah (17:9). One of the blessings and curses of human nature is that we use our power of reason not always and only to act rationally, but also to rationalise and make excuses for the things we do, even when we know we should not have done them. That, perhaps, is one of the lessons the Torah wishes us to draw from the story of the spies. Had they recalled what God had done to Egypt, the mightiest empire of the ancient world, they would not have said, "We cannot attack those people; they are stronger than we are" (Num. 13:31). But they were in the grip of fear. Strong emotion – fear especially – distorts our perception. It activates the amygdala, the source of our most primal reactions, causing it to override the prefrontal cortex that allows us to think rationally about the consequences of our decisions.

Tzitzit, with their thread of blue, remind us of heaven, and that is what we most need if we are consistently to act in accordance with the better angels of our nature.

Korah

When Truth Is
Sacrificed to Power

W hat was wrong with Korah and his fellow rebels? On the face of it, what they said was both true and principled. "You have gone too far," they said to Moses and Aaron. "The whole community is holy, every one of them, and God is with them. Why then are you setting yourselves above God's congregation?" (Num. 16:3–4).

They had a point. God had summoned the people to become "a kingdom of priests and a holy nation" (Ex. 19:6), that is, a kingdom every one of whose members was in some sense a priest, and a nation every one of whose members was holy. Moses himself had said, "Would that all God's people were prophets and that He would rest His spirit on each of them" (Num. 11:29). These are radically egalitarian sentiments. Why then was there a hierarchy, with Moses as leader and Aaron as high priest?

What was wrong with Korah's statement was that even at the outset it was obvious that Korah was duplicitous. There was a clear disconnection between what he claimed to want and what he really sought.

Korah did not seek a society in which everyone was the same, everyone a priest. He was not, as he sounded, a utopian anarchist, seeking to abolish hierarchy altogether. He was, instead, mounting a leadership challenge. As Moses' later words to him indicate, he wanted to be high priest himself. He was Moses' and Aaron's cousin, son of Yitzhar, the brother of Moses and Aaron's father Amram. He felt it unfair that both leadership positions had gone to a single family within the clan. He claimed to want equality – but in fact what he wanted was power.

That was Korah the Levite. But what was happening was more complex than that. There were two other groups involved: the Reubenites, Datan and Aviram, on one hand, and "250 Israelites who were men of rank within the community, representatives at the assembly, and famous," on the other. They too had their grievances. The Reubenites were aggrieved that as descendants of Jacob's firstborn, they had no special leadership roles. According to Ibn Ezra, the 250 "men of rank" were upset that, after the sin of the Golden Calf, leadership had passed from the firstborn within each tribe to the single tribe of Levi.

This was an unholy alliance, and bound to fail, since their claims conflicted. If Korah achieved his ambition of becoming high priest, the Reubenites and "men of rank" would have been disappointed. Had the Reubenites won, Korah and the "men of rank" would have been upset. Had the "men of rank" achieved their ambition, Korah and the Reubenites would be left dissatisfied. The disordered, fragmented narrative sequence in this chapter is a case of style mirroring substance. This was a disordered, confused rebellion, whose protagonists were united only in their desire to overthrow the existing leadership.

None of this, however, unsettled Moses. What caused him to become angry was something else altogether – the words of Datan and Aviram:

> Is it not enough that you brought us out of a land flowing with milk and honey to kill us in the desert! And now you want to lord it over us! What is more: you have not brought us to a land flowing with milk and honey or given us an inheritance of fields and vineyards. Do you think that you can pull something over our eyes? We will definitely not come! (Num. 16:13–14)

The monumental untruth of their claim – Egypt, where the Israelites were slaves and cried out to God to be saved, was not "a land flowing with milk and honey" – is what finally made Moses angry.

What is going on here? The sages defined it in one of their most famous statements:

> Any dispute for the sake of Heaven will have enduring value, but every dispute not for the sake of Heaven will not have enduring value. What is an example of a dispute for the sake of Heaven? The dispute between Hillel and Shammai. What is an example of one not for the sake of Heaven? The dispute of Korah and all his company. (Mishna Avot 5:21)

The rabbis did not conclude from the Korah rebellion that argument is wrong, that leaders are entitled to unquestioning obedience, that the supreme value in Judaism should be – as it is in some faiths – submission. To the contrary: *argument is the lifeblood of Judaism,* so long as it is rightly motivated and essentially constructive in its aims.

Judaism is a unique phenomenon: a civilisation all of whose canonical texts are anthologies of argument. In Tanakh, the heroes of faith – Abraham, Moses, Jeremiah, Job – argue with God. Midrash is founded on the premise that there are "seventy faces" – seventy legitimate interpretations – of Torah. The Mishna is largely constructed on the model of "Rabbi X says this, Rabbi Y says that." The Talmud, far from resolving these arguments, usually deepens them considerably. Argument in Judaism is a holy activity, the ongoing internal dialogue of the Jewish people as it reflects on the terms of its destiny and the demands of its faith.

What then made the argument of Korah and his co-conspirators different from that of the schools of Hillel and Shammai? Rabbenu Yona offered a simple explanation: an argument for the sake of Heaven is one that is about *truth.* An argument not for the sake of Heaven is about *power.* The difference is immense.

If I argue for the sake of truth, then if I win, I win. But if I lose, I also win, because being defeated by the truth is the only defeat that is also a victory. I am enlarged. I learn something I did not know before.

In a contest for power, if I lose, I lose. But if I win, I also lose, because in diminishing my opponents I have diminished myself.

Moses could not have had a more decisive vindication than the miracle for which he asked and was granted: that the ground open up and swallow his opponents. Yet not only did this not end the argument, it diminished the respect in which Moses was held: "The next day the whole Israelite community grumbled against Moses and Aaron. 'You have killed the Lord's people,' they said." (Num. 17:41). That Moses needed to resort to force was itself a sign that he had been dragged down to the level of the rebels. That is what happens when power, not truth, is at stake.

One of the aftermaths of Marxism, persisting in such movements as postmodernism and postcolonialism, is the idea that there is no such thing as truth. There is only power. The prevailing "discourse" in a society represents not the way things are, but the way the ruling power (the hegemon) wants things to be. All reality is "socially constructed" to advance the interests of one group or another. The result is a "hermeneutics of suspicion," in which we no longer listen to what anyone says; we merely ask what interest they are trying to advance. Truth, they say, is merely the mask worn to disguise the pursuit of power. To overthrow a "colonial" power, you have to invent your own "discourse," your own "narrative," and it does not matter whether it is true or false. All that matters is that people believe it.

That is what is now happening in the campaign against Israel on campuses throughout the world, and in the BDS (Boycott, Divestment, and Sanctions) movement in particular. Like the Korah rebellion, it brings together people who have nothing else in common. Some belong to the far left, a few to the far right; some are anti-globalists, while some are genuinely concerned with the plight of the Palestinians. Driving it all, however, are people who on theological and political grounds are opposed to the existence of Israel within any boundaries whatsoever, and are equally opposed to democracy, free speech, freedom of information, religious liberty, human rights, and the sanctity of life. What they have in common is a refusal to give the supporters of Israel a fair hearing – thus flouting the fundamental principle of justice, expressed in Roman law in the phrase, *Audi alteram partem,* "Hear the other side."

The flagrant falsehoods it sometimes utters – that Israel was not the birthplace of the Jewish people, that there never was a Temple in Jerusalem, that Israel is a "colonial" power, a foreign transplant alien to the Middle East – rival the claims of Datan and Aviram that Egypt was a land flowing with milk and honey and that Moses brought the people out solely in order to kill them in the desert. Why bother with truth when all that matters is power? Thus the spirit of Korah lives on.

All this is very sad indeed, since it is opposed to the fundamental principle of the university as a home for the collaborative search for truth. It also does little for the cause of peace in the Middle East, for the future of the Palestinians, or for freedom, democracy, religious liberty, and human rights. There are real and substantive issues at stake, which need to be faced by both sides with honesty and courage. Nothing is achieved by sacrificing truth to the pursuit of power – the way of Korah through the ages.

Ḥukkat

Anger Management

There are some, says the Talmud, who acquire their world in an hour and others who lose it in an hour. No example of the latter is more arresting and bewildering than the famous episode in *Parashat Ḥukkat*. The people have asked for water. God tells Moses to take a staff and speak to the rock and water will appear. This then follows:

> He and Aaron gathered the assembly together in front of the rock and Moses said to them, "Listen, you rebels, must we bring you water out of this rock?" Then Moses raised his arm and struck the rock twice with his staff. Water gushed out, and the community and their livestock drank.
>
> But the Lord said to Moses and Aaron, "Because you did not trust in Me enough to honour Me as holy in the sight of the Israelites, you will not bring this community into the land I give them." (Num. 20:10–12)

"Is this the Torah and this its reward?" we are tempted to say. What was Moses' sin that it merited such punishment? I have in the past expressed my view that Moses did not sin, nor was he punished. It was simply that each generation needs its own leaders. Moses was the right, indeed the only, leader capable of taking the Israelites out of Egypt. They needed another kind of leader and a different style of leadership to take the next generation into the Promised Land.

Within the framework of this book, though, as we discuss the ethics of the Bible, it seems more appropriate to look at a different explanation, the one given by Rambam in *Shemoneh Perakim*, the "Eight Chapters" that form the preface to his commentary to the Mishna, Tractate Avot, the Ethics of the Fathers.

In the course of these chapters Rambam sets out a surprisingly contemporary account of Judaism as a training in "emotional intelligence."[1] Healthy emotions are essential to a good and happy life, but temperament is not something we choose. Some people just happen to be more patient or calm or generous-spirited or optimistic than others. Emotions were at one stage called the "passions," a word that comes from the same root as "passive," implying that they are feelings that happen to us rather than reactions we choose to have. Despite this, Rambam believed that with sufficient training, we could overcome our destructive emotions and reconfigure our affective life.

In general, Rambam, like Aristotle, believed that emotional intelligence exists in striking a balance between excess and deficiency, too much and too little. Too much fear makes me a coward, too little makes me rash and foolhardy, taking unnecessary risks. The middle way is courage. There are, however, two exceptions, says Rambam: pride and anger. Even a little pride (some sages suggested "an eighth of an eighth") is too much. Likewise even a little anger is wrong.

That, says Rambam, is why Moses was punished: because he lost his temper with the people when he said, "Listen, you rebels." To be sure, there were other occasions on which he lost his temper – or at least looked as if he had. His reaction to the sin of the Golden Calf,

---

1. The term was introduced by Peter Salovey and John Mayer. See Peter Salovey, Marc A. Brackett, and John D. Mayer, *Emotional Intelligence: Key Readings on the Mayer and Salovey Model* (Port Chester, NY: Dude Pub., 2004), subsequently popularized by Daniel Goleman in, for instance, his book *Emotional Intelligence* (New York: Bantam, 1995).

which included smashing the tablets, was hardly eirenic or relaxed. But that case was different. The Israelites had committed a sin. God Himself was threatening to destroy the people. Moses had to act decisively and with sufficient force to restore order to a people wildly out of control.

Here, though, the people had not sinned. They were thirsty. They needed water. God was not angry with them. Moses' intemperate reaction was therefore wrong, says Rambam. To be sure, anger is something to which we are all prone. But Moses was a leader, and a leader must be a role model. That is why Moses was punished so heavily for a failure that might have been more lightly punished in someone less exalted.

In addition, says Rambam, by losing his temper Moses failed to respect the people and might have demoralised them. Knowing that Moses was God's emissary, the people might have concluded that if Moses was angry with them, so too was God. Yet they had done no more than ask for water. Giving the people the impression that God was angry with them was a failure to sanctify God's name. Thus one moment's anger was sufficient to deprive Moses of the reward surely most precious to him – seeing the culmination of his work by leading the people across the Jordan into the Promised Land.

The sages were outspoken in their critique of anger. They would thoroughly have approved of the modern concept of anger management. They did not like anger at all, and reserved some of their sharpest language to describe it. "The life of those who can't control their anger is not a life," they said (Pesaḥim 113b). Resh Lakish said, "When a person becomes angry, if he is a sage his wisdom departs from him; if he is a prophet his prophecy departs from him" (Pesaḥim 66b). Rambam said that when someone becomes angry it is as if he has become an idolater.[2]

What is dangerous about anger is that it causes us to lose control. It activates the most primitive part of the human brain that bypasses the neural circuitry we use when we reflect and choose on rational grounds. While in its grip we lose the ability to step back and judge the possible consequences of our actions. The result is that in a moment of irascibility we can do or say things we may regret for the rest of our lives.

2. *Mishneh Torah, Hilkhot Deot* 2:3.

For that reason, rules Rambam,[3] there is no "middle way" when it comes to anger. Instead we must avoid it under any circumstance. We must go to the opposite extreme. Even when anger is justified, we must avoid it. There may be times when it is necessary to *look as if* we are angry. That is what Moses did when he saw the Israelites worshipping the Golden Calf and broke the tablets of stone. Yet even then, says Rambam, inwardly we should be calm.

The *Orḥot Tzaddikim* (fifteenth century) notes that anger destroys personal relationships.[4] Short-tempered people scare others, who therefore avoid coming close to them. Anger drives out the positive emotions – forgiveness, compassion, empathy, and sensitivity. The result is that irascible people end up lonely, shunned, and disappointed. Bad-tempered people achieve nothing but their bad temper (Kiddushin 40b). They lose all else.

The classic role model of patience in the face of provocation was Hillel. The Talmud (Shabbat 31a) says that two people once made a wager with each other, saying, "He who makes Hillel angry shall receive four hundred *zuz*." One said, "I will go and provoke him." It was *erev* Shabbat and Hillel was washing his hair. The man stood by the door of his house and called, "Is Hillel here, is Hillel here?" Hillel robed himself and came out, saying, "My son, what do you seek?" "I have a question to ask," he said. "Ask, my son," replied Hillel. He said, "Why are the heads of the Babylonians round?" "My son, you ask a good question," said Hillel. "The reason is that they have no skilled midwives."

The man left, paused, then returned, crying out, "Is Hillel here? Is Hillel here?" Again, Hillel robed and came out, saying, "My son, what do you seek?" "I have another question." "Ask, my son." "Why are the eyes of the Palmyreans bleared?" Hillel replied, "My son, you ask a good question. The reason is that they live in sandy places."

He left, waited, then came back a third time, calling, "Is Hillel here? Is Hillel here?" Again, Hillel robed and came out, saying, "My son, what do you seek?" "I have another question." "Ask, my son." "Why are

3. Ibid.
4. *Orḥot Tzaddikim, Shaar Kaas*, "The Gate of Anger."

the feet of Africans wide?" "My son, you ask a good question. The reason is that they live in watery marshes."

"I have many questions to ask," said the man, "but I am worried that you might become angry." Hillel then robed himself and sat and said, "Ask all the questions you have to ask." "Are you the Hillel who is called the *nasi* [leader, prince] of Israel?" "Yes," said Hillel. "In that case," said the man, "may there not be many like you in Israel." "Why so, my son?" he asked. "Because I have just lost four hundred *zuz* because of you!" "Be careful of your moods," said Hillel. "You may lose four hundred *zuz* and yet another four hundred *zuz* through Hillel, yet Hillel will not lose his temper" (Shabbat 30b–31a).

It was this quality of patience under provocation that was one of the factors, according to the Talmud (Eiruvin 13b), that led the sages to rule according to the School of Hillel rather than that of Shammai.

The best way of defeating anger is to pause, stop, reflect, refrain, count to ten, and breathe deeply. If necessary, leave the room, go for a walk, meditate, or vent your toxic feelings alone. It is said about one of the rebbes of Lubavitch that whenever he felt angry, he would take down the *Shulḥan Arukh* to see whether anger was permitted under the circumstances. By the time he had finished studying, his anger had disappeared.

The moral life is one in which we grapple with anger but never let it win. The verdict of Judaism is simple: either we defeat anger or anger will defeat us.

Balak

A People That Dwells Alone?[1]

In the course of blessing the Jewish people, Balaam uttered words that have come to seem to many to encapsulate Jewish history:

> How can I curse whom God has not cursed?
> How can I doom whom God has not doomed?
> I see them from mountain tops,
> Gaze on them from the heights.
> Look: a people that dwells alone,
> Not reckoned among the nations. (Num. 23:8–9)

---

1. *A People That Dwells Alone* was the title given to the collection of essays by the late Jacob Herzog (London: Weidenfeld and Nicolson, 1975). It was also the theme of the autobiography of Israeli diplomat, and brother of Israel's former Chief Rabbi Israel Meir Lau, the late Naftali Lau-Lavie (*Balaam's Prophecy: Eyewitness to History* [Jerusalem: Toby Press, 2015]).

That is how it seemed during the persecutions and pogroms in Europe. It is how it seemed during the Holocaust. It is how it sometimes seems to Israel and its defenders today. We find ourselves alone. How should we understand this fact? How should we interpret this verse?

In my book *Future Tense*[2] I describe the moment when I first became aware of how dangerous a self-definition this can be. We were having lunch in Jerusalem on Shavuot 5761/2001. Present was one of the world's great fighters against anti-Semitism, Irwin Cotler, soon to become Canada's minister of justice, together with a distinguished Israeli diplomat. We were talking about the forthcoming United Nations Conference against Racism at Durban in 2001.

We all had reasons to know that it was going to be a disaster for Israel. It was there in the parallel sessions of the NGOs that Israel was accused of the five cardinal sins against human rights: racism, apartheid, crimes against humanity, ethnic cleansing, and attempted genocide. The conference became, in effect, the launch pad of a new and vicious anti-Semitism. In the Middle Ages, Jews were hated because of their religion. In the nineteenth and early twentieth century they were hated because of their race. In the twenty-first century they are hated because of their nation-state. As we were speaking of the likely outcome, the diplomat heaved a sigh and said, "'Twas ever thus. *Am levadad yishkon*: we are the nation fated to be alone."

The man who said this had the best of intentions. He had spent his professional life defending Israel, and he was seeking to comfort us. His words were meant no more than as a polite remark. But I suddenly saw how dangerous such an attitude is. If you believe your fate is to be alone, that is almost certainly what will happen. It is a self-fulfilling prophecy. Why bother to make friends and allies if you know in advance that you will fail? How then are we to understand Balaam's words?

First, it should be clear that this is a very ambiguous blessing. Being alone, from a Torah perspective, is not a good thing. The first time the words "not good" appear in the Torah is in the verse, "It is not good for man to be alone" (Gen. 2:18). The second time is when Moses' father-in-law Yitro sees him leading alone and says, "What you are doing

2. New York: Schocken, 2012.

is not good" (Ex. 18:17). We are social animals. We cannot live and thrive alone. Isolation is not a blessing but the opposite.

The word *badad* appears in two other profoundly negative contexts. First is the case of the leper: "He shall dwell alone; his place shall be outside the camp" (Lev. 13:46). The second is the opening line of the book of Lamentations: "How alone is the city once thronged with people" (Lam. 1:1). The only context in which *badad* has a positive sense is when it is applied to God (Deut. 32:12), for obvious theological reasons.

Second, Balaam who said those words was not a lover of Israel. Hired to curse them and prevented from doing so by God, he nonetheless tried a second time. This time he was successful, persuading the Moabite and Midianite women to seduce the Israelite men. As a result, 24,000 people died (Num. 25; 31:16). It was this second strategy of Balaam – after he had already said, "How can I curse whom God has not cursed? How can I doom whom God has not doomed?" (Num. 23:8) – that marks him out as a man profoundly hostile to the Israelites. The Talmud (Sanhedrin 105b) states that *all the blessings that Balaam bestowed on the Israelites eventually turned into curses,* with the sole exception of the blessing, "How goodly are your tents, Jacob, your dwelling places, Israel" (Num. 24:5). So in the rabbis' view, "a people that dwells alone" eventually became not a blessing but a curse.

Third, nowhere in Tanakh are we told that it will be the fate of Israel or Jews to be hated. To the contrary, the prophets foresaw that there would come a time when the nations would turn to Israel for inspiration. Isaiah envisaged a day on which

> Many peoples will come and say, "Come, let us go up to the mountain of the Lord, to the Temple of the God of Jacob. He will teach us His ways, so that we may walk in His paths." The law will go out from Zion, the word of the Lord from Jerusalem. (Is. 2:3)

Zechariah foresaw that "in those days ten people from all languages and nations will take firm hold of one Jew by the hem of his robe and say, 'Let us go with you, because we have heard that God is with you'" (Zech. 8:23). These are sufficient to cast doubt on the idea that anti-Semitism is eternal, incurable, woven into Jewish history and destiny.

Only in rabbinic literature do we find statements that seem to suggest that Israel is hated. Most famous is the statement of R. Shimon b. Yoḥai, "Halakha: it is well known that Esau hates Jacob."[3] R. Shimon b. Yoḥai was known for his distrust of the Romans, whom the rabbis identified with Esau/Edom. It was for this reason, says the Talmud, that he had to go into hiding for thirteen years (Shabbat 33b). His view was not shared by his contemporaries.

Those who quote this passage do so only partially and selectively. It refers to the moment at which Jacob and Esau meet after their long estrangement. Jacob feared that Esau would try to kill him. After taking elaborate precautions and wrestling with an angel, the next morning he sees Esau. The verse then says: "Esau ran to meet them. He hugged [Jacob], and throwing himself on his shoulders, kissed him. They [both] wept" (Gen. 33:4). Over the letters of the word "kissed" as it appears in a *sefer Torah*, there are dots, signalling some special meaning. It was in this context that R. Shimon b. Yoḥai said: "Even though it is well known that Esau hates Jacob, *at that moment he was overcome with compassion and kissed him with a full heart*" (Rashi ad loc.). In other words, precisely the text cited to show that anti-Semitism is inevitable proves the opposite: that at the crucial encounter, Esau did *not* feel hate towards Jacob. They met, embraced, and went their separate ways without ill will.

There is, in short, nothing in Judaism to suggest that it is the fate of Jews to be hated. It is neither written into the texture of the universe nor encoded in the human genome. It is not the will of God. Only in moments of deep despair have Jews believed this, most notably Leo Pinsker in his 1882 tract *Auto-emancipation*, in which he said of Judaeophobia, "As a psychic aberration, it is hereditary; as a disease transmitted for two thousand years, it is incurable."

Anti-Semitism is not mysterious, unfathomable, or inexorable. It is a complex phenomenon that has mutated over time, and it has identifiable causes – social, economic, political, cultural, and theological ones.

---

3. *Sifrei, Behaalotekha,* 89; Rashi to Gen. 33:4; see *Kreti* to *Yoreh De'ah* ch. 88 for the halakhic implications of this statement.

It can be fought; it can be defeated. But it will not be fought or defeated if people think that it is Jacob's fate to be hated by "Esau" or to be "the people that dwells alone," a pariah among peoples, a leper among nations, an outcast in the international arena.

What then does the phrase "a people that dwells alone" mean? It means a people prepared to stand alone if need be, living by its own moral code, having the courage to be different and to take the road less travelled.

Rabbi Samson Raphael Hirsch offered a fine insight by focusing on the nuance between "people" (*am*) and "nation" (*goy*) – or as we might say nowadays, "society" and "state."[4] Israel uniquely became a society before it was a state. It had laws before it had a land. It was a people – a group bound together by a common code and culture – before it was a nation, that is, a political entity. As I noted in *Future Tense*, the word *peoplehood* first appeared in 1992, and its early uses were almost entirely in reference to Jews.[5] What makes Jews different, according to Hirsch's reading of Balaam, is that *Jews are a distinctive people,* that is, a group defined by shared memories and collective responsibilities, "not reckoned among the nations" since they are capable of surviving even without nationhood, even in exile and dispersion. Israel's strength lies not in nationalism but in building a society based on justice and human dignity.

The battle against anti-Semitism can be won, but it will not be if Jews believe that they are destined to be alone. That is Balaam's curse, not God's blessing.

---

4. Samson Raphael Hirsch, Commentary to Numbers 23:9.
5. Sacks, *Future Tense*, 25.

Pinḥas

Elijah and the Still, Small Voice

Then the word of the Lord came to him: "Why are you here, Elijah?" He replied, "I am moved by the zeal for the Lord, God of hosts...." The Lord said to him, "Go out and stand on the mountain in the presence of the Lord, for the Lord is about to pass by." Then a great and powerful wind tore the mountains apart and shattered the rocks before the Lord. But the Lord was not in the wind. After the wind was an earthquake, but the Lord was not in the earthquake. After the earthquake came a fire. But the Lord was not in the fire. And after the fire – a still, small voice. (I Kings 19:9–12)

In 1165, an agonising question confronted Moroccan Jewry. A fanatical Muslim sect, the Almohads, had seized power and was embarking on a policy of forced conversion to Islam. The Jewish community was faced with a choice: to affirm Islamic faith or die. Some chose martyrdom. Others chose exile. But some acceded to terror and embraced another faith. Inwardly, though, they remained Jews and practised Judaism in secret. They were the *anusim*, Crypto-Jews, or as the Spanish were later to call such converts, the Marranos.

To other Jews, they posed a formidable moral problem. How were they to be viewed? Outwardly, they had betrayed their community and their religious heritage. Besides, their example was demoralising. It weakened the resolve of Jews who were determined to resist, come what may. Yet many of the Crypto-Jews still wished to remain Jewish, secretly fulfil the commandments and, when they could, attend the synagogue and pray.

One of them addressed this question to a rabbi. He had, he said, converted under coercion, but he remained at heart a faithful Jew. Could he obtain merit by observing in private as many of the Torah's precepts as possible? Was there, in other words, hope left for him as a Jew?

The rabbi's reply was emphatic. A Jew who had embraced Islam had forfeited membership in the Jewish community. He was no longer part of the House of Israel. For such a person to fulfil the commandments was meaningless. Worse, it was a sin. The choice was stark and absolute: to be or not to be a Jew. If you choose to be a Jew, you should be prepared to suffer death rather than compromise. If you choose not to be a Jew, then you must not seek to re-enter the house you deserted.

We can respect the firmness of the rabbi's stance. He set out, without equivocation, the moral choice. There are times when heroism is, for faith, a categorical imperative. Nothing less will do. His reply, though harsh, is not without courage. But another rabbi disagreed.

The name of the first rabbi is lost to us, but that of the second is not. He was Rambam, the greatest rabbi of the Middle Ages. Rambam was no stranger to religious persecution. Born in Cordova in 1135, he had been forced to leave, along with his family, some thirteen years later when the city fell to the Almohads. Twelve years were spent in wandering. In 1160, a temporary liberalisation of Almohad rule allowed the family to settle in Morocco. Within five years he was forced to move again, settling first in the land of Israel and ultimately in Egypt.

Rambam was so incensed by the rabbi's reply to the forced convert that he wrote a response of his own. In it, he frankly disassociates himself from the earlier ruling and castigates its author whom he describes as a "self-styled sage who has never experienced what so many Jewish communities had to endure in the way of persecution."

Rambam's reply, the *Iggeret HaShemad* ("Epistle on Forced Conversion"), is a substantial treatise in its own right.[1] What is striking, given
the vehemence with which it begins, is that its conclusions are hardly
less demanding than those of the earlier response. If you are faced with
religious persecution, says Rambam, you must leave and settle elsewhere.
"If he is compelled to violate even one precept it is forbidden to stay there.
He must leave everything he has, travel day and night until he finds a
spot where he can practise his religion."[2] This is preferable to martyrdom.

Nonetheless, one who chooses to go to his death rather than
renounce his faith "has done what is good and proper,"[3] for he has given
his life for the sanctity of God. What is unacceptable is to stay and excuse
oneself on the grounds that if one sins, one does so only under pressure.
To do this is to profane God's name, "not exactly willingly, but almost so."[4]

These are Rambam's conclusions. But surrounding them and
constituting the main thrust of his argument is a sustained defence of
those who had done precisely what Rambam had ruled they should not
do. The letter gives Crypto-Jews hope.

They have done wrong. But it is a forgivable wrong. They acted
under coercion and the fear of death. They remain Jews. The acts they
do as Jews still win favour in the eyes of God. Indeed doubly so, for
when they fulfil a commandment it cannot be to win favour in the eyes
of others. They know that when they act as Jews they risk discovery and
death. Their secret adherence has a heroism of its own.

What was wrong in the first rabbi's ruling was his insistence that a
Jew who yields to terror has forsaken his faith and is to be excluded from
the community. Rambam insists that it is not so. "It is not right to alienate,
scorn, and hate people who desecrate the Sabbath. It is our duty to befriend
them and encourage them to fulfil the commandments."[5] In a daring stroke
of interpretation, he quotes the verse: "Do not despise a thief if he steals to

1. An English translation and commentary is contained in Abraham S. Halkin and
David Hartman, *Crisis and Leadership: Epistles of Maimonides* (Philadelphia: Jewish
Publication Society of America, 1985), 15–35.
2. Ibid., 32.
3. Ibid., 30.
4. Ibid.
5. Ibid., 33.

satisfy his hunger when he is starving" (Prov. 6:30). The Crypto-Jews who come to the synagogue are hungry for Jewish prayer. They "steal" moments of belonging. They should not be despised, but welcomed.

This epistle is a masterly example of that most difficult of moral challenges: to combine prescription and compassion. Rambam leaves us in no doubt as to what he believes Jews should do. But at the same time he is uncompromising in his defence of those who fail to do it. He does not endorse what they have done – but he defends who they are. He asks us to understand their situation. He gives them grounds for self-respect. He holds the doors of the community open.

The argument reaches a climax as Rambam quotes a remarkable sequence of midrashic passages whose theme is that prophets must not condemn their people, but rather defend them before God. When Moses, charged with leading the people out of Egypt, replied, "But they will not believe me" (Ex. 4:1), ostensibly he was justified. The subsequent biblical narrative suggests that Moses' doubts were well founded. The Israelites were a difficult people to lead. But the Midrash says that God replied to Moses, "They are believers and the children of believers, but you [Moses] will ultimately not believe" (Shabbat 97a).

Rambam cites a series of similar passages and then says: If this is the punishment meted out to the pillars of the universe, the greatest of the prophets, because they briefly criticised the people – even though they were guilty of the sins of which they were accused – can we envisage the punishment awaiting those who criticise the Crypto-Jews who under threat of death and without abandoning their faith, confessed to another religion in which they did not believe?

In the course of his analysis, Rambam turns to the prophet Elijah and the text that forms the *haftara* for *Parashat Pinḥas*. Under the reign of Ahab and Jezebel, Baal worship had become the official cult. God's prophets were being killed. Those who survived were in hiding. Elijah responded by issuing a public challenge at Mount Carmel. Facing four hundred of Baal's representatives, he was determined to settle the question of religious truth once and for all.

Elijah told the assembled people to choose one way or another: for God or for Baal. They must no longer "halt between two opinions" (I Kings 18:21). Truth was about to be decided by a test. If it lay with

Baal, fire would consume the offering prepared by its priests. If it lay with God, fire would descend to Elijah's offering.

Elijah won the confrontation. The people cried out, "The Lord, He is God" (I Kings 18:39). The priests of Baal were routed. But the story does not end there. Jezebel issues a warrant for Elijah's death and he escapes to Mount Horeb. There he receives a strange vision. He witnesses a whirlwind, then an earthquake, then a fire. But he is led to understand that God is not in these things. Then God speaks to him in a "still, small voice," and tells him to appoint Elisha as his successor.

The episode is enigmatic. It is made all the more so by a strange feature of the text. Immediately *before* the vision, God asks, "What are you doing here, Elijah?" and Elijah replies, "I am moved by zeal for the Lord, the God of Hosts" (I Kings 9:9–10). Immediately *after* the vision, God asks the same question, and Elijah gives the same answer (I Kings 19:13–14). The Midrash turns the text into a dialogue:

> Elijah: The Israelites have broken God's covenant.
> God: Is it then your covenant?
> Elijah: They have torn down Your altars.
> God: But were they your altars?
> Elijah: They have put Your prophets to the sword.
> God: But you are alive.
> Elijah: I alone am left.
> God: Instead of hurling accusations against Israel, should you not have pleaded their cause?[6]

The meaning of the Midrash is clear. The zealot takes the part of God. But God expects His prophets to be defenders, not accusers.

The repeated question and answer is now to be understood in its tragic depth. Elijah declares himself to be zealous for God. He is shown that God is not disclosed in dramatic confrontation: not in the whirlwind or the earthquake or the fire. God now asks him again, "What are you doing here, Elijah?" Elijah *repeats* that he is zealous for God. He has not understood that religious leadership calls for another kind of virtue,

6.   Song of Songs Rabba 1:6.

the way of the still, small voice. God now indicates that someone else must lead. Elijah must hand his mantle on to Elisha.

In turbulent times, there is an almost overwhelming temptation for religious leaders to be confrontational. Not only must truth be proclaimed but falsehood must be denounced. Choices must be set out as stark divisions. Not to condemn is to condone. The rabbi who condemned the Crypto-Jews had faith in his heart, logic on his side, and Elijah as his precedent.

But the Midrash and Rambam set before us another model. A prophet hears not one imperative but two: guidance and compassion, a love of truth and an abiding solidarity with those for whom that truth has become eclipsed. To preserve tradition and at the same time defend those who others condemn is the difficult, necessary task of a moral religious leadership in an unreligious age.

Matot

Honouring the Word

The *parasha* of *Matot* begins with a passage about vows and oaths and their annulment. It uses vocabulary that was later to be adopted and adapted for *Kol Nidrei*, the annulment of vows on the eve of Yom Kippur. Its position here, though – near the end of the book of Numbers – is strange.

The Torah has been describing the last stages in the Israelites' journey to the Promised Land. The command has been given to divide the land by lot between the tribes. Moses has been told by God to prepare for his death. He asks God to appoint a successor, which He does. The role goes to Joshua, Moses' apprentice for many years. The narrative then breaks off to make way for an extended account of the sacrifices to be brought on the various days of the year. Following that comes the section with which *Parashat Matot* begins, about vows and oaths.

Why is it here? There is a superficial answer. There is a verbal link with the penultimate verse of the previous *parasha*: "These shall you offer to the Lord at the appointed times, in addition to *your vows and your freewill offerings*" (Num. 29:39). Having mentioned vows, the Torah now states the laws that apply to them. That is one explanation.

However there is another answer, one that goes to the very heart of the project on which the Israelites were about to embark once they had crossed the Jordan and conquered the land. One problem, perhaps *the* problem, to which the Torah is an answer is: *Can freedom and order coexist in the human sphere?* Can there be a society which is both free and just at the same time? The Torah sets out for us the other alternatives. There can be freedom and chaos. That was the world full of violence before the Flood. And there can be order without freedom. That was the Egypt from which the Israelites were liberated. Is there a third alternative? And if so, how is it created?

The answer the Torah gives has to do with *language*. Recall that it was with language that God created the world: "And God said, Let there be…and there was…." One of the first gifts God gave humanity was language. When the Torah says that "God formed man from the dust of the earth and breathed into him the breath of life and man became a living being" (Gen. 2:7), the *Targum* translates the last phrase as "and man became a *speaking* being." For Judaism, speaking is life itself.

However, Judaism is particularly interested in one unusual use of language. The Oxford philosopher J. L. Austin called it "performative utterance."[1] This happens when we use language not to *describe* something but to *do* something. So, for instance, when a groom says to his bride under the *ḥuppa*, "Behold you are betrothed to me," he is not *describing* a marriage, he is *getting married*. When in ancient times the beit din declared the New Moon, they were not making a statement of fact. They were *creating* a fact, they were *turning the day into* the New Moon.

The key example of a performative utterance is a promise. When I promise you that I will do something, I am creating something that did not exist before, namely an obligation. This fact, small though it might seem, turns out to be the foundation of Judaism.

A mutual promise – X pledges himself to do certain things for Y, and Y commits himself to do other things for X – is called a covenant, and Judaism is based on covenant, specifically the covenant made between God and the Israelites at Mount Sinai, which bound them and

1. J. L. Austin, *How to Do Things with Words* (Oxford: Clarendon Press, 1975).

still to this day binds us. In human history, it is the supreme case of a performative utterance.

Two philosophers understood the significance of the act of promising to the moral life. One was Nietzsche. This is what he said:

> To breed an animal with the prerogative to *promise* – is that not precisely the paradoxical task which nature has set herself with regard to humankind? Is it not the real problem *of* humankind? ... Man himself will really have to become *reliable, regular, necessary*, even in his own self-image, so that he, as someone making a promise is, is answerable to his own *future*! That is precisely what constitutes the long history of the origins of *responsibility*.[2]

The other was Hannah Arendt, who in essence explained what Nietzsche meant. Human affairs are fraught with unpredictability. That is because we are free. We do not know how other people will behave or how they will respond to an act of ours. So we can never be sure of the consequences of our own decisions. Freedom seems to rob the human world of order. We can tell how inanimate objects will behave under different conditions. We can be reasonably sure of how animals will behave. But we cannot tell in advance how humans will react. How then can we create an orderly society without taking away people's freedom?

The answer is *the act of promising*. When I promise to do something, I am freely placing myself under an obligation to do something in the future. If I am the kind of person who is known to keep his word, I have removed one element of unpredictability from the human world. You can rely on me, since I have given my word. When I promise, I voluntarily bind myself. It is this ability of humans to voluntarily commit themselves to do or refrain from doing certain acts that generates order in the relations between human beings without the use of coercive force.[3]

2. Friedrich Nietzsche, *On the Genealogy of Morality*, trans. Carol Diethe and ed. Keith Ansell-Pearson (Cambridge, UK: Cambridge University Press, 2007), 35–36.
3. Hannah Arendt, *The Human Condition* (Chicago: University of Chicago Press, 1958), 243–44.

"When a man makes a vow to the Lord or takes an oath to obligate himself by a pledge, he must not break his word but must do everything he said" (Num. 30:3). It is no accident that this, the second verse of *Parashat Matot*, is stated shortly before the Israelites approach the Promised Land. The institution of promising, of which vows and oaths to God are a supreme example, is essential to the existence of a free society. *Freedom depends on people keeping their word.*

One instance of how this plays out in real life appears later in the *parasha*. Two of the tribes, Reuben and Gad, decided that they would rather live to the east of the Jordan where the land was more suitable for their livestock. After a fraught conversation with Moses, who accused them of shirking their responsibilities to the rest of the people, they agreed to be on the front lines of the army until the conquest of the land was complete. Everything depended on their keeping their word.

All social institutions in a free society depend on trust, and trust means honouring our promises, doing what we say we will do. When this breaks down, the very future of freedom is at risk. There is a classic example of this in Tanakh. It appears in the book of Jeremiah, where the prophet is describing the society of his time, when people could no longer be trusted to keep their word:

> They bend their tongues like bows;
> They are valorous in the land for treachery, not for honesty;
> They advance from evil to evil.
> They do not heed Me – declares the Lord.
> Beware of your friends;
> Trust not even a brother,
> For every one of them is a deceiver, and every friend a slanderer.
> Friend deceives friend, and no one speaks the truth.
> They have taught their tongues to lie; they weary themselves with sinning.
> You live in the midst of deceit; in their deceit they refuse to heed Me – declares the Lord. (Jer. 9:2–5)

That was the condition of a society that was about to lose its freedom to the Babylonians. It never fully recovered.

If trust breaks down, social relationships break down. Society will then depend on law enforcement agencies or some other use of force. When force is widely used, society is no longer free. The only way free human beings can form collaborative and cooperative relationships without recourse to force is by the use of verbal undertakings honoured by those who make them.

Freedom needs trust. Trust needs people to keep their word, and keeping your word means treating words as holy, vows and oaths as sacrosanct. Only under very special and precisely formulated circumstances can you be released from your undertakings. That is why, as the Israelites approached the Holy Land where they were to create a free society, they had to be reminded of the sacred character of vows and oaths.

The temptation to break your word when it is to your advantage to do so can sometimes be overwhelming. That is why belief in God – a God who oversees all we think, say, and do and who holds us accountable to our commitments – is so fundamental. Although it sounds strange to us now, the father of toleration and liberalism, John Locke, held that citizenship should not be extended to atheists because, not believing in God, they could not be trusted to honour their word.[4]

So the appearance of laws about vows and oaths at the end of the book of Numbers, as the Israelites are approaching the land, is no accident, and the moral is still relevant today. A free society depends on trust. Trust depends on keeping your word. That is how humans imitate God – by using language to create. Words create moral obligations, and moral obligations, undertaken responsibly and honoured faithfully, create the possibility of a free society.

4. John Locke, *A Letter Concerning Toleration* (1689).

Masei

Retribution and Revenge

Near the end of the book of Numbers, we encounter the law of the cities of refuge: three cities to the east of the Jordan and, later, three more within the land of Israel itself. There, people who had committed homicide could flee and find protection until their case was heard by a court of law. If they were found guilty of murder in biblical times, they were sentenced to death. If found innocent – if the death happened by accident or inadvertently, with neither deliberation nor malice – then they were to stay in the city of refuge "until the death of the high priest" (Num. 35:28). There, they were protected against revenge on the part of the *goel hadam*, the blood-redeemer, usually the closest relative of the person who had been killed.

Homicide is never less than serious in Jewish law. But there is a fundamental difference between murder – deliberate killing – and manslaughter, accidental death. To kill someone who is not guilty of murder as an act of revenge, someone who is responsible for an accidental death, is not justice but further bloodshed; this must be prevented – hence the need for safe havens where people at risk could be protected.

The prevention of unjust violence is fundamental to the Torah. God's covenant with Noah and humankind after the Flood identifies murder as the ultimate crime: "Whoever sheds the blood of man, by man shall his blood be shed; for in the image of God has God made man" (Gen. 9:6). Blood wrongly shed cries to Heaven itself. God said to Cain after he murdered Abel, "Your brother's blood is crying to Me from the ground" (Gen. 4:10).

Here in Numbers we hear a similar sentiment: "You shall not pollute the land in which you live, for blood pollutes the land, and the land can have no expiation for blood that is shed on it, except by the blood of him who shed it" (Num. 35:33). The verb Ḥ-N-F, which appears twice in this verse and nowhere else in the Mosaic books, means to pollute, to soil, to dirty, to defile. There is something fundamentally blemished about a world in which murder goes unpunished. Human life is sacred. Even justified acts of bloodshed, as in the case of war, communicate impurity. A priest who has shed blood does not bless the people.[1] David is told that he may not build the Temple "because you shed much blood" (I Chr. 22:8). Death defiles.

That is what lies behind the idea of revenge. And though the Torah rejects revenge except when commanded by God,[2] something of the idea survives in the concept of the *goel hadam*, wrongly translated as "blood-avenger." It means, in fact, "blood-redeemer." A redeemer is someone who rights an imbalance in the world, who rescues someone or something and restores it to its rightful place. Thus Boaz redeems land belonging to Naomi.[3] Redeemers are people who restore relatives to freedom after they have been forced to sell themselves into slavery.[4] God redeems His people from bondage in Egypt. A blood-redeemer is one who ensures that murder does not go unpunished.

However, not all acts of killing are murder. Some are *bishgaga*, that is, unintentional, accidental, or inadvertent. These are the acts that lead to exile in the cities of refuge. Yet there is an ambiguity about this law. Was exile to the cities of refuge considered a way of *protecting* the

1. Berakhot 32b; Rambam, *Mishneh Torah, Hilkhot Tefilla* 15:3.
2. Only God, the giver of life, can command us to take life, and then often only on the basis of facts known to God but not to us.
3. See Ruth, chapters 3–4.
4. See Leviticus 25, where the verb appears nineteen times.

accidental killer, or was it itself *a form of punishment* – not the death sentence that would have applied to one guilty of murder, but punishment nonetheless? Recall that exile is a biblical form of punishment. Adam and Eve, after their sin, were exiled from Eden. Cain, after killing Abel, was told he would be "a restless wanderer on the face of the earth" (Gen. 4:12). We say in our prayers, "Because of our sins we were exiled from our land."

In truth both elements are present. On the one hand the Torah says, "The assembly must protect the one accused of murder from the redeemer of blood and send the accused back to the city of refuge to which he fled" (Num. 35:25). Here the emphasis is on protection. But on the other hand, we read that if the exiled person "ever goes outside the limits of the city of refuge to which he fled and the redeemer of blood finds him outside the city, the redeemer of blood may kill the accused without being guilty of murder" (Num. 35:26–27). Here an element of guilt is presumed; otherwise, why would the blood-redeemer be innocent of murder?[5]

We can see the difference by looking at how the Talmud and Rambam explain the provision that the exile must stay in the city of refuge until the death of the high priest. What had the high priest to do with accidental killing? According to the Talmud, the high priest "should have asked for mercy [i.e., should have prayed that there be no accidental deaths among the people] and he did not do so" (Makkot 11a). The assumption is that had the high priest prayed more fervently, God would not have allowed this accident to happen. Whether or not there is moral guilt, something wrong has occurred and there is a need for atonement, achieved partly through exile and partly through the death of the high priest. For the high priest atoned for the people as a whole, and when he died, his death atoned for the death of those who were accidentally killed.

Rambam, however, gives a completely different explanation in *The Guide for the Perplexed* (III:40). For him the issue at stake is not atonement but protection. The reason the man goes into exile in a city of refuge is

5. See Amnon Bazak, "Cities of Refuge and Cities of Flight," in *Torah MiEtzion, Devarim* (Jerusalem: Maggid, 2012), 229–236.

to allow the passions of the relative of the victim, the blood-redeemer, to cool. The exile stays there until the death of the high priest, because his death creates a mood of national mourning, which dissolves the longing for revenge – "for it is a natural phenomenon that we find consolation in our misfortune when the same misfortune or a greater one befalls another person. Amongst us no death causes more grief than that of the high priest."

The desire for revenge is basic. It exists in all societies. It leads to cycles of retaliation – represented in the fictional Montagues against the Capulets in *Romeo and Juliet*, the Corleones and Tattaglias in *The Godfather* – that have no natural end. Wars of the clans were capable of destroying whole societies.[6]

The Torah, understanding that the desire for revenge is natural, tames it by translating it into something else altogether. It recognises the pain, the loss, and the moral indignation of the victim's family. That is the meaning of the phrase *goel hadam*, the blood-redeemer, the figure who represents that instinct for revenge. The Torah legislates for people with all their passions, not for saints. It is a realistic code, not a utopian one.

Yet the Torah inserts one vital element *between* the killer and the victim's family: the principle of justice. There must be no direct act of revenge. The killer must be protected until his case has been heard in a court of law. If found guilty, he must pay the price. If found innocent, he must be given refuge. *This single act turns revenge into retribution.* This makes all the difference.

People often find it difficult to distinguish between retribution and revenge, yet they are completely different concepts. Revenge is an I-Thou relationship. You killed a member of my family so I will kill you. It is intrinsically personal. Retribution, by contrast, is *im*personal. It is no longer the Montagues against the Capulets but both under the impartial rule of law. Indeed the best definition of the society the Torah seeks to create is *nomocracy*: the rule of laws, not men.

Retribution is the principled rejection of revenge. It says that we are not free to take the law into our own hands. Passion may not override the due process of the law, for that is a sure route to anarchy and bloodshed.

6. See René Girard, *Violence and the Sacred* (Baltimore: Johns Hopkins University Press, 1977).

Wrong must be punished, but only after it has been established by a fair trial, and only on behalf not just of the victim but of society as a whole. It was this principle that drove the work of the late Simon Wiesenthal in bringing Nazi war criminals to trial. He called his autobiography *Justice, Not Vengeance.*[7] The cities of refuge were part of this process, by which vengeance was subordinated to, and replaced by, retributive justice.

This is not just ancient history. Almost as soon as the Berlin Wall fell and the Cold War came to an end in 1989, brutal ethnic war came to the former Yugoslavia, first in Bosnia and then in Kosovo. It has now spread to Iraq, Syria, and many other parts of the world. In his book *The Warrior's Honor: Ethnic War and the Modern Conscience*, Michael Ignatieff wondered how these regions descended so rapidly into chaos. This was his conclusion:

> The chief moral obstacle in the path of reconciliation is the desire for revenge. Now, revenge is commonly regarded as a low and unworthy emotion, and because it is regarded as such, its deep moral hold on people is rarely understood. But revenge – morally considered – is a desire to keep faith with the dead, to honor their memory by taking up their cause where they left off. Revenge keeps faith between the generations; the violence it engenders is a ritual form of respect for the community's dead – therein lies its legitimacy. Reconciliation is difficult precisely because it must compete with the powerful alternative morality of violence. Political terror is tenacious because it is an ethical practice. It is a cult of the dead, a dire and absolute expression of respect.[8]

It is foolhardy to act as if the desire for revenge does not exist. It does. But given free reign, it will reduce societies to violence and bloodshed without end. The only alternative is to channel it through the operation of law, fair trial, and then either punishment or protection. That is what was introduced into civilisation by the law of the cities of refuge, allowing retribution to take the place of revenge, and justice the place of retaliation.

7. New York: Grove Weidenfeld, 1989.
8. Michael Ignatieff, *The Warrior's Honor* (New York: Henry Holt, 2000), 188.

Deuteronomy
דברים

Devarim

Why Are There So Many Jewish Lawyers?

At the beginning of Deuteronomy, Moses reviews the history of the Israelites' experience in the wilderness, beginning with the appointment of leaders throughout the people, heads of thousands, hundreds, fifties, and tens. He continues:

> And I charged your judges at that time, "Hear the disputes between your people and judge fairly, whether the case is between two Israelites or between an Israelite and a foreigner residing among you. Do not show partiality in judging; hear both small and great alike. Do not be afraid of anyone, for judgement belongs to God. Bring me any case too hard for you, and I will hear it. (Deut. 1:16–17)

Thus at the outset of the book in which he summarised the entire history of Israel and its destiny as a holy people, he already gave priority to the administration of justice, something he would memorably summarise in a later chapter (Deut. 16:20) with the words, "Justice,

justice, shall you pursue." The words for justice, *tzedek* and *mishpat*, are recurring themes of the book. The root TZ-D-K appears eighteen times in Deuteronomy; the root SH-F-T, forty-eight times.

Justice has seemed, throughout the generations, to lie at the beating heart of the Jewish faith. In the course of a television programme I made for the BBC, I asked Hazel Cosgrove, the first woman to be appointed as a judge in Scotland, and an active member of the Edinburgh Jewish community, what had led her to choose law as a career. She replied as if it was self-evident, "Because Judaism teaches: 'Justice, justice, shall you pursue.'"

One of the great Jewish lawyers of our time, Alan Dershowitz, has recently published a book about Abraham,[1] whom he sees as the first Jewish lawyer, "the patriarch of the legal profession: a defence lawyer for the damned who is willing to risk everything, even the wrath of God, in defence of his clients,"[2] the founder not just of monotheism but of a long line of Jewish lawyers. Dershowitz gives a vivid description of Abraham's prayer on behalf of the people of Sodom ("Shall the Judge of all the earth not do justice?" [Gen. 18:25]) as a courtroom drama, with Abraham acting as lawyer for the citizens of the town, and God, as it were, as the accused. This was the forerunner of a great many such episodes in Torah and Tanakh, in which the prophets argued the cause of justice with God and with the people.

In modern times, Jews reached prominence as judges in America – among them Brandeis, Cardozo, and Felix Frankfurter. Ruth Bader Ginsburg was the first Jewish woman to be appointed to the Supreme Court. In Britain, between 1996 and 2008, two of Britain's three Lord Chief Justices were Jewish: Peter Taylor and Harry Woolf. In Germany in the early 1930s, though Jews made up 0.7 per cent of the population, they represented 16.6 per cent of lawyers and judges.

One feature of Tanakh is noteworthy in this context. Throughout the Hebrew Bible some of the most intense encounters between the prophets and God are represented as courtroom dramas. Sometimes, as in the cases of Moses, Jeremiah, and Habakkuk, the plaintiff is humanity

---

1. Alan Dershowitz, *Abraham: The World's First (But Certainly Not the Last) Jewish Lawyer* (New York: Schocken, 2015).
2. Ibid., 11.

or the Jewish people. In the case of Job it is an individual who has suffered unfairly. The accused is God Himself. The story is told by Elie Wiesel of how a case was brought against God by the Jewish prisoners in a concentration camp during the Holocaust.[3] At other times, it is God who brings a case against the Children of Israel.

The word the Hebrew Bible uses for these unique dialogues between heaven and earth[4] is *riv*, which means a lawsuit, and it derives from the idea that at the heart of the relationship between God and humanity – both in general and specifically in relation to the Jewish people – is *covenant*. The covenant is a binding agreement, a mutual pledge, based on obedience to God's law on the part of humans, and on God's promise of loyalty and love on the part of Heaven. Thus either side can, as it were, bring the other to court on grounds of failure to fulfil their undertakings.

Three features mark Judaism as a distinctive faith. First is the radical idea that when God reveals Himself to humans He does so in the form of law. In the ancient world, God was power. In Judaism, God is order, and order presupposes law. In the natural world of cause and effect, order takes the form of scientific law. But in the human world, where we have free will, order takes the form of moral law. We have noted before that Torah means "direction, guidance, teaching"; another meaning is "law." The most basic meaning[5] of the most fundamental principle of Judaism, *Torah min haShamayim*, "Torah from Heaven," is that God, not humans, is the source of binding law.

Second, we are charged with being interpreters of the law. That is our responsibility as heirs and guardians of the *Torah Shebe'al Peh*, the Oral Tradition. The phrase in which Moses describes the voice the people heard at the Revelation at Sinai, *kol gadol velo yasaf*, is understood by the commentators in two seemingly contradictory ways. On the one hand it means "the voice that was *never* heard again"; on the other, it means "the voice that did not cease," that is, the voice that was *ever* heard again.[6]

---

3. Elie Wiesel, *The Trial of God* (New York: Schocken, 1995). The story is believed to be fictional, though on one occasion Wiesel said that it happened and that he was there.
4. On the subject in general, see Anson Laytner, *Arguing with God: A Jewish Tradition* (Northvale, NJ: Jason Aronson, 1977).
5. Not the only meaning, to be sure. See Rambam, *Mishneh Torah, Hilkhot Teshuva* 3:5.
6. Deut. 5:19, and see Rashi ad loc., who gives both interpretations.

There is, though, no contradiction. The voice that was never heard again is the one that represents the Written Torah. The voice that is ever heard again is that of the Oral Torah.

The Written Torah is *min haShamayim*, "from Heaven," but about the Oral Torah the Talmud insists: *Lo bashamayim hi*, "It is not in heaven" (Bava Metzia 59b). Hence Judaism is a continuing conversation between the Giver of the law and the interpreters of the law. That is part of what the Talmud means when it says that "every judge who delivers a true judgement becomes a partner with the Holy One, Blessed Be He in the work of creation" (Shabbat 10a).

Third, fundamental to Judaism is education, and fundamental to education is instruction in Torah, that is, the law. That is what Isaiah meant when he said, "Listen to Me, you who know justice, *the people in whose heart is My law*; do not fear the reproach of men, nor be afraid of their insults" (Is. 51:7). It is what Jeremiah meant when he said, "'This is the covenant I will make with the House of Israel after those days,' says the Lord. '*I will put My law within them, and I will write it on their hearts*; and I will be their God, and they shall be My people'" (Jer. 31:33). It is what Josephus meant when he said, nineteen hundred years ago, "Should any one of our nation be asked about our laws, he will repeat them as readily as his own name. The result of our thorough education in our laws from the very dawn of intelligence is that they are, as it were, *engraved on our souls*."[7] To be a Jewish child is to be, in the British phrase, "learned in the law." We are a nation of constitutional lawyers.

Why? Because Judaism is not just about spirituality. It is not simply a code for the salvation of the soul. It is a set of instructions for the creation of what the late Rabbi Aharon Lichtenstein called "societal beatitude." It is about bringing God into the shared spaces of our collective life. That needs law: law that represents justice, honouring all humans alike regardless of colour or class; law that judges impartially between rich and poor, powerful and powerless, even *in extremis* between humanity and God; law that links God, its giver, to us, its interpreters; law that alone allows freedom to coexist with order, so that my freedom is not bought at the cost of yours.

Small wonder, then, that there are so many Jewish lawyers.

---

7. *Against Apion* 2.178.

Va'ethanan

The Right and the Good

Buried among the epic passages in *Va'ethanan* – among them the *Shema* and the Ten Commandments – is a brief passage with large implications for the moral life in Judaism. Here it is together with the preceding verse:

> You shall diligently keep the commandments of the Lord your God, and His testimonies and His statutes, which He has commanded you. *And you shall do what is right and good in the sight of the Lord,* that it may go well with you, and that you may go in and take possession of the good land that the Lord swore to give to your fathers. (Deut. 6:17–18)

The difficulty is obvious. The preceding verse makes reference to commandments, testimonies, and statutes. This, on the face of it, is the whole of Judaism as far as conduct is concerned. What then is meant by the phrase "the right and the good" that is not already included within the previous verse?

Rashi says that it refers to "compromise [that is, not strictly insisting on your rights] and action within or beyond the letter of the law [*lifnim mishurat hadin*]." The law, as it were, lays down a minimum threshold: this we must do. But the moral life aspires to more than simply doing what we must.[1] The people who most impress us with their goodness and rightness are not merely people who keep the law. The saints and heroes of the moral life go beyond. They do more than they are commanded. They go the extra mile. That, according to Rashi, is what the Torah means by "the right and the good."

Ramban, while citing Rashi and agreeing with him, goes on to say something slightly different in his commentary on the same passage:

> At first Moses said that you are to keep His statutes and His testimonies which He commanded you, and now he is stating that even where He has not commanded you, give thought as well to do what is good and right in His eyes, for He loves the good and the right.
>
> Now this is a great principle, for it is impossible to mention in the Torah all aspects of man's conduct with his neighbours and friends, all his various transactions and the ordinances of all societies and countries. But since He mentioned many of them, such as, "You shall not go around as a talebearer," "You shall not take vengeance nor bear a grudge," "You shall not stand idly by the blood of your neighbour," "You shall not curse the deaf," "You shall rise before the hoary head," and the like, He went on to state in a general way that in all matters one should do what is good and right, including even compromise and going beyond the strict requirement of the law....Thus one should behave in every sphere of activity, until he is worthy of being called "good and upright."

1. See Lon Fuller, *The Morality of Law* (New Haven, CT: Yale University Press, 1969), and Rabbi Aharon Lichtenstein's much reprinted article, "Does Jewish Tradition Recognize an Ethic Independent of the Halakhah?" in *Modern Jewish Ethics*, ed. Marvin Fox (Columbus: Ohio State University Press, 1975), 62–88.

Ramban is going beyond Rashi's point, that the right and the good refer to a higher standard than the law strictly requires. It seems as if Ramban is telling us that there are aspects of the moral life that are not caught by the concept of law at all. That is what he means by saying, "It is impossible to mention in the Torah all aspects of man's conduct with his neighbours and friends."

Law is about universals, principles that apply in all places and times: Do not murder. Do not rob. Do not steal. Do not lie. Yet there are important features of the moral life that are not universal at all. They have to do with specific circumstances and the way we respond to them. What is it to be a good husband or wife, a good parent, a good teacher, a good friend? What is it to be a great leader, or follower, or member of a team? When is it right to praise, and when is it appropriate to say, "You could have done better"? There are aspects of the moral life that cannot be reduced to rules of conduct, because what matters is not only what we do, but the way in which we do it – with humility or gentleness or sensitivity or tact.

Morality is about persons, and no two persons are alike. When Moses asked God to appoint a successor, he began his request with the words, "Lord, God of the spirits of all flesh" (Num. 27:16). On this the rabbis commented: what Moses was saying was that because each person is different, he asked God to appoint a leader who would relate to each individual as an individual, knowing that what is helpful to one person may be harmful to another.[2] This ability to judge the right response to the right person at the right time is a feature not only of leadership, but of human goodness in general.

Rashi begins his commentary to Genesis with the question: If the Torah is a book of law, why does it not start with the first law given to the People of Israel as a whole, which does not appear until Exodus 12? Why does it include the narratives about Adam and Eve, Cain and Abel, the patriarchs and matriarchs and their children? Rashi gives an answer that has nothing to do with morality – he says it has to do with the Jewish people's right to their land. But Netziv (Rabbi Naftali Zvi Yehuda Berlin; 1816–1893) writes that the stories of Genesis are there

2. *Sifrei Zuta, Midrash Tanḥuma,* and Rashi to Numbers ad loc.

to teach us how the patriarchs were upright in their dealings, even with people who were strangers and idolaters. That, he says, is why Genesis is called by the sages "the book of the upright."[3]

Morality is not just a set of rules, even a code as elaborate as the 613 commandments and their rabbinic extensions. It is also about the way we respond to people as individuals. The story of Adam and Eve in the Garden of Eden is at least in part about what went wrong in their relationship when the man referred to his wife as *isha*, "woman," a generic description, a type. Only when he gave her a proper name, Ḥava, Eve, did he relate to her as an individual in her individuality, and only then did God "make [them] garments of skin and clothed them" (Gen. 3:21). This too is the difference between the god of Aristotle and the God of Abraham. Aristotle thought that God knew only universals, not particulars. This is the god of science, of the Enlightenment, of Spinoza. The God of Abraham is the God who relates to us in our singularity, in what makes us different from others as well as what makes us the same.

This ultimately is the difference between the two great principles of Judaic ethics: justice and love. Justice is universal. It treats all people alike, rich and poor, powerful and powerless, making no distinctions on the basis of colour or class. But love is particular. A parent loves his or her children for what makes them each unique. The moral life is a combination of both. That is why it cannot be reduced solely to universal laws. That is what the Torah means when it speaks of "the right and the good" over and above the commandments, statutes, and testimonies.

A good teacher knows what to say to a weak student who, through great effort, has done better than expected, and to a gifted student who has come to the top of the class but is still performing below his or her potential. A good employer knows when to praise and when to challenge. We all need to know when to insist on justice and when to exercise forgiveness. The people who have had a decisive influence on our lives are almost always those we feel understood us in our singularity. We were not, for them, a mere face in the crowd. That is why, though morality involves universal rules and cannot exist without them, it also involves interactions that cannot be reduced to rules.

3. *Haamek Davar* to Genesis, Introduction.

Rabbi Israel of Ruzhin (1796–1850) once asked a student how many sections there were in the *Shulḥan Arukh*. The student replied, "Four." "What," asked the Ruzhiner, "do you know about the fifth section?" "But there is no fifth section," said the student. "There is," said the Ruzhiner. "It says: always treat a person like a mensch."

The fifth section of the code of law is the conduct that cannot be reduced to law. That is what it takes to do the right and the good.

Ekev

The Power of Gratitude

In the early 1990s, one of the great medical research exercises of modern times took place. It became known as the Nun Study. Some seven hundred American nuns, all members of the School Sisters of Notre Dame in the United States, agreed to allow their records to be accessed by a research team investigating the process of ageing and Alzheimer's Disease. At the start of the study the participants were aged between seventy-five and 102.[1]

What gave this study its unusual longitudinal scope is that in 1930, the nuns, then in their twenties, had been asked by the Mother Superior to write a brief autobiographical account of their life and their reasons for entering the convent. These documents were now analysed by the researchers using a specially devised coding system to register, among other things, positive and negative emotions. By annually assessing the nuns' current state of health, the researchers were able to test whether their emotional state in 1930 had an effect on their health some sixty years

---

1.   See Robert Emmons, *Thanks!: How the New Science of Gratitude Can Make You Happier* (Boston: Houghton Mifflin, 2007).

later. Because they had all lived a very similar lifestyle during these six decades, they formed an ideal group for testing hypotheses about the relationship between emotional attitudes and health.

The results, published in 2001, were startling.[2] The more positive emotions – contentment, gratitude, happiness, love, and hope – the nuns expressed in their autobiographical notes, the more likely they were to be alive and well sixty years later. The difference was as much as seven years in life expectancy. So remarkable was this finding that it has led, since then, to a new field of gratitude research, as well as a deepening understanding of the impact of emotions on physical health.

What medicine now knows about individuals, Moses knew about nations. Gratitude – *hakarat hatov* – is at the heart of what he has to say about the Israelites and their future in the Promised Land. Gratitude had not been their strong point in the desert. They complained about lack of food and water, about the manna and the lack of meat and vegetables, about the dangers they faced from the Egyptians as they were leaving, and about the inhabitants of the land they were about to enter. They lacked thankfulness during the difficult times. A greater danger still, said Moses, would be a lack of gratitude during the good times. This is what he warned:

> When you have eaten your fill and have built fine houses and live in them, and when your herds and flocks have multiplied, and your silver and gold is multiplied, and all that you have is multiplied, do not exalt yourself, forgetting the Lord your God, who brought you out of the land of Egypt, out of the house of slavery.... Do not say to yourself, "My power and the might of my own hand have gained me this wealth." (Deut. 8:11–17)

The worst thing that could happen to them, warned Moses, would be that they would forget how they came to the land, how God had promised it to their ancestors and taken them from slavery to freedom,

---

2. Deborah D. Danner, David A. Snowdon, and Wallace V. Friesen, "Positive Emotions in Early Life and Longevity: Findings from the Nun Study," *Journal of Personality and Social Psychology* 80, no. 5 (2001): 804–13.

sustaining them during the forty years in the wilderness. This was a revolutionary idea. The nation's history, it asserted, should be engraved on people's souls and re-enacted in the annual cycle of festivals; the nation, as a nation, should never attribute its achievements to itself – "my power and the might of my own hand" – but should always ascribe its victories, indeed its very existence, to something higher than itself: God. This is a dominant theme of Deuteronomy, and it echoes throughout the book time and again.

Since the publication of the Nun Study and the flurry of further research it inspired, we now know of the multiple effects of developing an attitude of gratitude. It improves physical health and immunity against disease. Grateful people are more likely to take regular exercise and go for regular medical check-ups. Thankfulness reduces toxic emotions such as resentment, frustration, and regret, and makes depression less likely. It helps people avoid overreacting to negative experiences by seeking revenge. It even tends to make people sleep better. It enhances self-respect, making it less likely that you will envy others for their achievements or success. Grateful people tend to have better relationships. Saying "thank you" enhances friendships and elicits better performance from employees. It is also a major factor in strengthening resilience. One study of Vietnam War veterans found that those with higher levels of gratitude suffered lower incidence of Post-Traumatic Stress Disorder. Remembering the many things we have to be thankful for helps us survive painful experiences, from losing a job to bereavement.[3]

Jewish prayer is an ongoing seminar in gratitude. *Birkhot HaShaḥar*, the "Dawn Blessings" said at the start of morning prayers each day, form a litany of thanksgiving for life itself: for the human body, the physical world, land to stand on, and eyes to see with. The first words we say each morning – *Modeh/Moda ani*, "I thank You" – mean that we begin each day by giving thanks.

Gratitude also lies behind a fascinating feature of the *Amida*. When the leader of prayer repeats the *Amida* aloud, we are silent

---

3. Much of the material in this paragraph is to be found in articles published on the website "Greater Good: The Science of a Meaningful Life." See www.greatergood. berkeley.edu.

other than the responses of *Kedusha* and saying "Amen" after each blessing – with one exception. When the leader says the words *Modim anaḥnu Lakh*, "We give thanks to You," the congregation says a parallel passage known as *Modim DeRabbanan*. For every other blessing of the *Amida*, it is sufficient to assent to the words of the leader by saying "Amen." The one exception is *Modim*, "We give thanks." Rabbi Elijah Spira (1660–1712) in his work *Eliyahu Rabba*,[4] explains that when it comes to saying thank you, we cannot delegate it to someone else to do on our behalf. Thanks must come directly from us.

Part of the essence of gratitude is that it recognises that we are not the sole authors of what is good in our lives. The egoist, says André Comte-Sponville, "is ungrateful because he doesn't like to acknowledge his debt to others and gratitude is this acknowledgement."[5] La Rochefoucald put it more bluntly: "Pride refuses to owe, self-love to pay."[6] Thankfulness has an inner connection with humility. It recognises that what we are and what we have is due to others, above all to God. Comte-Sponville adds: "Those who are incapable of gratitude live in vain; they can never be satisfied, fulfilled or happy: they do not live, they get ready to live, as Seneca puts it."[7]

Though you do not have to be religious to be grateful, there is something about belief in God as creator of the universe, shaper of history, and author of the laws of life that directs and facilitates our gratitude. It is hard to feel grateful to a universe that came into existence for no reason and is blind to us and our fate. It is precisely our faith in a personal God that gives force and focus to our thanks.

It is no coincidence that the United States, founded by Puritans – Calvinists steeped in the Hebrew Bible – should have a day known as Thanksgiving, recognising the presence of God in American history. On October 3, 1863, at the height of the Civil War, Abraham Lincoln issued a Thanksgiving Proclamation, thanking God that though

---

4. Eliyahu Rabba, *Oraḥ Ḥayim* 127:1.
5. André Comte-Sponville, *A Small Treatise on the Great Virtues: The Uses of Philosophy in Everyday Life* (New York: Holt, 2001), 133.
6. Ibid., 135.
7. Ibid., 137.

the nation was at war with itself, there were still blessings for which both sides could express gratitude: a fruitful harvest, no foreign invasion, and so on. He continued:

> No human counsel hath devised nor hath any mortal hand worked out these great things. They are the gracious gifts of the Most High God, who, while dealing with us in anger for our sins, hath nevertheless remembered mercy.... I do therefore invite my fellow citizens in every part of the United States ... to set apart and observe the last Thursday of November next, as a day of Thanksgiving and Praise to our beneficent Father who dwelleth in the Heavens. And I recommend to them that while offering up the ascriptions justly due to Him for such singular deliverances and blessings, they do also, with humble penitence for our national perverseness and disobedience, commend to His tender care all those who have become widows, orphans, mourners or sufferers in the lamentable civil strife in which we are unavoidably engaged, and fervently implore the interposition of the Almighty Hand to heal the wounds of the nation and to restore it as soon as may be consistent with the Divine purposes to the full enjoyment of peace, harmony, tranquillity and Union.

What might such a declaration made today – in Israel, or the United States, or indeed anywhere – do to heal the wounds that so divide nations today? Thanksgiving is as important to societies as it is to individuals. It protects us from resentments and the arrogance of power. It reminds us of how dependent we are on others and on a force greater than ourselves. As with individuals so with nations: thanksgiving is essential to happiness and health.

Re'eh

The Second Tithe and the Making of a Strong Society

Biblical Israel from the time of Joshua until the destruction of the Second Temple was a predominantly agricultural society. Accordingly, it was through agriculture that the Torah pursued its religious and social programme. It has three fundamental elements.

The first was the alleviation of poverty. For many reasons the Torah accepts the basic principles of what we now call a market economy. But though market economics is good at creating wealth it is less good at distributing it equitably. Thus the Torah's social legislation aimed, in the words of Henry George, "to lay the foundations of a social state in which deep poverty and degrading want should be unknown."[1]

Hence institutions that left parts of the harvest for the poor: *leket, shikheḥa,* and *pe'ah* – fallen ears of grain, the forgotten sheaf, and

---

1. "Moses: Apostle of Freedom" (address first delivered to the Young Men's Hebrew Association of San Francisco, June, 1878).

the corners of the field. There was the produce of the seventh year, which belonged to no one and everyone, and *maaser ani*, the tithe for the poor given in the third and sixth years of the seven-year cycle. *Shemitta* and *Yovel*, the seventh and fiftieth years with their release of debts, manumission of slaves, and return of ancestral property to its original owners restored essential elements of the economy to their default position of fairness. So the first principle was: no one should be desperately poor.

The second, which included *teruma* and *maaser rishon*, the priestly portion and the first tithe, went to support, respectively, the priests and the Levites. These were a religious elite within the nation in biblical times, whose role was to ensure that the service of God, especially in the Temple, continued at the heart of national life. They had other essential functions, among them education and the administration of justice, as teachers and judges.

The third was more personal and spiritual. There were laws such as the bringing of first fruits to Jerusalem, and the three pilgrimage festivals – Passover, Shavuot, and Sukkot – as they marked seasons in the agricultural year that had to do with driving home the lessons of gratitude and humility. They taught that the land belongs to God and we are merely His tenants and guests. The rain, the sun, and the earth itself yield their produce only because of His blessing. Without such regular reminders, societies slowly but inexorably become materialistic and self-satisfied. Rulers and elites forget that their role is to serve the people, and instead they expect the people to serve them. That is how nations at the height of their success begin their decline, unwittingly laying the ground for their defeat.

All this makes one law in *Parashat Re'eh* – the law of the second tithe – hard to understand. As we noted above, in the third and sixth years of the septennial cycle, this was given to the poor. However, in the first, second, fourth, and fifth years, it was to be taken by the farmer to Jerusalem and eaten there in a state of purity:

> You shall eat the tithe of your grain, new wine, and olive oil, and the firstborn of your herds and flocks in the presence of the Lord your God at the place He will choose as a dwelling for

His Name, so that you may learn to revere the Lord your God always. (Deut. 14:23)

If the farmer lived at a great distance from Jerusalem, he was allowed an alternative:

> You may exchange your tithe for silver, and take the silver with you and go to the place the Lord your God will choose. Use the silver to buy whatever you like: cattle, sheep, wine or other fermented drink, or anything you wish. (Deut. 14:25–26)

The problem is obvious. The second tithe did not go to the poor, or to the priests and Levites, so it was not part of the first or second principle. It may have been part of the third, to remind the farmer that the land belonged to God, but this too seems unlikely. There was no declaration, as happened in the case of first fruits, and no specific religious service, as took place on the festivals. Other than being in Jerusalem, the institution of the second tithe seemingly had no cognitive or spiritual content. What then was the logic of the second tithe?

The sages,[2] focusing on the phrase, "so that *you may learn* to revere the Lord your God," said that it was to encourage people to study. Staying for a while in Jerusalem while they consumed the tithe or the food bought with its monetary substitute, they would be influenced by the mood of the holy city, with its population engaged either in divine service or sacred study.[3] This would have been much as happens today for synagogue groups that arrange study tours to Israel.

Rambam, however, gives a completely different explanation.

> The second tithe was commanded to be spent on food in Jerusalem: in this way the owner was compelled to give part of it away as charity. As he was not able to use it otherwise than by way of eating and drinking, he must have easily been induced to give

---

2. *Sifrei* ad loc. A more extended version of this interpretation can be found in the *Sefer HaḤinnukh*, command 360.

3. See also *Tosafot, Bava Batra* 21a, s.v. *Ki MiTzion.*

it gradually away. This rule brought multitudes together in one place, and strengthened the bond of love and brotherhood among the children of men.[4]

For Rambam, the second tithe served a social purpose. It strengthened civil society. It created bonds of connectedness and friendship among the people. It encouraged visitors to share the blessings of the harvest with others. Strangers would meet and become friends. There would be an atmosphere of camaraderie among the pilgrims. There would be a sense of shared citizenship, common belonging, and collective identity. Indeed Rambam says something similar about the festivals themselves:

> The use of keeping festivals is plain. Man derives benefit from such assemblies: the emotions produced renew the attachment to religion; they lead to friendly and social intercourse among the people.[5]

The atmosphere in Jerusalem, says Rambam, would encourage public-spiritedness. Food would always be plentiful, since the fruit of trees in their fourth year, the tithe of cattle, and the corn, wine, and oil of the second tithe would all have been brought there. They could not be sold and they could not be kept for the next year; therefore much would be given away in charity, especially (as the Torah specifies) to "the Levite…and the stranger, and the orphan, and the widow" (Deut. 14:29).

Writing about America in the 1830s, Alexis de Tocqueville found that he had to coin a new word for the phenomenon he encountered there and saw as one of the dangers in a democratic society. The word was *individualism*. He defined it as "a mature and calm feeling which disposes each member of the community to sever himself from the mass of his fellows and to draw apart with his family and his friends," leaving "society at large to itself."[6] Tocqueville believed that democracy

4. *The Guide for the Perplexed*, III:39.
5. Ibid., III:46.
6. Alexis de Tocqueville, *Democracy in America*, abridged with an introduction by Thomas Bender (New York: Vintage Books, 1954), 2:104.

encouraged individualism. As a result, people would leave the business of the common good entirely to the government, which would become ever more powerful, eventually threatening freedom itself.

It was a brilliant insight. Two recent examples illustrate the point. The first was charted by Robert Putnam, the great Harvard sociologist, in his study of Italian towns in the 1990s.[7] During the 1970s all Italian regions were given local government on equal terms, but over the next twenty years, some prospered, others stagnated; some had effective governance and economic growth, while others were mired in corruption and underachievement. The key difference, he found, was the extent to which the regions had an active and public-spirited citizenry.

The other is the experiment, known as the "free rider game," that we saw in our discussion of *Parashat Tetzaveh*. As you will recall, each of the participants is given a certain amount of money and invited to contribute to a common pot, which is then multiplied and returned in equal parts to the players. If one does not put in money, the other players soon notice that not everyone is contributing equally. The unfairness makes them all contribute less to the shared pot. If, however, the other players are given the chance to punish the suspected cheat by paying a dollar to make him lose three dollars, they tend to do so. The experiment demonstrates that there is always a potential conflict between self-interest and the common good. The group suffers and no one gains. The free rider stops free-riding, and everyone benefits.

As I was writing this essay in 2015, the Greek economy was in a state of collapse. Years earlier, in 2008, an economist, Benedikt Herrmann, had tested people in different cities throughout the world to see whether there were geographical and cultural variations in the way people played the free rider game. He found that in places like Boston, Copenhagen, Bonn, and Seoul, voluntary contributions to the common pot were high. They were much lower in Istanbul, Riyadh, and Minsk, where the economy was less developed. But they were lowest of all in Athens, Greece. What is more, when players in Athens penalised the free riders, those penalised did not stop free-riding. Instead they took

---

7. Robert D. Putnam, Robert Leonardi, and Raffaella Nanetti, *Making Democracy Work: Civic Traditions in Modern Italy* (Princeton, NJ: Princeton University Press, 1993).

revenge by punishing their punishers.[8] Where public-spiritedness is low, society fails to cohere and the economy fails to grow.

Hence the brilliance of Rambam's insight that the second tithe existed to create social capital, meaning bonds of trust and reciprocal altruism among the population, which came about through sharing food with strangers in the holy precincts of Jerusalem. Loving God helps make us better citizens and more generous people, thus countering the individualism that eventually makes democracies fail.

8. B. Herrmann, C. Thoni, and S. Gachter, "Antisocial Punishment Across Societies," *Science* 319, no. 5868 (2008): 1362–67.

Shofetim

Environmental
Responsibility

Some commands in the Torah were understood so narrowly by the sages that they were rendered almost inapplicable. One example is the *ir hanidaḥat*, the city led astray into idolatry, about which the Torah states that "you must kill all the inhabitants of the city by the sword" (Deut. 13:16). Another is the *ben sorer umoreh*, the stubborn and rebellious child, brought by his parents to the court and, if found guilty, put to death (Deut. 21:18–21).

In both these cases, some sages interpreted the law so restrictively that they said "there never was and never will be" a case in which the law was applied (Sanhedrin 71a). As for the condemned city, R. Eliezer said that if it contained a single *mezuza*, the law was not enforced (ibid.). In the case of the rebellious child, R. Yehuda taught that if the mother and father did not sound or look alike, the law did not apply (Mishna Sanhedrin 8:4). According to these interpretations, the two laws were never meant to be put into practice, but were written solely "so that we should expound them and receive reward."[1] They had only an educational – not a legal – function.

In the opposite direction, some laws were held to be far more extensive than they seemed at first sight. One striking example occurs in *Parashat Shofetim*. It refers to the conduct of a siege in the course of war. The Torah states:

> When you lay siege to a city for a long time, fighting against it to capture it, do not destroy its trees by putting an ax to them, because you can eat their fruit. Do not cut them down. Are the trees people, that you should besiege them? However, you may cut down trees that you know are not fruit trees and use them to build siege works until the city at war with you falls. (Deut. 20:19–20)

This prohibition against destroying fruit-bearing trees was known as the rule of *bal tashḥit*, "do not destroy." On the face of it, it is highly limited in scope. It does no more than forbid a "scorched earth" policy in the conduct of war. It seems to have no peacetime application. However, the sages understood it very broadly as including any act of needless destruction. Rambam states the law thus: "Not only does this apply to trees, but also whoever breaks vessels or tears garments, destroys a building, blocks a wellspring of water, or destructively wastes food transgresses the command of *bal tashḥit*."[2] This is the halakhic basis of an ethic of environmental responsibility.

Why did the Oral Tradition, or at least some of its exponents, narrow the scope of the law in some cases and broaden it in others? The short answer is: we do not know. The rabbinic literature does not tell us. But we can speculate. A *posek*, seeking to interpret divine law in specific cases, will seek to do so in a way consistent with the total structure of biblical teaching. If a text seems to conflict with a basic principle of Jewish law, it will be understood restrictively, at least by some. If it exemplifies such a principle, it will be understood broadly.

1. Tosefta Sanhedrin 11:6; 14:1.
2. *Mishneh Torah, Hilkhot Melakhim* 6:10.

The law of the condemned city, where all the inhabitants were sentenced to death, seems to conflict with the principle of individual justice. When Sodom was threatened with such a fate, Abraham argued that if there were only ten innocent people, the destruction of the entire population would be manifestly unfair: "Shall the Judge of all the earth not do justice?" (Gen. 18:25).

The law of the stubborn and rebellious son was explained in the Talmud by R. Yose the Galilean on the grounds that: "The Torah foresaw his ultimate destiny." He had begun with theft. The likelihood was that he would go on to violence and then to murder. "Therefore the Torah ordained: let him die innocent rather than die guilty" (Mishna Sanhedrin 8:5). This is preemptive punishment. The child is punished less for what he has done than for what he may go on to do. R. Shimon b. Yoḥai, who said the law never was or would be applied, may have believed that in Judaism there is a contrary principle, that people are only judged for what they have done, not for what they will do. Retributive punishment is justice; preemptive punishment is not.

To repeat: this is speculative. There may have been other reasons at work. But it makes sense to suppose that the sages sought as far as possible to make their individual rulings consistent with the value-structure of Jewish law as they understood it. On this view, the law of the condemned city exists to teach us that idolatry, once accepted in public, is contagious, as we see from the history of Israel's kings. The law of the stubborn and rebellious child is there to teach us how steep is the downward slope from juvenile delinquency to adult crime. Law exists not just to regulate but also to educate.

In the case of *bal tashḥit*, however, there is an obvious fit with much else in Jewish law and thought. The Torah is concerned with what we would nowadays call "sustainability." This is particularly true of the three commands ordaining periodic rest: Shabbat, the Sabbatical year, and the Jubilee year. On Shabbat all agricultural work is forbidden "so that your ox and your donkey may rest" (Ex. 23:12). It sets a limit to our intervention in nature and the pursuit of economic growth. We become conscious that we are creations, not just creators. The earth is not ours but God's. For six days it is handed over to us, but on the seventh we symbolically abdicate that power. We may perform no "work," which is to say, an act that alters the state of something for human purposes. Shabbat is a weekly reminder of the integrity of nature and the boundaries of human striving.

What Shabbat does for humans and animals, the Sabbatical and Jubilee years do for the land. The earth too is entitled to its periodic rest. The Torah warns that if the Israelites do not respect this, they will suffer exile: "Then shall the land make up for its Sabbatical years throughout the time that it is desolate and you are in the land of your enemies; then shall the land rest and make up for its sabbath years" (Lev. 26:34). Behind this are two concerns. One is environmental. As Rambam points out, land which is overexploited eventually erodes and loses its fertility. The Israelites were therefore commanded to conserve the soil by giving it periodic fallow years, not pursuing short-term gain at the cost of long-term desolation.[3] The second, no less significant, is theological: "The land," says God, "is Mine; you are but strangers resident with Me" (Lev. 25:23). We are guests on earth.

Another group of commands is directed against over-interference with nature. The Torah forbids crossbreeding livestock, planting a field with mixed seeds, and wearing a garment of mixed wool and linen. These rules are called *ḥukkim* or "statutes." Ramban understood this term to mean laws that respect the integrity of nature. To mix different species, he argued, is to presume to be able to improve on creation, and is thus an affront to the Creator. Each species has its own internal laws of development and reproduction, and these must not be tampered with: "One who combines two different species thereby changes and defies the work of creation, as if he believes that the Holy One, Blessed Be He has not completely perfected the world and he now wishes to improve it by adding new kinds of creatures."[4] Deuteronomy also contains a law forbidding taking a young bird together with its mother. Ramban sees this as having the same underlying concern, namely of protecting species. Though the Bible permits us to use some animals for food, we must not cull them to extinction.

Samson Raphael Hirsch in the nineteenth century gave the most forcible interpretation of biblical law. The statutes relating to

3. *The Guide for the Perplexed*, III:39.
4. Ramban, commentary to Lev. 19:19.

environmental protection, he said, represent the principle that "the same regard which you show to man you must also demonstrate to every lower creature, to the earth which bears and sustains all, and to the world of plants and animals." They are a kind of social justice applied to the natural world: "They ask you to regard all living things as God's property. Destroy none; abuse none; waste nothing; employ all things wisely.... Look upon all creatures as servants in the household of creation."[5]

Hirsch also gave a novel interpretation to the phrase in Genesis 1, "Let us make mankind in our image, in our likeness" (Gen. 1:26). The passage is puzzling, for at that stage, prior to the creation of man, God was alone. The "us," says Hirsch, refers to the rest of creation. Because man alone would develop the capacity to change and possibly endanger the natural world, nature itself was consulted as to whether it approved of such a being. The implied condition is that man may use nature only in such a way as to enhance it, not put it at risk. Anything else is *ultra vires*, outside the remit of our stewardship of the planet.

In this context, a phrase in Genesis 2 is decisive. Man was set in the Garden of Eden "to work it and take care of it" (Gen. 2:15). The two Hebrew verbs are significant. The first – *le'avda* – literally means "to serve it." Man is not just a master but also a servant of nature. The second – *leshamra* – means "to guard it." This is the verb used in later Torah legislation to describe the responsibilities of a guardian of property that does not belong to him. He must exercise vigilance in his protection and is liable for loss through negligence. This is perhaps the best short definition of man's responsibility for nature as the Bible conceives it.

Man's dominion over nature is thus limited by the requirement to serve and conserve. The famous story of Genesis 2–3 – eating the forbidden fruit and the subsequent exile from Eden – makes just this point. Not everything that we can do, may we do. Transgress the limits, and disaster follows. All of this is summed up by a simple midrash:

> When God made man, He showed him the panoply of creation and said to him: "See all My works, how beautiful they are. All I have made, I have made for you. Take care, therefore, that you

5. S. R. Hirsch, *The Nineteen Letters*, Letter 11.

do not destroy My world, for if you do, there will be no one left to mend what you have destroyed."[6]

We know much more than we once did about the dangers to the earth's ecology by the ceaseless pursuit of economic gain. The guidance of the Oral Tradition in interpreting "do not destroy" expansively, not restrictively, should inspire us now. We should expand our horizons of environmental responsibility for the sake of generations not yet born, and for the sake of God whose guests on earth we are.

6. Ecclesiastes Rabba 7:13.

Ki Tetzeh

To the Third and Fourth Generations

There is, on the face of it, a fundamental contradiction in the Torah. On the one hand we hear, in the passage known as the Thirteen Attributes of Mercy, the following words:

> The Lord, the Lord, compassionate and gracious God, slow to anger, abounding in love and faithfulness.... Yet He does not leave the guilty unpunished; *He punishes the children and their children for the sin of the parents to the third and fourth generation.* (Ex. 34:7)

The implication is clear. Children suffer for the sins of their parents.

On the other hand we read in *Parashat Ki Tetzeh*: "Parents are not to be put to death for their children, nor children put to death for their parents; each will die for their own sin" (Deut. 24:16).

The book of Kings records a historic event when this principle proved decisive.

When Amaziah was well established as king, he executed the officials who had assassinated his father. However, he did not kill the children of the assassins, for he obeyed the command of the Lord as written by Moses in the Book of the Law: "Parents are not to be put to death for their children, nor children put to death for their parents; each will die for their own sin." (II Kings 14:5–6)

There is an obvious resolution. The first statement refers to divine justice, "at the hands of Heaven." The second, in Deuteronomy, refers to human justice as administered in a court of law. How can mere mortals decide the extent to which one person's crime was induced by the influence of others? Clearly the judicial process must limit itself to the observable facts. The person who committed the crime is guilty. Those who may have shaped his character are not.

Yet the matter is not so simple, because we find Jeremiah and Ezekiel, the two great prophets of exile in the sixth century BCE, restating the principle of individual responsibility in strong and strikingly similar ways. Jeremiah says:

In those days people will no longer say, "The parents have eaten sour grapes, and the children's teeth are set on edge." Instead, everyone will die for their own sin; whoever eats sour grapes – their own teeth will be set on edge. (Jer. 31:29–30)

Ezekiel says:

The word of the Lord came to me: "What do you people mean by quoting this proverb about the land of Israel: 'The parents eat sour grapes, and the children's teeth are set on edge'? As surely as I live," declares the Sovereign Lord, "you will no longer quote this proverb in Israel. For everyone belongs to Me, the parent as well as the child – both alike belong to Me. The one who sins is the one who will die." (Ezek. 18:1–4)

Here the prophets are not speaking about judicial procedures and legal responsibility. They are talking about divine judgement and justice. They are giving the people hope at one of the lowest points in Jewish history: the Babylonian conquest and the destruction of the First Temple. The people, sitting and weeping by the waters of Babylon, might have given up hope altogether. They were being judged for the failings of their ancestors that had brought the nation to this desperate plight, and their exile seemed to stretch endlessly into the future. Ezekiel, in his vision of the valley of dry bones, hears God reporting that the people were saying, "Our bones are dried up, our hope is lost" (Ezek. 37:11). He and Jeremiah were counselling against despair. The people's future was in their own hands. If they returned to God, God would return to them and bring them back to their land. The guilt of previous generations would not be attached to them.

But if this is so, then the words of Jeremiah and Ezekiel really do conflict with the idea that God punishes sins to the third and fourth generation. Recognising this, the Talmud makes a remarkable statement:

> Said R. Yose b. Ḥanina: Our master Moses pronounced four [adverse] sentences on Israel, but four prophets came and revoked them.... Moses said, "The Lord ... *punishes the children and their children for the sin of the parents to the third and fourth generation.*" Ezekiel came and declared, "The one who sins is the one who will die." (Makkot 24b)

In general the sages rejected the idea that children could be punished, even at the hands of Heaven, for the sins of their parents. As a result, they systematically re-interpreted every passage that gave the opposite impression, that children were indeed being punished for their parents' sins. Their general position was this:

> Are not children then to be put to death for the sins committed by their parents? Is it not written, "Visiting the iniquities of the fathers upon the children"? – There the reference is to children who follow in their parents' footsteps [literally, "seize their parents' deeds in their hands," i.e., commit the same sins themselves]. (Berakhot 7a; Sanhedrin 27b)

Specifically, they explained biblical episodes in which children were punished along with their parents by saying that in these cases the children "had the power to protest/prevent their parents from sinning, but they failed to do so" (Sanhedrin 27b; *Yalkut Shimoni*, I:290). As Rambam says, whoever has the power to prevent someone from committing a sin but does not do so, he is seized (i.e., punished, held responsible) for that sin.[1]

Did, then, the idea of individual responsibility come late to Judaism, as some scholars argue? This is highly unlikely. During the rebellion of Korah, when God threatened to destroy the people, Moses said, "Shall one man sin and will You be angry with the whole congregation?" (Num. 16:22). When people began dying after David had sinned by instituting a census, he prayed to God: "I have sinned. I, the shepherd, have done wrong. These are but sheep. What have they done? Let Your hand fall on me and my family" (II Sam. 24:17). The principle of individual responsibility is as basic to Judaism as it was to other cultures in the ancient Near East.[2]

Rather, what is at stake is the deep understanding of the scope of responsibility we bear if we take seriously our roles as parents, neighbours, townspeople, citizens, and children of the covenant. Judicially, only the criminal is responsible for his crime. But, implies the Torah, we are also our brother's keeper. We share collective responsibility for the moral and spiritual health of society. "All Israelites," said the sages, "are responsible for one another" (Shevuot 39a). Legal responsibility is one thing, and relatively easy to define. But moral responsibility is something altogether larger, if necessarily more vague. "Let a person not say, 'I have not sinned, and if someone else commits a sin, that is a matter between him and God.' This is contrary to the Torah," writes Rambam in *Sefer HaMitzvot*.[3]

This is particularly so when it comes to the relationship between parents and children. Abraham was chosen, says the Torah, solely so that "he will instruct his children and his household after him that they may keep the way of the Lord by doing what is right and just" (Gen. 18:19).

1. *Mishneh Torah, Hilkhot Deot* 6:7.
2. See Yehezkel Kaufmann, *The Religion of Israel* (New York: Schocken, 1972), 329–33.
3. *Sefer HaMitzvot*, positive command 205.

The duty of parents to teach their children is fundamental to Judaism. It appears in both the first two paragraphs of the *Shema*, as well as the various passages cited in the "Four Sons" section of the Haggada. Rambam counts as one of the gravest of all sins – so serious that God does not give us an opportunity to repent – "one who sees his son falling into bad ways and does not stop him." The reason, he says, is that "since his son is under his authority, had he stopped him the son would have desisted." Therefore it is accounted to the father as if he had actively caused his son to sin.[4]

If so, then we begin to hear the challenging truth in the Thirteen Attributes of Mercy. To be sure, we are not legally responsible for the sins of either our parents or our children. But in a deeper, more amorphous sense, what we do and how we live do have an effect on the future to the third and fourth generation.

Rarely has that effect been more devastatingly described than in recent books by two of America's most insightful social critics: Charles Murray of the American Enterprise Institute and Robert Putnam of Harvard. Notwithstanding their vastly different approaches to politics, Murray in *Coming Apart* and Putnam in *Our Kids* have issued essentially the same prophetic warning of a social catastrophe in the making. For Putnam, "the American dream" is "in crisis."[5] For Murray, the division of the United States into two classes with ever-decreasing mobility between them "will end what has made America America."[6]

Their argument is roughly this: At a certain point, in the late 1950s or early 1960s, a whole series of institutions and moral codes began to dissolve. Marriage was devalued. Families began to fracture. More and more children grew up without stable association with their biological parents. New forms of child poverty began to appear, as well as social dysfunctions such as drug and alcohol abuse, teenage pregnancies, and crime and unemployment in low-income areas. Over time, an upper class

4. *Mishneh Torah, Hilkhot Teshuva* 4:1. The reference is of course to a son under the age of thirteen.
5. Robert Putnam, *Our Kids: The American Dream in Crisis* (New York: Simon & Schuster, 2015).
6. Charles Murray, *Coming Apart: The State of White America, 1960–2010* (New York: Crown Forum, 2012), 11.

pulled back from the brink and is now intensively preparing its children for high achievement, while on the other side of the tracks children are growing up with little hope for educational, social, and occupational success. The American dream of opportunity for all is wearing thin.

What makes this development so tragic is that for a moment, people forgot the biblical truth that what we do does not affect us alone. It affects our children to the third and fourth generation. Even the greatest libertarian of modern times, John Stuart Mill, was emphatic on the responsibilities of parenthood. He wrote:

> The fact itself, of causing the existence of a human being, is one of the most responsible actions in the range of human life. To undertake this responsibility – to bestow a life which may be either a curse or a blessing – unless the being on whom it is to be bestowed will have at least the ordinary chances of a desirable existence, is a crime against that being.[7]

If we fail to honour our responsibilities as parents, then – though no law will hold us responsible – society's children will pay the price. They will suffer because of our sins.

7. *On Liberty and Other Writings*, ed. Stefan Collini (New York: Cambridge University Press, 1989), 117.

Ki Tavo

The Pursuit of Joy

Happiness, said Aristotle, is the ultimate good at which all humans aim.[1] But in Judaism it is not necessarily so. Happiness is a high value. *Ashrei*, the closest Hebrew word to happiness, is the first word of the book of Psalms. We say the prayer known as *Ashrei* three times each day. We can surely endorse the phrase in the American Declaration of Independence that among the inalienable rights of humankind are life, liberty, and the pursuit of happiness.

But *Ashrei* is not the central value of the Hebrew Bible. Occurring almost ten times as frequently is the word *simḥa*, joy. It is one of the fundamental themes of Deuteronomy as a book. The root s-m-ḥ appears only once in each of Genesis, Exodus, Leviticus, and Numbers, but no fewer than twelve times in Deuteronomy. It lies at the heart of the Mosaic vision of life in the land of Israel. That is where we serve God with joy.

Joy plays a key role in two contexts in *Parashat Ki Tavo*. One has to do with the bringing of first fruits to the Temple in Jerusalem. After describing the ceremony that took place, the Torah concludes: "Then

---

1. Aristotle, *Nicomachean Ethics*, Book 1.

you will rejoice in all the good things that the Lord your God has given you and your family, along with the Levites and the stranger in your midst" (Deut. 26:11).

The other context is quite different and astonishing. It occurs within the curses. There are two passages of curses in the Torah, one in Leviticus 26, the other here in Deuteronomy 28. The differences are notable. The curses in Leviticus end on a note of hope. Those in Deuteronomy end in bleak despair. The Leviticus curses speak of a total abandonment of Judaism by the people. The people walk *bekeri* with God, variously translated as "with hostility," "rebelliously," or "contemptuously." But the curses in Deuteronomy are provoked simply "because you did not serve the Lord your God with joy and gladness of heart out of the abundance of all things" (Deut. 28:47).

Now, joylessness may not be the best way to live, but it is surely not even a sin, let alone one that warrants a litany of curses. What does the Torah mean when it attributes national disaster to a lack of joy? Why does joy seem to matter in Judaism more than happiness? To answer these questions we have first to understand the difference between happiness and joy. This is how the first psalm describes the happy life:

> Happy is the man who has not walked in the counsel of the wicked, nor stood in the way of sinners, nor sat where scoffers sit. But his desire is in the Torah of the Lord; on his Torah he meditates day and night. He shall be like a tree planted by streams of water, bearing its fruit in its season, and its leaf does not wither; and in all that he does he prospers. (Ps. 1:1–3)

This is a serene and blessed life, granted to one who lives in accordance with the Torah. Like a tree, such a life has roots. It is not blown this way and that by every passing wind or whim. Such people bear fruit, stay firm, survive, and thrive. Yet for all that, happiness is the state of mind of an individual.

Simḥa in the Torah is never about individuals. It is always about something we share. A newly married man does not serve in the army for a year, says the Torah, so that he can stay at home "and bring joy to the wife he has married" (Deut. 24:5). You shall bring all your offerings to the central Sanctuary, says Moses, so that "there, in the presence of the Lord your God, you and your families shall eat and rejoice in all you have put your hand to, because the Lord your God has blessed you" (Deut. 12:7). The festivals as described in Deuteronomy are days of joy, precisely because they are occasions of collective celebration: "you, your sons and daughters, your male and female servants, the Levites in your towns, and the strangers, the fatherless and the widows living among you" (Deut. 16:11). *Simḥa* is joy shared. It is not something we experience in solitude.

Happiness is an attitude to life as a whole while joy lives in the moment. J. D. Salinger once said: happiness is a solid, joy is a liquid. Happiness is something you pursue. But joy is not. It discovers you. It has to do with a sense of connection to other people or to God. It comes from a different realm than happiness. It is a social emotion. It is the exhilaration we feel when we merge with others. It is the redemption of solitude.

Paradoxically, the biblical book most focused on joy is precisely the one often thought of as the unhappiest of all: *Kohelet*, Ecclesiastes. Ecclesiastes is notoriously the man who has everything, yet describes it all as *hevel*, a word he uses almost forty times in the space of the book. *Hevel* is variously translated as "meaningless," "pointless," "futile," "empty," or as the King James Bible famously rendered it, "vanity." In fact, though, Ecclesiastes uses the word *simḥa* seventeen times, that is, more than the whole of the Mosaic books together. After every one of his meditations on the pointlessness of life, Ecclesiastes ends with an exhortation to joy:

> I know that there is nothing better for people than to rejoice and do good while they live. (3:12)

> So I saw that there is nothing better for a person than to rejoice in his work, because that is his lot. (3:22)

> So I commend rejoicing in life, because there is nothing better for a person under the sun than to eat and drink and rejoice. (8:15)

> However many years anyone may live, let him rejoice in them all. (11:8)

I argue in the Koren Sukkot *Maḥzor* that Ecclesiastes can only be understood if we realise that *hevel* does not mean "pointless," "empty," or "futile." It means "a shallow breath." Ecclesiastes is a meditation on mortality. However long we live, we know we will one day die. Our lives are a mere microsecond in the history of the universe. The cosmos lasts forever while we living, breathing mortals are a mere fleeting breath.

Ecclesiastes is obsessed by this because it threatens to rob life of any certainty. We will never live to see the long-term results of our endeavours. Moses did not lead the people into the Promised Land. His sons did not follow him to greatness. Even he, the greatest of prophets, could not foresee that he would be remembered for all time as the greatest leader the Jewish people ever had. *Lehavdil*, Van Gogh sold only one painting in his lifetime. He could not have known that he would eventually be hailed as one of the greatest painters of modern times. We do not know what our heirs will do with what we leave them. We cannot know how, or if, we will be remembered. How then are we to find meaning in life?

Ecclesiastes eventually finds it not in happiness but in joy – because joy lives not in thoughts of tomorrow, but in the grateful acceptance and celebration of today. We are here; we are alive; we are among others who share our sense of jubilation. We are living in God's land, enjoying His blessings, eating the produce of His earth, watered by His rain, brought to fruition under His sun, breathing the air He breathed into us, living the life He renews in us each day. And yes, we do not know what tomorrow may bring; and yes, we are surrounded by enemies; and yes, it was never the safe or easy option to be a Jew. But when we focus on the moment, allowing ourselves to dance, sing, and give thanks, when we do things for their own sake rather than for any other reward, when we let go of our separateness and become a voice in the holy city's choir, then there is joy.

Kierkegaard once wrote: "It takes moral courage to grieve; it takes religious courage to rejoice."[2] It is one of the most poignant facts about Judaism and the Jewish people that though our history has been

2. *Journals and Papers* (Bloomington: Indiana University Press, 1967), 2:493.

shot through with tragedy, Jews never lost the capacity to rejoice, to celebrate in the heart of darkness, to sing the Lord's song even in a strange land. There are Eastern faiths that promise peace of mind if we can train ourselves into habits of acceptance. Epicurus taught his disciples to avoid risks like marriage or a career in public life. Neither of these approaches is to be negated, yet Judaism is not a religion of acceptance, nor have Jews tended to seek the risk-free life. We can survive the failures and defeats if we never lose the capacity for joy. On Sukkot, we leave the security and comfort of our houses and live in a shack exposed to the wind, the cold, and the rain. Yet we call it *zeman simḥatenu*, our season of joy. That is no small part of what it is to be a Jew.

Hence Moses' insistence that the capacity for joy is what gives the Jewish people the strength to endure. Without it, we become vulnerable to the multiple disasters set out in the curses in this *parasha*. Celebrating together binds us as a people – that and the gratitude and humility that come from seeing our achievements not as self-made but as the blessings of God. The pursuit of happiness can lead, ultimately, to self-regard and indifference to the sufferings of others. It can lead to risk-averse behaviour and a failure to "dare greatly." Not so joy. Joy connects us to others and to God. Joy is the ability to celebrate life as such, knowing that whatever tomorrow may bring, we are here today, under God's heaven, in the universe He made, to which He has invited us as His guests.

Towards the end of his life, having been deaf for twenty years, Beethoven composed one of the greatest pieces of music ever written, his *Ninth Symphony*. Intuitively he sensed that this work needed the sound of human voices. It became the West's first choral symphony. The words he set to music were Schiller's *Ode to Joy*. I think of Judaism as an ode to joy. Like Beethoven, Jews have known suffering, isolation, hardship, and rejection, yet they never lacked the religious courage to rejoice. A people that can know insecurity and still feel joy is one that can never be defeated, for its spirit can never be broken nor its hope destroyed. As individuals we may aspire to the goodness that leads to happiness, but as part of a moral and spiritual community, even in hard times we find ourselves lifted on the wings of joy.

Nitzavim

Why Judaism?

Parashat *Nitzavim* raises a question that goes to the heart of Judaism, but which was not asked for many centuries until raised by a great Spanish scholar of the fifteenth century, Rabbi Isaac Arama. Moses is almost at the end of his life. The people are about to cross the Jordan and enter the Promised Land. Moses knows he must do one thing more before he dies. He must renew the covenant between the people and God.

Their parents had entered into that commitment almost forty years before when they stood at Mount Sinai and said, "We will do and obey all that God has declared" (Ex. 24:7). But now Moses has to ensure that the next generation *and all future generations* will be bound by it. He wants no one to be able to say, "God made a covenant with my ancestors but not with me. I did not give my consent. I was not there. I am not bound." That is why Moses says:

> It is *not with you alone* that I am making this sworn covenant, but with whoever is standing here with us today before the Lord our God, and *with whoever is not here* with us today. (Deut. 29:13–14)

"Whoever is not here" cannot mean Israelites alive at the time who were somewhere else. The entire nation was present at the assembly. It means "generations not yet born." That is why the Talmud says: we are all *mushba veomed meHar Sinai*, "foresworn from Sinai" (Yoma 73b; Nedarim 8a).

Hence one of the most fundamental facts about Judaism: converts excepted, we do not choose to be Jews. We are born as Jews. We become legal adults, subject to the commands, at age twelve for girls, thirteen for boys. But we are part of the covenant from birth. A bat or bar mitzva is not a "confirmation." It involves no voluntary acceptance of Jewish identity. That choice took place more than three thousand years ago when Moses said, "It is *not with you alone* that I am making this sworn covenant, but with ... *whoever is not here* with us today," meaning all future generations.

But how can this be so? There is no obligation without consent. How can we be subject to a commitment on the basis of a decision taken long ago by our distant ancestors? To be sure, in Jewish law you can confer a benefit on someone else without their consent. But though it is surely a benefit to be a Jew, it is also in some sense a liability, a restriction on our range of legitimate choices. Why then are we bound now by what the Israelites said then?

Jewishly, this is the ultimate question. How can religious identity be passed on from parent to child? If identity were merely ethnic, we could understand it. We inherit many things from our parents – most obviously our genes. But being Jewish is not a genetic condition. It is a set of religious obligations.

The sages gave an answer in the form of a tradition about *Parashat Nitzavim*. They said that the souls of all future generations were present at Sinai. As souls, they freely gave their consent, generations before they were born (Shevuot 39a). However, Arama argues that this cannot answer our question, since God's covenant is not with souls only, but also with embodied human beings. We are physical beings with physical desires. We can understand that the soul would agree to the covenant. What does the soul desire if not closeness to God?[1]

But the assent that counts is that of living, breathing human beings with bodies, and we cannot assume that they would agree to the

---

1. Isaac Arama, *Akedat Yitzḥak*, Deuteronomy, *Nitzavim*.

Torah with its many restrictions on eating, drinking, sexual relations, and the rest. Not until we are born and are old enough to understand what is being asked of us can we give our consent in a way that binds us. Therefore the fact that the unborn generations were present at Moses' covenant ceremony does not give us the answer we need.

In essence, Arama is asking: Why be Jewish? What is fascinating is that he was the first to ask this question since the age of the Talmud. Why was it not asked before? Why was it first asked in fifteenth-century Spain? For many centuries, the question "Why be Jewish?" did not arise. The answer was self-evident. I am Jewish because that is what my parents were and theirs before them, back to the dawn of Jewish time. Existential questions arise only when we feel there is a choice. For much of history, Jewish identity was not a choice. It was a fact of birth, a fate, a destiny. It was not something you chose any more than you choose to be born.

In fifteenth-century Spain, Jews were faced with a choice. Spanish Jewry experienced its Kristallnacht in 1391, and from then on until the expulsion in 1492, Jews found themselves excluded from more and more areas of public life. There were immense pressures on them to convert, and some did so. Of these, some maintained their Jewish identity in secret, but others did not. For the first time in many centuries, staying Jewish came to be seen not just as a fate but as a choice. That is why Arama raised the question that had been unasked for so long. It is also why, in an age in which everything significant seems open to choice, it is being asked again in our time.

Arama gave one answer. I gave my own in my book *A Letter in the Scroll*.[2] But I also believe a large part of the answer lies in what Moses himself said at the end of his address: "I call heaven and earth as witnesses that I have set before you life and death, the blessing and the curse. Therefore, choose life, that you and your children may live" (Deut. 30:19).

Choose life. No religion, no civilisation, has insisted so strenuously and consistently that *we can choose*. We have it in us, says Rambam, to

2. *A Letter in the Scroll: Understanding Our Jewish Identity and Exploring the Legacy of the World's Oldest Religion* (New York: Free Press, 2000). Published in Britain as *Radical Then, Radical Now: The Legacy of the World's Oldest Religion* (London: HarperCollins, 2001).

be as righteous as Moses or as evil as Jeroboam.[3] We can be great. We can be small. We can choose.

The ancients – with their belief in fate, fortune, *Moira, Ananke,* the influence of the stars, or the arbitrariness of nature – did not fully believe in human freedom. For them true freedom meant, if you were religious, accepting fate, or, if you were philosophical, the conscious-ness of necessity. Nor do most scientific atheists believe in it today. We are determined, they say, by our genes. Our fate is scripted in our DNA. Choice is an illusion of the conscious mind. It is the fiction we tell ourselves.

Judaism says no. Choice is like a muscle: use it or lose it. Jewish law is an ongoing training regime in willpower. Can you eat this, not that? Can you exercise spiritually three times a day? Can you rest one day in seven? Can you defer the gratification of instinct – what Freud took to be the mark of civilisation? Can you practise self-control – according to the "marshmallow test," the surest sign of future success in life?[4] To be a Jew means not going with the flow, not doing what others do just because they are doing it. It gives us 613 exercises in the power of will to shape our choices. That is how we, with God, become co-authors of our lives.

Choose *life.* In many other faiths, life down here on earth with its loves, losses, triumphs, and defeats, is not the highest value. Heaven is to be found in life after death, or the soul in unbroken communion with God, or in acceptance of the world-that-is. Life is eternity, life is serenity, life is free of pain. But that, for Judaism, is not quite life. It may be noble, spiritual, sublime – but it is not life in all its passion, respon-sibility, and risk.

Judaism teaches us how to find God down here on earth, not up there in heaven. It means engaging with life, not taking refuge from it. It seeks not so much happiness as joy: the joy of being with others and together with them making a blessing over life. It means taking the risk of love, commitment, loyalty. It means living for something larger than the pursuit of pleasure or success. It means daring greatly.

3. *Mishneh Torah, Hilkhot Teshuva* 5:2.
4. Walter Mischel, *The Marshmallow Test: Mastering Self-Control* (London: Bantam Press, 2014).

It does not deny pleasure. Judaism is not ascetic. It does not worship pleasure. Judaism is not hedonist. Instead it sanctifies pleasure. It brings the Divine Presence into the most physical acts: eating, drinking, intimacy. We find God not just in the synagogue but in the home, the house of study, and acts of kindness; we find God in community, hospitality, and wherever we mend some of the fractures of our human world.

No religion has ever held the human person in higher regard. We are not tainted by original sin. We are not a mere bundle of selfish genes. We are not an inconsequential life form lost in the vastness of the universe. We are the being on whom God has set His image and likeness. We are the people God has chosen to be His partners in the work of creation. We are the nation God married at Sinai with the Torah as our marriage contract. We are the people God called on to be His witnesses. We are the ambassadors of heaven in the country called earth.

We are not better, or worse, than others. We are simply different, because God values difference whereas for most of the time, human beings have sought to eliminate difference by imposing one faith, one regime, or one empire on all humanity. Ours is one of the few faiths to hold that the righteous of all nations have a share in heaven because of what they do on earth.

Choose life. Nothing sounds easier, yet nothing has proven more difficult over time. Instead, people choose substitutes for life. They pursue wealth, possessions, status, power, fame, and to these gods they make the supreme sacrifice, realising too late that true wealth is not what you own but what you are thankful for, that the highest status is not to care about status, and that influence is more powerful than power.

That is why, though few faiths are more demanding, most Jews at most times have stayed faithful to Judaism, living Jewish lives, building Jewish homes, and continuing the Jewish story. That is why, with a faith as unshakable as it has proven true, Moses was convinced that "not with you alone do I make this covenant and this oath... but also with those who are not with us today." His gift to us is that through worshipping something so much greater than ourselves, we become so much greater than we would otherwise have been.

Why Judaism? Because there is no more challenging way of choosing life.

Torah as Song

oses' long and tempestuous career is about to end.
With words of blessing and encouragement, he hands on the mantle
of leadership to his successor Joshua, saying, "I am one hundred and
twenty years old today. I may no longer go out and come in, since the
Lord has said to me, 'You will not cross this Jordan'" (Deut. 31:2). As
Rashi notes, he says, "I may not," not "I cannot." He is still in full bodily
vigour, "his eye...undimmed and his natural energy unabated" (34:7).
But he has reached the end of his personal road. The time has come for
another age, a new generation, and a different kind of leader.

But before he takes his leave of life, God has one last command
for him, and through him, for the future: "And now write for yourselves
this song and teach it to the Children of Israel, put it in their mouths,
that this song may be a witness for Me among the Children of Israel"
(Deut. 32:19). The plain sense of the verse is that God is commanding
Moses and Joshua to write out the song that follows, that of *Haazinu*
(32:1–43). So Rashi and Ramban understand it. But the Oral Tradition
read it differently.

According to the sages, "And now write for yourselves" applies to the Torah as a whole. Thus the last of all the 613 commands is to write – or at least take part in writing, if only a single letter – a Torah scroll. Here is Rambam's statement of the law:

> Every Israelite is commanded to write a Torah scroll for himself, as it says, "Now therefore write this song," meaning, "Write for yourselves [a complete copy of] the Torah that contains this song," since we do not write isolated passages of the Torah [but only a complete scroll]. Even if one has inherited a Torah scroll from his parents, nonetheless it is a mitzva to write one for oneself, and one who does so is as if he had received [the Torah] from Mount Sinai. One who does not know how to write a scroll may engage [a scribe] to do it for him, and whoever corrects even one letter is as if he has written a whole scroll.[1]

Why this command? Why, then, at the end of Moses' life? Why make it the last of all the commands? And if the reference is to the Torah as a whole, why call it a "song"?

The Oral Tradition is here hinting at a set of very deep ideas. First, it is telling the Israelites, and us in every generation, that it is not enough to say, "We received the Torah from Moses" or "from our parents." We have to take the Torah and make it new in every generation. We have to write our own scroll. The point about the Torah is not that it is old but that it is new; it is not just about the past but about the future. It is not simply some ancient document that comes from an earlier era in the evolution of society. It speaks to us, here, now – but not without our making the effort to write it again.

There are two Hebrew words for an inheritance: *naḥala* and *yerusha/morasha*. They convey different ideas. *Naḥala* is related to the word *naḥal*, meaning a river, a stream. As water flows downhill, so an inheritance flows down the generations. It happens naturally. It needs no effort on our part.

1. *Mishneh Torah, Hilkhot Tefillin, Mezuza, VeSefer Torah* 7:1.

A *yerusha/morasha* is different. Here the verb is active. *It means to take possession of something by a positive deed or effort.* The Israelites received the land as a result of God's promise to Abraham. It was their legacy, but they nonetheless had to fight battles and win wars. *Lehavdil,* Mozart and Beethoven were both born to musical fathers. Music was in their genes, but their art was the result of almost endless hard work. Torah is a *morasha,* not a *naḥala.* We need to write it for ourselves, not merely inherit it from our ancestors.

And why call the Torah a song? Because if we are to hand on our faith and way of life to the next generation, it must sing. Torah must be affective, not just cognitive. It must speak to our emotions. As Antonio Damasio showed empirically in *Descartes' Error,*[2] though the reasoning part of the brain is central to what makes us human, it is the limbic system, the seat of the emotions, that leads us to choose this way, not that. If our Torah lacks passion, we will not succeed in passing it on to the future. Music is the affective dimension of communication, the medium through which we express, evoke, and share emotion. Precisely because we are creatures of emotion, music is an essential part of the vocabulary of mankind.

Music has a close association with spirituality. As Rainer Maria Rilke put it:

> Words still go softly out towards the unsayable.
> And music always new, from palpitating stones
> Builds in useless space its godly home.[3]

Song is central to the Judaic experience. We do not pray; we *daven,* meaning that we sing the words we direct towards heaven. Nor do we read the Torah. Instead we chant it, each word with its own cantillation. Even rabbinical texts are never merely studied; we chant them with the particular sing-song known to all students of Talmud. Each time and text has its specific melodies. The same prayer may be sung to half a

---

2. Antonio Damasio, *Descartes' Error: Emotion, Reason, and the Human Brain* (London: Penguin, 2005).
3. "Sonnets to Orpheus," book II, sonnet 10.

dozen different tunes depending on whether it is part of the morning, afternoon, or evening service, and whether the day is a weekday, Shabbat, festival, or one of the High Holy Days. There are different cantillations for biblical readings, depending on whether the text comes from the Torah, the Prophets, or the *Ketuvim*, "the Writings." Music is the map of the Jewish spirit, and each spiritual experience has its own distinctive melodic landscape.

Judaism is a religion of words, and yet whenever the language of Judaism aspires to the spiritual, it modulates into song, as if the words themselves seek escape from the gravitational pull of finite meanings. Music speaks to something deeper than the mind. If we are to make Torah new in every generation, we have to find ways of singing its song a new way. The words never change, but the music does.

A previous chief rabbi of Israel, Rabbi Avraham Shapiro, once told me a story about two great rabbinic sages of the nineteenth century, equally distinguished scholars, one of whom lost his children to the secular spirit of the age, the other of whom was blessed with children who followed in his path. The difference between them was this, he said: when it came to *Seuda Shelishit*, the third Shabbat meal, the former spoke words of Torah while the latter sang songs. His message was clear. Without an affective dimension – without music – Judaism is a body without a soul. It is the songs we teach our children that convey our love of God.

Some years ago, one of the leaders of world Jewry wanted to find out what had happened to the "missing Jewish children" of Poland, those who, during the war, had been adopted by Christian families and brought up as Catholics. He decided that the easiest way was through food. He organised a large banquet and placed advertisements in the Polish press, inviting whoever believed he or she had been born a Jew to come to this free dinner. Hundreds came, but the evening was on the brink of disaster since none of those present could remember anything of their earliest childhood – until the man asked the person sitting next to him if he could remember the song his Jewish mother had sung to him before going to sleep. He began to sing *Rozhinkes mit mandlen* ("Raisins and almonds"), the old Yiddish lullaby. Slowly others joined in, until the whole room was a chorus. Sometimes all that is left of Jewish identity is a song.

Rabbi Yechiel Michel Epstein (1829–1908), in the introduction to the *Arukh HaShulḥan, Ḥoshen Mishpat*, writes that the Torah is compared to a song because, to those who appreciate music, the most beautiful choral sound is a complex harmony with many different voices singing different notes. So, he says, it is with the Torah and its myriad commentaries, its "seventy faces." Judaism is a choral symphony scored for many voices, the written text its melody, the Oral Tradition its polyphony.

So it is with a poetic sense of closure that Moses' life ends with the command to begin again in every generation, writing our own scroll, adding our own commentaries, the people of the book endlessly reinterpreting the book of the people and singing its song. The Torah is God's libretto, and we, the Jewish people, are His choir. Collectively we have sung God's song. We are the performers of His choral symphony. And though when Jews speak they often argue, when they sing, they sing in harmony, because words are the language of the mind but music is the language of the soul.

Haazinu

The Arc of the Moral Universe

In majestic language, Moses breaks into song, investing his final testament to the Israelites with all the power and passion at his command. He begins dramatically but gently, calling heaven and earth to witness what he is about to say, sounding ironically very much like "The quality of mercy is not strained," Portia's speech in *The Merchant of Venice*.

> Listen, you heavens, and I will speak;
>> hear, you earth, the words of my mouth.
> Let my teaching fall like rain
>> and my words descend like dew,
> like showers on new grass,
>> like abundant rain on tender plants. (Deut. 32:1–2)

But this is a mere prelude to the core message Moses wants to convey. It is the idea known as *tzidduk hadin*, vindicating God's justice. The way Moses puts it is this:

> He is the Rock, His works are perfect,
>> and all His ways are just.
> A faithful God who does no wrong,
>> upright and just is He. (Deut. 32:4)

This is a doctrine fundamental to Judaism and its understanding of evil and suffering in the world – a difficult but necessary doctrine. God is just. Why then do bad things happen?

> Is He corrupt? No – the defect is in His children,
>> a crooked and perverse generation. (Deut. 32:5)

God requites good with good, evil with evil. When bad things happen to us it is because we have been guilty of doing bad things ourselves. The fault lies not in our stars but ourselves.

Moving into the prophetic mode, Moses foresees what he has already predicted, even before they have crossed the Jordan and entered the land. Throughout the book of Deuteronomy he has been warning of the danger that, in their land, once the hardships of the desert and the struggles of battle have been forgotten, the people will become comfortable and complacent. They will attribute their achievements to themselves and they will drift from their faith. When this happens they will bring disaster on themselves:

> Jeshurun grew fat and kicked –
>> you became fat, thick, gross –
> They abandoned the God who made them
>> and scorned the Rock their Saviour...
> You deserted the Rock, who fathered you;
>> forgot the God who gave you birth. (Deut. 32:15–18)

This, the first use of the word *Yeshurun* in the Torah – from the root *yashar*, upright – is deliberately ironic. Israel once knew what it was to be upright, but it will be led astray by a combination of affluence, security, and assimilation to the ways of its neighbours. It will betray the terms of the covenant, and when that happens it will find that God is no longer with it. It will discover that history is a ravening wolf. Separated from the source of its strength, it will be overpowered by its enemies. All that the nation once enjoyed will be lost. It is a stark and terrifying message.

Yet Moses is here bringing the Torah to a close with a theme that has been there from the beginning. God, creator of the universe, made a world that is fundamentally *good*, the word that echoes seven times in the first chapter of Genesis. It is humans, granted free will as God's image and likeness, who introduce evil into the world and then suffer its consequences. Hence Moses' insistence that when trouble and tragedy appear, we should search for the cause within ourselves and not blame God. God is upright and just. The defect is in us, His children.

This is perhaps the most difficult idea in the whole of Judaism. It is open to the simplest of objections, one that has sounded in almost every generation. If God is just, why do bad things happen to good people? This is the question asked not by sceptics and doubters, but by the very heroes of faith. We hear it in Abraham's plea, "Shall the Judge of all the earth not do justice?" (Gen. 18:25). We hear it in Moses' challenge, "Why have You done evil to this people?" (Ex. 5:22). It sounds again in Jeremiah: "Lord, You are always right when I dispute with You. Yet I must plead my case before You: Why are the wicked so prosperous? Why are evil people so happy?" (Jer. 12:1).

It is an argument that has never ceased. It continued through the rabbinic literature. It was heard again in the *kinot*, the laments, prompted by the persecution of Jews in the Middle Ages. It sounds in the literature produced in the wake of the Spanish expulsion, and echoes still when we recall the Holocaust.

The Talmud says that of all the questions Moses asked God, this was the one to which God did not give an answer (Berakhot 7a). The simplest, deepest interpretation is given in Psalm 92, "The song of the Sabbath day." Though "the wicked spring up like grass" (Ps. 92:7), they will eventually be destroyed. The righteous, by contrast, "flourish like a palm tree and grow tall like a cedar in Lebanon" (92:13). Evil wins in the short term but never in the long. The wicked are like grass, the righteous like a tree. Grass grows overnight but it takes years for a tree to reach its full height. In the long run, tyrannies are defeated. Empires decline and fall, goodness and rightness win the final battle. As Martin Luther King said in the spirit of the psalm: "The arc of the moral universe is long, but it bends towards justice."[1]

It is a difficult belief, this commitment to seeing justice in history under the sovereignty of God. Yet consider the alternatives. They are three. The first is to say that there is no meaning in history whatsoever. *Homo hominis lupus est,* "Man is wolf to man." History is a Darwinian struggle to survive, and justice is no more than the name given to the will of the stronger party.

The second, about which I write in my new book *Not In God's Name,*[2] is dualism, the idea that evil comes not from God but from an independent force: Satan, the Devil, the Antichrist, Lucifer, the Prince of Darkness, and the many other names given to the force that is not God but is opposed to Him and those who worship Him. This idea, which has surfaced in sectarian forms in each of the Abrahamic monotheisms, as well as in modern, secular totalitarianisms, is one of the most dangerous in all of history. It divides humanity into the unshakably good and the irredeemably evil, giving rise to a long history of bloodshed and barbarism of the kind we see being enacted today in many parts of the world in the name of holy war against the greater and lesser Satan. This is dualism, not monotheism, and the sages, who called it *shetei reshuyot,* "two powers" or "two domains" (Berakhot 33b), were right to reject it utterly.

The third, debated extensively in rabbinic literature, is to say that justice ultimately exists in the World to Come, in life after death. Yet though this is an essential element of Judaism, it is striking how relatively little Judaism had recourse to it, recognising that the central thrust of Tanakh is on this world and life before death. For it is here that we must work for justice, fairness, compassion, decency, the alleviation of poverty, and the perfection, as far as lies within our power, of society and our individual lives. Tanakh almost never takes this option. God does not say to Jeremiah or Job that the answer to their question exists in heaven and they will see it as soon as they end their stay on earth. The

1. "Out of the Long Night," *The Gospel Messenger,* February 8, 1958, 14.
2. New York: Schocken, 2015.

passion for justice so characteristic of Judaism would dissipate entirely were this the only answer.

Difficult though Jewish faith is, it has had the effect through history of leading us to say: if bad things have happened, let us blame no one but ourselves, and let us labour to make them better. It was this that led Jews, time and again, to emerge from tragedy, shaken, scarred, limping like Jacob after his encounter with the angel, yet resolved to begin again, to rededicate ourselves to our mission and faith, to ascribe our achievements to God and our defeats to ourselves.

Out of such humility, a momentous strength is born.

Moses' Death, Moses' Life

And so Moses dies, alone on a mountain with God as he had been all those years ago when, as a shepherd in Midian, he caught sight of a bush in flames and heard the call that changed his life and the moral horizons of the world.

It is a scene affecting in its simplicity. There are no crowds. There is no weeping. The sense of closeness yet distance is almost overwhelming. He sees the land from afar but has known for some time that he will never reach it. Neither his wife nor his children are there to say goodbye; they disappeared from the narrative long before. His sister Miriam and his brother Aaron, with whom he shared the burdens of leadership for so long, have predeceased him. His disciple Joshua has become his successor. Moses has become the lonely man of faith, except that with God no man, or woman, is lonely even if they are alone.

It is a profoundly sad moment, yet the obituary the Torah gives him – whether Joshua wrote it, or whether he wrote it himself at God's behest with tears in his eyes (Bava Batra 15a) – is unsurpassed:

> Never again did there arise a prophet in Israel like Moses, whom
> the Lord knew face to face, in all the signs and wonders that the
> Lord sent him to display in the land of Egypt to Pharaoh and
> all his servants and all his land, and for all the mighty acts and
> awesome sights that Moses displayed in the sight of all Israel.
> (Deut. 34:10–12)

Moses rarely figures in the lists people make from time to time
of the most influential people in history. He is harder to identify with
than Abraham in his devotion, David in his charisma, or Isaiah in his
symphonies of hope. The contrast between Abraham's and Moses' deaths
could not be more pointed. Of Abraham, the Torah says, "Then Abraham breathed his last and died at a good old age, an old man and full of
years; and he was gathered to his people" (Gen. 25:8). Abraham's death
was serene. Though he had been through many trials, he had lived to
see the first fulfilment of the promises God had given him. He had a
child, and he had acquired at least the first plot of land in Israel. In the
long journey of his descendants he had taken the first step. There is a
sense of closure.

By contrast, Moses' old age is anything but serene. In the last
month of his life he challenged the people with undiminished vigour
and unvarnished candour. At the very moment that they were getting
ready to cross the Jordan and enter the land, Moses warned them of the
challenges ahead. The greatest trial, he said, would not be poverty but
affluence, not slavery but freedom, not homelessness in the desert but
the comfort of home. Reading these words, one is reminded of Dylan
Thomas's poem, "Do not go gentle into that good night." There is as
much passion in his words in his hundred and twentieth year as at any
earlier stage of his life. This is not a man ready to retire. Until the very
end he continued to challenge both the people and God.

What do we learn from the death of Moses?

1. For each of us, even for the greatest, there is a Jordan we will not
   cross, a promised land we will not enter, a destination we will not
   reach. That is what R. Tarfon meant when he said: "It is not for
   you to complete the task, but neither are you free to desist from it"

(Mishna Avot 2:16). What we began, others will continue. What matters is that we undertook the journey. We did not stand still.

2. "No man knows his burial place" (Deut. 34:6). What a contrast between Moses and the heroes of other civilisations whose burial places become monuments, shrines, places of pilgrimage. It was precisely to avoid this that the Torah insists explicitly that no one knows where Moses is buried. We believe that the greatest mistake is to worship human beings as if they were gods. We admire human beings; we do not worship them. That difference is anything but small.

3. God alone is perfect. That is what Moses wanted people never to forget. Even the greatest human is not perfect. Moses sinned. We still do not know what his sin was – there are many opinions. But that is why God told him he would not enter the Promised Land. No human is infallible. Perfection belongs to God alone. Only when we honour this essential difference between heaven and earth can God be God and humans, human.

4. Nor does the Torah hide Moses' sin. "Because you did not sanctify Me…" (Num. 20:12). The Torah does not hide anyone's sin. It is fearlessly honest about the greatest of the great. Bad things happen when we try to hide people's sins. That is why there have been so many recent scandals in the world of religious Jews, some sexual, some financial, some of other kinds. When religious people hide the truth they do so from the highest of motives. They seek to prevent a *ḥillul Hashem*. The result, inevitably, is a greater *ḥillul Hashem*. Such sanctimony, denying the shortcomings of even the greatest, leads to consequences that are ugly and evil and turn decent people away from religion. The Torah does not hide people's sins. Neither may we.

5. There is more than one way of living a good life. Even Moses, the greatest of men, could not lead alone. He needed the peacemaking skills of Aaron, the courage of Miriam, and the support of the seventy elders. We should never ask: Why am I not as great as X? We each have something – a skill, a passion, a sensitivity – that makes, or could make, us great. The greatest mistake is trying to be someone else instead of being yourself. Do what you are best

at, then surround yourself with people who are strong where you are weak.

6. Never lose the idealism of youth. The Torah says of Moses that at the age of 120, "his eye was undimmed and his natural energy unabated" (Deut. 34:7). I used to think these were two complementary phrases until I realised that the first is the explanation of the second. That Moses' "eye was undimmed" means that he never lost the passion for justice that he had as a young man. It is there, as vigorous in Deuteronomy as it was in Exodus. We are as young as our ideals. Give way to cynicism and you rapidly age.

7. At the burning bush, Moses said to God: "I am not a man of words. I am heavy of speech and tongue" (Ex. 4:10). By the time we reach Deuteronomy, the book named "Words," *Devarim*, Moses has become the most eloquent of prophets. Some are puzzled by this. They should not be. God chose one who was not a man of words, so that when he spoke, people realised that *it was not he who was speaking but God who was speaking through him*. What he spoke were not his words but God's words. That is why He chose a couple who could not have children – Abraham and Sarah – to become parents of the first Jewish child. That is why He chose a people not conspicuous for their piety to become God's witnesses to the world. *The highest form of greatness is to open ourselves to God so that His blessings flow through us to the world*. That is how the priests blessed the people. It was not their blessing. They were the channel of God's blessing. The highest achievement to which we can aspire is to open ourselves to others and to God in love so that something greater than ourselves flows through us.

8. Moses defended the people. Did he like them? Did he admire them? Was he liked by them? The Torah leaves us in no doubt as to the answers to those questions. Yet he defended them with all the passion and power at his disposal. Even when they had sinned. Even when they were ungrateful to God. Even when they made a Golden Calf. He risked his life to do so. He said to God: "And now, forgive them, and if not, blot me out of the book You have written" (Ex. 32:32). According to the Talmud, God taught

Moses this lesson at the very outset of his career. When Moses said about the people, "They will not believe in me" (Ex. 4:1), God said, "They are the believers, children of believers, and in the end it will be you who does not believe" (Shabbat 97a). The leaders worthy of admiration are those who defend the people – even the non-Orthodox, even the secular, even those whose orthodoxy is a different shade from theirs. The people worthy of respect are those who give respect. Those who hate will be hated, those who look down on others will be looked down on, and those who condemn will be condemned. That is a basic principle of Judaism: *midda kenegged midda*. The people who are great are those who help others to become great. Moses taught the Jewish people how to become great.

The greatest tribute the Torah gives Moses is to call him *eved Hashem*, the servant of God. That is why Rambam writes that we can all be as great as Moses.[1] Because we can all serve. We are as great as the causes we serve, and when we serve with true humility, a force greater than ourselves flows through us, bringing the Divine Presence into the world.

---

1. *Mishneh Torah, Hilkhot Teshuva* 5:2.

About the Author

A n international religious leader, philosopher, award-winning author, and respected moral voice, Rabbi Lord Jonathan Sacks was recently named the winner of the 2016 Templeton Prize in recognition of his "exceptional contributions to affirming life's spiritual dimension." Described by HRH The Prince of Wales as "a light unto this nation" and by former British Prime Minister Tony Blair as "an intellectual giant," Rabbi Sacks is a frequent and sought-after contributor to radio, television, and the press, both in Britain and around the world.

He served as chief rabbi of the United Hebrew Congregations of the Commonwealth for twenty-two years, between 1991 and 2013. He holds seventeen honorary degrees, including a Doctor of Divinity conferred to mark his first ten years in office as chief rabbi, by the then-archbishop of Canterbury, Lord Carey.

In recognition of his work, Rabbi Sacks has won several international awards, including the Jerusalem Prize in 1995 for his contribution to Diaspora Jewish life, the Ladislaus Laszt Ecumenical and Social Concern Award from Ben-Gurion University in Israel in 2011, the Guardian of Zion Award from the Ingeborg Rennert Center for Jerusalem Studies at

Bar-Ilan University, and the Katz Award in recognition of his contribution to the practical analysis and application of halakha in modern life in Israel in 2014. He was knighted by Her Majesty the Queen in 2005 and made a Life Peer, taking his seat in the House of Lords in October 2009.

The author of more than twenty-five books, Rabbi Sacks has published a new English translation and commentary for the *Koren Sacks Siddur*, the first new Orthodox siddur in a generation, as well as powerful commentaries for the *Rosh HaShana, Yom Kippur, Pesaḥ, Shavuot,* and *Sukkot Maḥzorim*. A number of his books have won literary awards. His most recent work, *Not in God's Name*, was awarded a 2015 National Jewish Book Award in America and was a top ten Sunday Times bestseller in the UK. Others include *The Dignity of Difference*, winner of the Grawemeyer Award in Religion in 2004 for its success in defining a framework for interfaith dialogue between people of all faiths and of none, and National Jewish Book Awards for *A Letter in the Scroll* in 2000, *Covenant & Conversation: Genesis* in 2009, and the *Koren Sacks Pesaḥ Maḥzor* in 2013. His Covenant & Conversation commentaries on the weekly Torah portion, which are translated into Hebrew, Spanish, Portuguese, and Turkish, are read in Jewish communities around the world.

After achieving first-class honours in philosophy at Gonville and Caius College, Cambridge, he pursued post-graduate studies in Oxford and London, gaining his doctorate in 1981 and receiving rabbinic ordination from Jews' College and Yeshivat Etz Chaim. He served as the rabbi for Golders Green Synagogue and Marble Arch Synagogue in London before becoming principal of Jews' College.

Born in 1948 in London, he has been married to Elaine since 1970. They have three children and several grandchildren.

www.rabbisacks.org / @RabbiSacks

The fonts used in this book are from the Arno family

The Covenant & Conversation Series:

Genesis: The Book of Beginnings

Exodus: The Book of Redemption

Leviticus: The Book of Holiness

Numbers: The Wilderness Years (forthcoming)

Deuteronomy (forthcoming)

Lessons in Leadership

Maggid Books
The best of contemporary Jewish thought from
Koren Publishers Jerusalem Ltd.